D1277510

BROKER *to* BROKER

REALTOR MAGAZINE

BROKER to BROKER

Management Lessons from America's Most Successful Real Estate Companies

Edited by Robert Freedman,
Senior Editor, *Realtor® Magazine*

WILEY

JOHN WILEY & SONS, INC.

Copyright © 2006 by National Association of REALTORS®. All rights reserved.

Published by John Wiley & Sons, Inc., Hoboken, New Jersey.
Published simultaneously in Canada.

No part of this publication may be reproduced, stored in a retrieval system, or transmitted in any form or by any means, electronic, mechanical, photocopying, recording, scanning, or otherwise, except as permitted under Section 107 or 108 of the 1976 United States Copyright Act, without either the prior written permission of the Publisher, or authorization through payment of the appropriate per-copy fee to the Copyright Clearance Center, Inc., 222 Rosewood Drive, Danvers, MA 01923, (978) 750-8400, fax (978) 646-8600, or on the web at www.copyright.com. Requests to the Publisher for permission should be addressed to the Permissions Department, John Wiley & Sons, Inc., 111 River Street, Hoboken, NJ 07030, (201) 748-6011, fax (201) 748-6008, or online at http://www.wiley.com/go/permissions.

Limit of Liability/Disclaimer of Warranty: While the publisher and author have used their best efforts in preparing this book, they make no representations or warranties with respect to the accuracy or completeness of the contents of this book and specifically disclaim any implied warranties of merchantability or fitness for a particular purpose. No warranty may be created or extended by sales representatives or written sales materials. The advice and strategies contained herein may not be suitable for your situation. You should consult with a professional where appropriate. Neither the publisher nor author shall be liable for any loss of profit or any other commercial damages, including but not limited to special, incidental, consequential, or other damages.

For general information on our other products and services or for technical support, please contact our Customer Care Department within the United States at (800) 762-2974, outside the United States at (317) 572-3993 or fax (317) 572-4002.

Wiley also publishes its books in a variety of electronic formats. Some content that appears in print may not be available in electronic books. For more information about Wiley products, visit our web site at www.wiley.com.

Library of Congress Cataloging-in-Publication Data:
Broker to Broker: Management Lessons From America's Most Successful Real Estate Companies / REALTOR® Magazine.
    p. cm.
  ISBN-13: 978-0-471-78318-3 (cloth)
  ISBN-10: 0-471-78318-8 (cloth)
  1. Real estate business—United States. 2. Real estate business—United States—Management. 3. Real estate agents—United States. I. REALTOR® magazine.
  HD255.B755 2006
  333.33'068—dc22

                                    2005023679

Printed in the United States of America.

10 9 8 7 6 5 4 3 2 1

Contents

CHAPTER   Risk Management   242

12

Foreword

There's no shortage of management resources for brokers and owners of residential real estate offices, but searching for what's available is time consuming. Every minute you spend combing the Internet or flipping through books and magazines looking for ways to respond to a problem or to get ideas for helping your associates ramp up their business is time spent away from your core activities—the activities through which you add value to your business.

It's in the pursuit of solving this time problem that the editors of REALTOR® Magazine, the flagship publication of the National Association of REALTORS®, bring you this brokerage management compilation of best practices. By packaging together articles from REALTOR® Magazine on the latest thinking in the business, the editors have conducted much of your research for you. You'll find articles on shoring up your brokerage's bottom line, planning for changes in your marketplace, attracting and retaining sales associates, and implementing sound risk management policies, among dozens of other articles on a wide range of essential topics.

At the same time, throughout the compilation the editors direct you to additional resources online, from the National Association of REALTORS® and elsewhere. In that way the compilation goes beyond the pages of REALTOR® Magazine to the latest thinking throughout the real estate industry—all brought to you in a format that puts a premium on one of the most scarce resources you have: your time.

—*Thomas M. Stevens, 2006 president, National Association of REALTORS®, and senior vice president, NRT Inc., Parsippany, New Jersey.*

Bringing Management Best Practices to You

Tod Beaty, broker-owner of two Hammond GMAC Real Estate offices in Cambridge, Massachusetts, has people strolling up to his storefront on Brattle Square at all hours to stare at his front window. Yes, he has pictures of his listings there, like virtually every other broker in his market. But his pictures are on a big television monitor and anyone on the sidewalk outside his office with a cell phone can scroll through the listings, pull up detailed information, and, if they like what they see, send a message to the listing agent whom they'd like to talk to.

The application is still so new—it launched in mid-May 2005, and his is the first company to use it, either in the United States or elsewhere, he says—that it's too soon to tell how much it will boost his foot traffic, if at all.

But it couldn't be a better way to reach out to people who are thinking about buying but aren't yet ready to walk into a real estate office to start the process.

"It's a nice bridge people can take without having to come into the office to get more information," says Beaty.

Equally innovative, Matthew Widdows, broker-owner of HomeSmart Real Estate in Phoenix, uses one employee to staff the receptionist desk in his four offices. Operating out of the HomeSmart headquarters, the receptionist appears on a flat-screen TV in the reception area of the branch offices and, through the use of cameras, interacts with customers remotely. The result is tech wizardry that appeals to young customers and enables Widdows to pay for the reception function at several offices with a single paycheck.

"The savings from not having to hire people for each office, train and manage them, and provide benefits offsets the upfront costs of the technology," says Widdows.

Welcome to the way brokers are operating residential real estate offices today. Fueled by years of strong home sales and a stream of new licensees entering the business, broker-owners and their managers are tapping technology innovation to stay ahead of the competition. But the dynamism in the industry isn't just about technology aimed at boosting customer traffic, although that's a big part of it. In their efforts to attract customers and help their sales associates prosper, brokers are pushing the envelope in every way they run their business. Consider these few ideas:

- Leeann Iacino, CRB, GRI, and Jack O'Connor, CRB, founders of Prestige Real Estate Group LLC, in Denver, make company equity shares available to their associates. Nothing new in that, but they're taking the opportunity to a level that, O'Connor thinks, is the highest in the industry. About a third of their more than 300 associates have an equity stake, with some owning as much as 8 percent of the company. *Why they do it:* O'Connor says the opportunity to take a large equity stake encourages associates to build the company's performance into their calculus for personal success.

- Mark Dandrea of A-List Realty in Columbus, Ohio, in a move that goes against mainstream thinking in the industry, encourages his sales associates to affiliate with his company part-time. Dandrea doesn't subscribe to the idea that part-timers aren't professional and should be discouraged from affiliating. *Why he does it:* Dandrea thinks letting associates launch their careers part-time helps them build sound sales habits for the long term because they're not under as much financial pressure to get up to speed quickly.

- Debbie D'Valentine, CEO of Tomie Raines Inc., in Lansing, Michigan, requires her associates to tell customers up front what services to expect and to get customer feedback after closing on how well they delivered on those services. *Why she does it:* Implementing a rigid process like this isn't something some associates like to do because it goes against their sense of independence, D'Valentine says. But by creating conditions for accountability, associates acquire a strong incentive to make customer-service a top-of-mind practice, and that boosts repeat business, she says.

- Marianne Barkman, senior vice president at John L. Scott Real Estate in Bellevue, Washington, talks books with her sales associates at regular get-togethers. She has more than literature on her mind, though. *Why she does it:* The discussions give her and her associates a chance to bond in a relaxed environment and, more importantly, help them learn that sales performance isn't everything. That realization is a starting point for her associates to achieve the work-life balance that's necessary to avoid burnout, she says.

- Bill Mathers, owner of MathersRealty.com, in Charlotte, North Carolina, gets recruiting help from minority and immigrant leaders in his market. He makes regular stops at churches and community groups. *Why he does it:* The recruiting effort creates a win-win situation, he believes. The community leaders learn of opportunities for their members, who might otherwise consider only nonprofessional work, and he gets credibility with recruits who are crucial for his success in an increasingly multicultural market.

"The range of innovation in how brokers and managers build business and run their offices has never been greater," says Thomas M. Stevens, 2006 president of the National Association of REALTORS® (NAR) and senior vice president of NRT Inc., Parsippany, New Jersey.

Keeping up with fast-paced innovation isn't easy. Anyone tackling the day-to-day challenges of running a brokerage has little time to spare for a strategic survey of what others in the business are doing to get ahead. And yet keeping abreast of brokerage innovation, and charting your business course for the future based on what you find, isn't optional for long-term success, brokers say.

"You should spend some time thinking about what isn't right in front of you," says Harold (Hal) Kahn, CRB, CRS®, broker-owner of Kahn Inc., REALTORS®, in Newburgh, New York. "Timing is the critical component in executing any business plan, so knowing what's taking place in your marketplace is crucial."

It's with this challenge in mind that the editors of REALTOR® Magazine, the flagship publication of the National Association of REAL-

TORS®, bring you this compilation of brokerage management best practices. The 70 pieces here, culled from articles featured in the "For Brokers" section of the magazine over the past two years, have been selected based on their usefulness to you.

The "For Brokers" section appears each month in an edition of REALTOR® Magazine that goes to the approximately 160,000 brokers and managers in the REALTOR® community. The content is targeted exclusively at meeting the needs of those who manage the people who do the selling.

In this compilation, you'll read about how much it cost Beaty to install and operate his interactive window display and how effective he thinks it will be in boosting his office traffic. In a piece on HomeSmart, Widdows talks about bottom-line issues such as the cost of his virtual receptionist. That kind of practical information, loaded with ideas for you, is what we try to provide in the "For Brokers" section, and we believe the pieces selected for this compilation do a solid job meeting that test. They won't provide you with all of the information you will need to make a decision, of course. But we think you'll get enough to know whether what one broker is doing is right for you, and whether it's practical for you to try it in your market.

What's more, we try to give you direction for getting more information or for making a first contact so you can get the ball rolling in your own company. A piece on the latest thinking in office design, for example ("Office design that keeps associates on top," p. 163), lets you know how much various design ideas cost, and sends you to our magazine's sister publication on the Internet, REALTOR® Magazine Online, for resources compiled by NAR information specialists on office design.

Best of all, these ideas are coming to you from your colleagues in the brokerage community, the professionals on the ground. As in all REALTOR® Magazine articles, the voice of the practitioner is front and center, reflecting what's actually happening in markets today. In this way, the pieces are part of the larger conversation you have with your colleagues each day on what works and what doesn't when it comes to improving your business. But because you can't take time out from running your business to talk to everyone you'd like to, we bring those conversations to you, edited and organized to meet your busy schedule.

The compilation is built around three sections: Managing Operations, Managing People, and Managing Risk. In each is a selection of articles that gives you a snapshot of ideas. In Managing Operations, for example, there are five chapters—finances, operations, marketing, planning, and technology categories—and each includes a handful of short pieces on what companies are doing to tackle a problem or meet a need—centralizing closing services through video conferencing, for example, or expanding your business through the use of virtual assistants.

Each section closes with profiles of companies whose operations offer ideas for you. An example is Realty Select, Inc., in Lancaster County, Pennsylvania, a brokerage launched in 2003 that aims to compete for talent with established area companies by hiring new licensees as employees. It offers them a salary with small commission split plus health and retirement plans. It also hands them significant business right off the bat by pulling in sellers at high volume with low flat-fee pricing.

If you have companies doing something similar in your market, you gain by getting insight into how a company like this works.

We hope you enjoy reading through these selections and, even better, finding something that sparks an idea for your company. For those of you who've already read some of these pieces in the magazine, you'll find value in the way we've organized the selections in an easy-reference format, broken out some high-impact material for quick accessibility, and updated information on the people we quote. There are also a few pieces that hadn't yet appeared in the magazine at the time this compilation went to press, so the content is as fresh as can be.

We think this brokerage management tool is a resource you'll go back to again and again. You can read the sections and the pieces within them in any order. We thus invite you to browse the contents then dip into the selections that pique your interest. You're sure to stumble on some interesting ideas and companies that you weren't expecting to find.

—ROBERT FREEDMAN

Washington, D.C.

Managing Operations

Smart Moves

It's never been more challenging to operate a residential real estate office. Thanks to strong markets, the number of people earning—and
looking for a place to hang—their real estate license is on a sharp in-
cline. The number of new licensees in my state of California, for example, was 500 to 1,500 a month at the end of 2004, a rate that's expected
to continue through 2005 and into 2006, regulators here say. This surge
in new licensees, many of them young adults with tech savvy but little
sales experience, heightens the importance of the training, technology,
and performance incentives you offer.

At the same time, as managers, we must stay attuned to new ways of
keeping our operations profitable, even as bargain-shopping consumers
put downward pressure on commissions. For some of us, that means
structuring commission plans that help ensure that our overhead for
each associate is covered. It also means staying on top of the latest in
risk-management strategies and technology security.

Here, you'll find dozens of ideas from specialists in finances, operations,
marketing, planning, and technology to give you a leg up as you tackle today's management's challenges. You'll also find case studies of companies
trying out ideas that you might want to try in your own operations.

—*Larry Knapp, CRB, e-PRO, president and COO,
Alain Pinel, REALTORS®, Saratoga, California.*

Finances

Boosting Your Bottom Line

QUICK TIPS

Double up associates.

Add rookies.

Toughen criteria for higher splits.

Give associates more responsibility for ads—on both content and cost.

Diversify income streams.

Gene Ward, CRS®, added 15 associates in two years without expanding his office space. How'd he do it? The managing broker of the Lincolnshire office of Woods Bros. Realty in Lincoln, Nebraska, puts two, sometimes three, associates into a single office and also doubles them up in cubicles.

Cozy quarters wasn't the most popular move among the sales force, which numbered 130 at the time, but no one has left in search of solitude, he says. That's because he's made it clear to his associates that such cost-cutting is crucial for his office's survival in today's environment of rising business costs. And now, Ward says, he has the largest real estate office in his market.

At a time when sales associates are demanding greater commission splits and technology and marketing costs are eating more of the company dollar, brokers and managers are embarking on a variety of strategies to grow their profitability. Among other things, they're adding services to boost revenue and shifting more costs to associates. Some are also recruiting rookies to push down the average commission split they pay their associates.

"Our business is so competitive today and has so many more costs than it did years ago that you have to continually evaluate your operations to stay profitable," says Nancy Kinney, GRI, manager of Real Living Premier in Marion, Ohio.

The rise in the average commission split for veteran associates is at a crisis level in many markets, say some brokers and managers.

Years ago, the typical split for veteran associates was 60 percent to 65 percent of commissions. Today it's not unusual for associates to quickly earn 80 percent or more—sometimes as much as 95 percent. "Associates make a lot of money; brokers don't," says Ronda Needham, CRB, who oversees the Highland Park office of Ebby Halliday, REALTORS® in Dallas.

To combat the problem, Needham's company makes generous splits something to strive for, not a given. Most new associates start with a 50–50 split, but once they bring in $87,000 in gross commissions their split grows to 80 percent. The split increases to 90 percent once they bring in gross commissions of $260,000. Reaching that level is a reasonable challenge, Needham says, because the average sale price in her market is $583,000.

Chris Harris, GRI, who in 2004 oversaw the main office of Keystone Realty in Reno, Nevada, used a similar strategy for keeping splits down. He scouted real estate schools with the express purpose of affiliating rookie salespeople and quickly brought on 25 new associates at a 55–45 split. Veteran associates received an 80 percent split once they brought in $50,000 in gross commissions.

The result? An immediate jump in the company dollar, from about 22 percent to 27 percent, Harris says. He estimated that the lower commission splits of new recruits more than compensated for the fewer sales they generated and the added training and other costs they incurred. At the same time, given the strong market during that period, even newbies were quickly generating robust sales, as well as showing a lot of loyalty. "The new licensees appreciated what the brokerage was doing for them in terms of training and potential for greater splits," Harris said. "We lost few people."

Harris is now a broker with Coldwell Banker Village Realty in Reno.

Cost Cutting

Ebby Halliday's Needham is pleased to see associates reach the upper ranks of her tiered commission structure, because it shows they're performing well. But to keep costs down, she shifts some key expenses, including most property advertising, to associates, no matter at what level they're performing.

Her associates are generally amenable to absorbing the ad costs, because "they'd rather have the opportunity to make choices in how their properties are advertised," she says.

What's more, the company uses its big size to negotiate favorable rates for graphics work, so associates can get professionally designed materials at a discount. Plus, her office saves by not having to hire staff to create ads or stock paper. Needham estimates she'll save at least $35,000 annually by contracting with a design company rather than hiring someone to do it.

Kinney of Marion, Ohio, says she practices the meticulous art of analyzing her business—where her sales come from and where her expenses go—to better calibrate her costs. For example, within the past year she's pulled significant amounts of money out of newspaper advertising and plowed it into Internet and cable TV advertising, because those sources were generating more efficient uses of her ad dollars than newspapers.

"We're paying $14 a week for each house we show on a local cable channel. That represents 1,200 potential viewers of the listing a day and our biggest value," she says. "A lot of people in our market shop for houses on cable."

Expand Your Interests

Cost-cutting is an obvious source of increased profits, but many companies are looking at the revenue side, too, diversifying their services to reduce their reliance on sales as their main income source.

Ancillary services account for 28 percent of Realty Executives of Phoenix's bottom line, says John Foltz, CRB, president. Specifically, the company generates revenue through mortgage and title services, even though it doesn't own the providers. Instead, it works through affiliated business arrangements with partners and takes a percentage of their net revenues. "That way we don't have to become experts in mortgage and title services," says Foltz. His company generates gross annual sales of some $5 billion and 30,000 transactions in 17 offices.

Long & Foster Real Estate, the mid-Atlantic regional giant headquartered in Fairfax, Virginia, takes a different approach to ancillary services. The company, which has about 10,600 associates in 200 offices in eight states and Washington, D.C., owns a mortgage company with Wells Fargo, the banking giant. The income adds "a lot" to Long & Foster's bottom line, says Wes Foster, president.

Foster's company also partners with a title company and owns an insurance business, both of which add some but not a huge amount to company revenue.

For big companies such as Realty Executives of Phoenix and Long & Foster, offering ancillary services is largely beyond debate. Consumers have come to expect large real estate companies to offer something close to one-stop shopping. But adding ancillary services can pay off for smaller companies, too.

Kerry Veach, broker-owner of RE/MAX Southern Realty, a three-office brokerage in Fort Walton Beach, Florida, launched a title company two years ago. The move is paying off well, generating about 10 percent of his company's bottom line this past year, he says.

Associates can buy stock in the title company in amounts based on the volume of sales they generate, giving them a stake in the affiliate's performance. The title service has about a 40 percent capture rate of the sales the associates bring in.

For the smallest brokerages, ancillary services may not be in the cards, unless they partner with an affiliated business. And even then small brokers may just prefer to stay focused on brokerage services. "I've been approached with opportunities to add services over the years, but I like to keep my operation as simple as possible," says Lydia A. Odle, broker-owner of Lydia A. Odle, REALTOR®, in Alexandria, Virginia, with 11 sales associates.

Whether you're running a one-stop shop or a boutique that focuses exclusively on brokerage, boosting profits requires constant vigilance over your operations. Analyzing every expense and every potential new revenue source is the surest path to greater profits.

—Robert Freedman, with additional reporting by Pat Taylor. This piece
originally appeared in the July 2003 issue of REALTOR® Magazine.

SIX SMALL WAYS TO ACHIEVE BIG PROFITS

How are brokers and managers maintaining a healthy income? Here are a few ideas.

1. *Float commissions.* Every day John Foltz of Realty Executives of Phoenix deposits funds used to pay commissions into an interest-bearing account. That way, the funds draw interest between the time a commission check is written and the associate cashes the check. The practice contributes five percent to his company's bottom line.

2. *Balance your associate mix.* Nancy Kinney, GRI, manager of Real Living Premier in Marion, Ohio, says concentrating on a niche market can gain you visibility in that market. But it can be risky to your cash flow if sales in the niche take a turn for the worse. Affiliate associates whose market specialties fill gaps in your ranks. Several strong associates working middle-market sales can keep your cash flow strong, while a few strong performers in high-end homes can generate nice profits.

3. *Purchase advertising, such as classified space, in bulk to obtain price discounts.* Parcel out the costs with a small markup to associates who advertise their listings in the ads. Foltz's company charges his associates $5.50 per line, a nominal increase over the bulk rate the company receives.

4. *Charge consumers a set transaction fee.* It helps offset administrative costs per transaction, says Wes Foster of Long & Foster Real Estate in Fairfax, Virginia. "It's rare that consumers don't pay the fee," he says. But if they don't, the company and salesperson share the cost.

5. *Manage risk.* Apply tough, standardized quality control measures to each transaction to reduce liability and costs for E&O insurance and litigation, suggests Foltz. His company maintains a staff of three who review

every purchase contract to ensure all disclosures and other requirements are met.

6. *Charge online referral fees.* Foltz charges $800 to associates who receive qualified leads from the company's web site. The fee applies only to leads generated from houses not listed by the company but made available for viewing on its Internet Data Exchange (IDX)-enabled web site, and salespeople pay only if the deal closes and they receive a commission.

MORE ONLINE

Brokerage Financial Management Courses

The Council of Real Estate Brokerage (CRB) Managers, an affiliate of the National Association of REALTORS®, offers a two-day financial management and planning course that provides help understanding financial statements, forecasting revenues, and developing an expense budget, among other finance areas. Learn about this and other CRB financial management courses, including instruction online and on CD-ROM, at the CRB web site, www.crb.com. You'll find information on the group's courses under "Education."

Taking Control of Your Accounting

QUICK TIPS

Digitalize your bookkeeping.

Stay abreast of ever-changing business tax deductions.

Know which IRS business-entity structure makes sense.

Orson Woodhouse, GRI, broker-owner of Woodhouse Group in Boise, Idaho, is paying 50 percent more for accounting services than he was at the end of 2002. He couldn't be happier.

That's because he replaced his old accounting firm with one that brings real estate and small-business experience to the table. His experience shows how critical it is to understand the ways accounting and tax issues can impact your bottom line.

The new firm proved its worth quickly by saving Woodhouse money on his taxes and creating more efficiency in his operations. "I didn't have a bad experience with my old firm," says Woodhouse, whose company specializes in new-home sales and relocation. "It just wasn't leading-edge in our industry."

Right off the bat, the new firm—Balukoff, Lindstrom & Co., in Boise—replaced Woodhouse's manual bookkeeping system with Quick-Books, which enables the brokerage to tabulate everything electronically, then e-mail quarterly and annual reports to the accounting firm. When there's a problem, the electronic system makes it easy to make changes. "We've seen a fivefold increase in bookkeeping efficiency," Woodhouse says.

The accounting firm also recommended changes in how Woodhouse categorizes expenses, saving him money on his 2002 taxes. Among other things, it recommended that Woodhouse take advantage of tax laws favorable to real estate professionals for income-property investment losses. "Practitioners can write off 100 percent of their income-property losses, an option not open to passive investors," says Michael Lindstrom, who was president of Balukoff when it worked with Woodhouse. Lindstrom is now a tax partner with Eide Bailly LLC.

The firm also recommended strategies that make sense for brokerages with independent contractors and a handful of employees. Among them:

Asset growth. Changes to federal deduction laws enacted a couple of years ago enable business owners to deduct $100,000 a year, up from $24,000, on business assets such as software. "We recommended that Woodhouse spend money on assets rather than pay taxes," says Lindstrom.

Family savings. Federal laws provide favorable tax treatment for employing family members to do odd jobs such as post For Sale signs. A certain amount of compensation to family members isn't subject to payroll tax. And children's income is typically taxed at a lower rate. At Woodhouse Group, Woodhouse's wife keeps the company books.

Large vehicle deduction. A business car weighing more than 6,000 pounds can be written off, although tax-law changes enacted in 2004 place new limits on depreciation amounts.

An accounting firm also can advise on how to structure your business entity, whether as an S, C, or limited-liability corporation. Each has advantages under certain conditions, and owners can change their structure as company goals change. (See "Match Company Structure to Your Goals.")

So, how do you pick the right accounting firm? Woodhouse assembled leads by talking to colleagues in his market. He interviewed five companies before settling on Balukoff. "You can always find someone who can get your taxes done correctly," he says. "It's worth it to pay more for someone who has your long-term health in mind."

—*Robert Freedman. This article originally appeared in the November 2003 issue of REALTOR® Magazine.*

MATCH COMPANY STRUCTURE TO YOUR GOALS

Here are three examples of how to structure your business to respond to your company's changing goals, according to Michael Lindstrom, a tax partner with Eide Bailly LLC, Boise, Idaho. For specific advice, consult an accountant.

C Corporation

Advantage: Put yourself on a salary and get 100 percent of employee medical insurance costs deducted from your taxes. Helpful if anticipating high medical bills.

Disadvantage: May be expensive if there are more than a few employees.

Limited-Liability Corporation

Advantage: Maximize retirement benefits up to a certain point.

Disadvantage: Benefits are limited if the owner reaches $200,000 in income. In these cases, it may make sense to adopt an S corporation structure.

S Corporation

Advantage: Get favorable payroll-tax treatment.

Disadvantage: Lose out on the ability to fund retirement plans.

MORE ONLINE

Finding an Accountant

The National Association of Small Business Accountants maintains a database of member accountants, searchable by state, on its web site, www.smallbizaccountants.com. Before you select an accountant, the association recommends you check first about the types of businesses they specialize in, the accounting services they provide, and the amount of experience they have. The database is under "Find an Accountant."

Preparing for a Financial Turn for the Worse

In the college town of Amherst, Massachusetts, where the tide of real estate business ebbs and flows with the rhythm of the academic calendar, a broker's finances can sometimes be as barren as a New England winter. Between September and February, area home sales tend to drop by half, a major hit to brokers' bottom line, says Gerald L. Jones, CRB, GRI, broker-owner of Jones Town & Country Realty in Amherst.

To make sure his company is financially prepared to weather the annual fall-off in business, Jones:

Keeps higher amounts of working capital on hand than would otherwise be necessary. How? By making fewer draws for profit-taking or profit-sharing during the flush months. That way, in lean months, there's money available to cover costs, including profit-taking and profit-sharing.

Pays a year's premium for errors and omissions insurance in an upfront lump sum. You can negotiate a better rate that way, he says.

Buys (in cash) rather than leases some office equipment, such as copiers and the phone system.

Sets up a company line of credit during flush periods, when the money isn't needed, to handle unexpected costs, rather than waiting until lean months. The timing puts you in a better position for shopping around and negotiating the terms. "It's just a matter of living below your means rather than to the maximum of your means," says Jones, whose three-office company has 75 associates.

Even if your company doesn't face the sales extremes of a college town, preparing your bottom line to absorb unexpected hits is crucial for long-term viability.

Alan Mauldin, GRI, and Michelle Mauldin, CRS®, GRI, co-owners of Signature Realty in Edmond, Oklahoma, were surprised in 2002 to find that they faced a 100 percent increase in E&O insurance. They'd had no prior claims, but in the three years since they'd locked in a contract term, their sales volume had increased 65 percent. The Mauldins have been finding savings in other areas:

Health insurance. They took out a policy with a maximum $5,000 deductible and maintain a health savings account to pay for costs incurred up to the deductible. That has saved them hundreds in monthly insurance premiums while allowing them to build up a savings account that's exempt from federal income taxes.

Vendor costs. They've reduced their advertising costs with local print publications 20 percent to 25 percent, for example, by leveraging the volume of business they give the publications.

Other tips from brokers include:

Own your office and lease it back to your company. You build your equity while locking in your lease payments. My company is a Subchapter S corporation. An LLC owns the real estate itself.

> Reed Simmons, CRB, broker-owner,
> Dickson Realty Inc., Reno, Nevada

Accumulate reserves during flush months and make loans to yourself to cover unexpected costs or capital projects.

> William D. Seawell Jr., CRS®, GRI, broker-owner,
> Seawell, REALTORS®, Greensboro, North Carolina

Face it: Real estate business income is in constant flux. But a few simple moves may be all you need to prepare your company's bottom line for those financial cold spells.

> —*Robert Freedman. This article originally appeared in the August 2004 issue of REALTOR® Magazine.*

Calculating Associate Compensation— The New Rules

QUICK TIPS

Separate fixed from variable office costs.

Calculate amount each associate adds to variable costs.

Match splits to costs.

Factor in costs of teams, personal assistants.

Don't overpay for top performers.

Janice Grupido, CRB, GRI, would like to rely on a little less art and a little more science in setting compensation plans each year for the dozens of associates who work in her offices in the Troy and Rochester areas of Michigan. Ideally, the broker-owner of Countryside GMAC Real Estate would look at what each salesperson consumes in brokerage resources to generate revenue.

That's a challenging thing to do. Yet, it's becoming more important as brokers look more to treating each sales associate as a separate profit center, each of whom comes with a unique set of costs and an ability to generate revenue.

"Start with a view that each associate operates as an individual company; then you try to determine if each individual generates more revenue than it costs to keep the person on board," says David Cocks, managing partner of Charlotte, North Carolina-based Compensation-Master, a consultant on real estate brokerage compensation plans.

That approach differs from what's done typically in residential real estate brokerages, where setting compensation plans requires a bit of alchemy—part art, part science. For the most part, brokers apply a desk-cost approach that might be likened to the way a manufacturer sets the price of a product based on its per-unit production costs. If each unit costs $1 to manufacture, then to earn a profit the manufacturer must charge something above $1 for each unit.

That's more or less the approach taken by Shorewest, REALTORS®, an 18-office independent brokerage based in Brookfield, Wisconsin—although what goes into the calculation is more complex. "All of our costs are divided by the number of desks," says Rick Murry, CRB, GRI, sales director. "That's how we establish the minimum income we need."

In taking this approach, brokers isolate their fixed costs and then peg commission splits to the amount of variable costs associates are responsible for. In general, the more variable costs covered by the broker, the bigger the broker's share of the commission split.

Thus, you often see brokers splitting commissions on something close to a 50–50 basis at the beginning of the year, then raising that split once associates' revenue covers their share of fixed costs and they can assume responsibility for more of their variable costs.

Looking Closer at Associate Costs

Treating each associate as a separate profit center goes beyond the desk-cost approach by identifying variable as well as fixed costs.

Although zeroing in on precise amounts is difficult, brokers aren't entirely in the dark about what their associates cost them.

Marian Benton, GRI, operating principal of Keller Williams Realty in Ann Arbor, Michigan, says she needs to generate $18,000 each from at least a third of her 176 associates to ensure her fixed costs are covered. "We look at rent, overhead, leased equipment—everything—to see how much money we need to break even," says Benton.

To create an income cushion, she sets her annual budget assuming that one-third will earn enough in gross commissions to meet the $18,000 in commission splits to the company, the splits of another third will reach about half that, and the splits of the remaining third—mainly newer associates—will reach a few thousand dollars.

The splits to the brokerage are set annually as a percentage of gross commission income (GCI), and there's flexibility in how the percentage is set. Many associates take a 70 percent split until the 30 percent contribution to the broker equates to $18,000. Once that happens, they get 100 percent of their commissions. They may also opt for a higher, 80–20, split up front in exchange for guaranteeing the $18,000 to the brokerage before the end of the calendar year. On top of the $18,000, each associate pays a franchise fee, which is capped at $3,000.

Unlike offices in many other real estate companies, though, Benton doesn't need to worry too much about the amount of variable costs generated by her associates. In the Keller Williams model associates mostly pay variable costs themselves, even making spending decisions collectively through a salesperson council. The council works with the broker to determine the services it wants and how to allocate the costs among the ranks. "If they want a color copier or an extra fax line, they can have those, but they pay for those types of costs," she says.

Getting the commission split right becomes more important when the broker pays all or a portion of associates' variable costs. Those are harder to peg to individual associates than fixed costs, which can simply be allocated on a per-person basis.

At the same time, brokers can face market pressures on where to set commission splits, and those pressures can lead to split levels that won't necessarily accord with what makes sense for your company.

"If every other broker in your area is offering associates a 90 percent split, you must consider offering a 90 percent split, whether or not that makes sense from a cost standpoint," says Grupido. "About five years ago, we had a 50–50 split that graduated up to 80 percent depending on volume; then there was a big push in the market to drive that up, and that push still hasn't dissipated," she says. "Now associates can get up to 90 percent." But she's not bringing in new people at that split; they have to work for it.

Identifying Actual Costs

Getting compensation right becomes particularly important when associates seek help from brokers on big-ticket items, such as personal assistants, or when they have sales teams.

A desk-cost approach to compensating associates with a personal assistant can miss the mark, even if the associates pay the assistants from their share of commissions, because of the way the assistants raise costs to the brokerage.

"The associates may say the assistants don't cost the broker any more, but those assistants need to have a phone line and they use other services," says Cocks. "In the accounting department, someone has to cut them a check, and the broker is still responsible for them, even though they're working under other associates."

Costs from personal assistants can be even more of an issue if an associate taps a less-productive associate in the office to be the assistant. That's because the broker's increased commissions from the associate with the assistant might not be enough to compensate for the loss of the commission from the low producer.

"If the low producer is doing $12,000 in gross commissions a year and is paying the broker a 50–50 split, that's $6,000 you would need to recover if that person goes to work for another associate," says Cocks. And that may not be that easy to do. "If the other associate is on an 80–20 split, that person would have to generate much more business from the assistant than $12,000 for the broker to recover the $6,000."

Match Splits to Costs

When it comes to top producers, splits can require even more finesse.

To be sure, the large volume that top producers generate can help a brokerage in many ways, including intangibles such as the increased visibility that comes from getting more signage out into the market. Go-getters can also help you up your ancillary income by sending more referrals to, say, your mortgage services. But if splits don't adequately reflect costs, top performers can still be a losing proposition for brokers.

Cocks recounts one case in which a broker gave a highly advantageous split and other perks, including use of a company car, to a top performer. The salesperson in fact brought in tremendous volume, but when the broker analyzed the arrangement, the findings were startling: The brokerage was absorbing a $45,000 annual loss on the person. It wasn't until the broker conducted a detailed accounting review that it became clear the costs of the perks were far more than the company splits the associate generated. It made more sense to let the associate go and bring in other associates, at lower splits, to replace the lost volume. And that's what the broker did.

Realistic Look at Savings

You need to look carefully at associate savings as well as costs. Clearly, an associate working from home costs a broker less than one occupying office space. But how you price such savings is tricky.

With the exception of lower occupancy costs—maybe a few thousand dollars a year, depending on where the office is and whether the company owns or rents its space—costs tend not to drop, says Cocks. That's because the associates are still big consumers of brokerage resources, and the fixed costs for such services as phone lines and utilities don't change.

Plus, the drain on some resources can increase, such as the time a broker spends supervising. "You're making more calls, sending more e-mail," says Grupido.

Cocks says it's possible for brokers to get a relatively clear picture of what each associate costs them and to customize compensation plans to each associate based on those figures. His company sells a proprietary software program that calculates what each associate generates in variable costs. The company also touts a survey it conducted among a sample of its clients, both 100 percent and commission-split companies, finding broker revenue increasing almost by a third in the first year of implementing compensation plans for associates based on estimates of what those associates cost to maintain.

Some of CompensationMaster's Findings

Average pretax profit: 6.1 percent (not counting ancillary income).

Average company dollar: 39.1 percent.

Average revenue increase: 31.3 percent.

Those are strong figures when pegged against comparable industry figures, Cocks claims. Anecdotally, average company pretax profit industrywide is 2 percent to 3 percent, according to David Colmar, head of Colmar and Associates in Rancho Santa Fe, California, a real estate research firm. Average pretax profit tends to be higher, near 6 percent, for the country's top performing companies, Colmar says.

Limiting brokerage costs to just fixed costs can also produce stronger brokerage profitability.

At Keller Williams, average brokerage share of gross commission income is considerably less than in the 500 largest brokerages in the country—16.8 percent at Keller Williams offices compared with 29.2 percent for other companies—according to David Jenks, vice president of research and development at Keller Williams Realty International, based in Austin, Texas. Jenks compared Keller Williams figures with industry figures compiled by REAL Trends, a residential real estate information provider.

But Jenks says the company's pretax profits are higher because its brokerage expenses are lower. For the 500 largest companies, brokerage costs average 25.7 percent, leaving a 3.5 percent pretax profit. Costs at Keller Williams offices are 9.6 percent of GCI, which leaves a 5 percent pretax profit after 2.2 percent of income is taken off the top for a company profit-sharing program.

The analyses suggest that accounting for variable costs is the key to setting compensation plans that maximize brokerage income. So, whatever mix of art and science you use to set your plans, make sure you have a clear picture of how much your associates cost you.

—*Robert Freedman. This article originally appeared in the January 2004 issue of REALTOR® Magazine.*

MORE ONLINE

Latest Thinking on Compensation Planning

The National Association of REALTORS®' Information Central maintains a field guide on compensation plans that includes links to more than a dozen articles and books on setting compensation plans for sales professionals. Access to some of the material requires a fee or a site user name and password, available only to NAR members. The field guide is at www.realtor.org, under "Library."

Calculating the Right Compensation Split

A title that's been around for many years is *Compensation Planning: The Key to Profitability*, by David Cocks and Larry Laframboise, 1995, of CompensationMaster. Originally published by the Council of Real Estate Brokerage Managers, an affiliate of the National Association of REALTORS®, the book is now available as a PDF file online at the web site of CompensationMaster, www.compensationmasterusa.com, under "Resources."

2

Operations

Running Multi-Office Loan and Title Companies

> ### QUICK TIPS
>
> Centralize mortgage and title processing.
> Tap video conferencing to handle multiple brokerage offices.
> Let marketing reps attend closings, freeing up sales associates' time.

Whether you're looking into providing ancillary services or you already offer them, it's a challenge to provide the services cost effectively when you operate multiple offices.

Should you place loan and title officers in each location? Or should loan and title officers move from office to office, enabling them to interact with customers and participate in closings as needed?

Before you answer, consider a third option: Centralize your loan and title professionals in one office and have them interact with your customers, including during closings, through videoconferences.

Gary Yarbrough, regional director for Realty Executives in Texas, did just that two years ago, situating a team of loan and title officers at the company's Southlake headquarters. They participate in closings for a number of company-owned and franchised offices. Of course, they don't participate in all deals—only those in which the customers are using Realty Executives' mortgage finance or title services.

Given the technology involved, you can bet setting up the system won't be cheap. In Yarbrough's operation, startup costs totaled about $10,000 per office. That was in 2002, and covered the television hardware and high-speed T1 lines.

But you can count on savings and better quality control over time, Yarbrough believes. A handful of mortgage and title professionals consolidated in a single office can do the work of a number of duplicative staff at each office, and it's easier to ensure uniform work quality. "Your team is smaller but more highly trained," says Yarbrough.

In Yarbrough's operation, 15 mortgage officers and 7 title professionals handle closings for 410 associates working out of 16 offices around the state.

Yarbrough posts a marketing representative in each office to attend the closings. The reps, who are licensed as notaries, facilitate the closings and witness as documents are signed.

With the reps as facilitators, the sales associates who handled the transaction can attend the closings or not, as they see fit, giving them flexibility to concentrate on more value-producing activities, such as prospecting, says Yarbrough.

Loan and title officers and the buyers and sellers each have copies of all documents at a closing. Once buyers and sellers sign the documents, the notary scans and e-mails them to the loan and title officers. The signed originals are also sent by overnight mail to the title officer.

To find videoconference providers, search the Internet for the term "videoconferencing." Yarbrough installed Polycom 323 TV monitors and video hardware. And he recommends investing in sufficient bandwidth to ensure fast video transmission. Look for bandwidth capable of handling at least 384 kilobits of data per second. Yarbrough also recommends installing T1 rather than DSL data transmission lines. You can typically obtain bandwidth service directly from the videoconferencing provider.

In the first year after the launch, some 1,500 transactions—about a third of all Realty Executives transactions in the state—were closed using Yarbrough's videoconferencing equipment and the reaction from buyers has been positive. "The customers love it," says Yarbrough.

Thanks to the favorable reviews, other corporate-owned Realty Executives offices are looking to put their offices on the air, too.

—*Robert Freedman. This article originally appeared in the February 2003 issue of REALTOR® Magazine.*

MORE ONLINE

Videoconferencing Services

REALTOR VIP® Alliance Program partner Conference Plus Inc. offers video, audio, and Web conferencing services. The REALTOR VIP® Alliance Program is operated by the National Association of REALTORS® to link services to NAR members at a discounted group rate. Information on Conference Plus Inc. is at www.realtor.org under "REALTOR VIP®."

Growing without Adding Staff

When Kathy Drewien, ABR®, CRS®, launched North Atlanta Realty Group in Marietta, Georgia, in February 2003, she brought with her a habit from her days as a sales associate that she thought was too valuable to break: using virtual assistants to help her manage leads and market listings, and to coordinate transactions. Now she makes virtual assistants available to her associates.

"Virtual assistants enable me to offer my associates support services so they can focus on income-producing activities without my having to add staff to my payroll," says Drewien. She has even ensconced a VA in her office who works for noncompeting brokers. In exchange for a desk, the VA pays a portion of her earnings to Drewien.

VAs are typically home-based administrative support specialists who, in real estate, use the Internet to do everything in-house support staff do except post signs and hang lockboxes. And because geography is no barrier, you can choose from a national, or even international, talent pool.

The services of real estate specialists typically fall into two categories: listing coordination and transaction coordination. Listing coordination, which can include lead management and marketing support, is generally charged on a per-hour basis and sometimes on retainer, requiring a minimum number of hours per month, typically 10. The usual rate is $30–$60 per hour. Tasks include:

Creating a Web presence for listings.

Creating and sending just-listed postcards to consumers and practitioners.

Managing leads.

Transaction coordination is generally charged on a per-transaction basis, usually $250–$350 per transaction, but brokers might negotiate a discount based on the number of associates using the services. A reasonable workload is 30–40 transactions a month. Tasks include:

Uploading contract information to an online platform.

Monitoring deadlines.

Maintaining and monitoring transaction files.

If you're ready to contract with a virtual assistant:

Hire different assistants for different types of tasks. "Don't expect a listing coordinator to also do transaction coordination," says Kim Hughes, president of Kim Hughes and Co., a virtual assistant company based in Mineola, Texas. "The tasks call for different skills, and each can be time-consuming." If you want both types of service, see whether the assistant has a relationship with another who has a different specialty. Many virtual assistants form teams of complementary specialties.

Assess how the virtual assistant responds to your initial contact. If your first contact is during business hours, a virtual assistant should respond within an hour or two if not immediately. "If a virtual assistant takes 12 hours to respond, that's unprofessional," says Hughes.

Don't lock yourself into a long-term contract. There's no reason a contract should require more than 5 to 10 days' notice before termination, says Karen Ann Drebes, president of Source for Sources Inc., a Scottsdale, Arizona, virtual assistant company specializing in transaction management.

Demand confidentiality. Your agreement should include a clause binding the virtual assistant to confidentiality because the person will be handling proprietary information, says Hughes.

Don't subsidize a virtual assistant's training. It's not your job to pay virtual assistants to learn a particular computer application. If the assistant you're considering doesn't know the application, there are others who do, says Drebes.

> —*Robert Freedman. This article originally appeared in the January 2005 issue of REALTOR® Magazine.*

MORE ONLINE

Finding Real Estate Virtual Assistants

The Real Estate Virtual Assistant Network, at www.revanetwork.com, and the International Virtual Assistants Association, at www.ivaa.org, offer search tools to help you find virtual assistants specializing in real estate.

Researching the Pros and Cons of Virtual Assistants

REALTOR® Magazine Online maintains articles that aim to help you decide whether virtual assistants are right for your brokerage. Read these pieces at www.realtor.org/realtormag and enter search keyword "virtual assistants."

Disaster-Proofing Your Brokerage

QUICK TIPS

Maintain remote access to your office programs, records.

Don't skimp on record keeping.

Involve associates in decision making.

Put contingency planning on your radar screen.

Misfortune often strikes a business without clear warning—whether in the form of an accident to you or a key employee, an act of nature, a disgruntled customer, or a management predicament of your own making. Are you ready to deal with the unexpected? Here's how four fast-thinking brokers reacted decisively to keep calamity from putting their business on the skids.

Case #1: Ship Shape

Under a gleaming summer sky, with a whiff of sea breeze coming in from the coast near his home in Sayreville, New Jersey, Ken Stanley, CRB, took a step back as he wrapped up some repairs on his boat.

The boat had been in dry dock, and he hoped to spruce it up before putting it up for sale in the next few weeks.

Then his foot slipped, and he fell 10 feet to the ground. An hour later, he was in emergency care with his knee broken, blood clots in one leg, and facing a three-week stay in the hospital.

As the broker-owner of a small residential real estate brokerage—Realty Executives Home Group in Edison, New Jersey—the veteran Coast Guard reservist found the accident, which occurred in 1999, to be more than a painful trauma; it was a disaster in the making for his business.

With only one full-time and one part-time support staffer and more than a dozen sales associates depending on him for everything from their commission checks to sales advice, much of his operation could effectively have been shut down by the hospital stay. But, not long before the accident, Stanley had upgraded his office computer system, facilitating remote access to his office files. He was able to move his operation to his hospital bed and continue working.

"I was able to generate checks, pay bills—basically, do just about everything I could from the office," says Stanley, an 18-year veteran in the industry. "If I'd had to do everything by hand, it would've been a real mess."

For Stanley, network technology was the answer to keeping his accident from spiraling into a business disaster. But disasters can take any shape, from costly and dispiriting lawsuits to sudden losses of sales associates to office fires. By planning for contingencies and organizing your operations to respond flexibly to unforeseen events, you can turn disasters into stories with a happy ending, say brokers who've navigated their offices through crises.

Case #2: Suited for Battle

For even the most carefully managed real estate brokerage, the threat of lawsuits is a fact of life. At a minimum, the key to disaster-proofing your brokerage is your errors and omissions insurance, say real estate attorneys. That insurance kicks in when you're sued and gives you the resources to defend yourself.

But setting up a thoughtful risk-management plan is equally important, because it reduces the likelihood of your being sued in the first place and gives you a basis for negotiating lower E&O premiums, says Robert Bass, a broker defense lawyer in Phoenix.

At its most basic level, risk management means instituting a sound record keeping policy.

For Duane Fouts, broker-owner of Dan Schwartz Realty Inc. in Phoenix, record keeping is proving to be key to mold litigation he's been fighting for two years.

To the credit of one of his sales associates, who followed company policy and kept a copy of an inspection report giving a clean bill of health to the house that's the subject of the suit, Fouts can document that his associate was unaware of any mold problem. The buyer, who filed the lawsuit, claims the seller and the associate failed to disclose mold spreading under the kitchen sink.

"There's really no way a broker or a manager could have avoided a lawsuit like this," says Fouts, "but there's no doubt we're well prepared for it because our associate did his job."

Adequate documentation is clearly just as crucial in lawsuits you initiate. Thanks to meticulous record retention, David Bronson, broker-owner of Bronson America, REALTORS®, in Binghamton, New York, prevailed in a lawsuit he filed two years ago to secure his commission on a sale he worked on in Ithaca, New York.

Per an agreement he had entered into with the seller, a nonprofit organization, he procured a ready, willing, and able buyer. Then the nonprofit decided not to sell the property. But the nonprofit turned around and sold it a short while later without him. When Bronson filed a lawsuit to claim his commission, the seller argued that the deal Bronson put together was for less than the asking price. But Bronson was able to counter this by producing a handwritten note from the nonprofit organization's treasurer authorizing him to reduce the price of the property to the appraised value, which was the price his buyer had agreed to pay.

"The key document was the price reduction authorization," says Bronson, who received financial help on the case from the New York State Association of REALTORS®. "The treasurer gave a sworn deposition that the organization wanted to sell the property at the appraised value," and the note supported that contention, he says.

Case #3: Mutiny Averted

When a lawsuit strikes, it can feel as if the office is under siege. But there are other disasters that erupt from inside the brokerage. In some cases, personality conflicts or misunderstandings can be a recipe for disaster if the problem isn't diagnosed quickly and treated, say brokers.

When Michael Morelli, a broker with John L. Scott Real Estate in Puyallup, Washington, brought a handful of go-getters into his 35-associate office, the chemistry between him and the newcomers was bad from the beginning. Within weeks, the new group was disparaging him behind his back about even minor problems, such as copier malfunctions. The situation persisted for months, bringing down morale among his other associates. Morelli was tempted to throw up his hands and tender his resignation.

Instead, working with a consultant, he completed a painful self-assessment and rebuilt his management approach from the ground up, with a new focus on building better relationships with the associates.

Morelli now involves associates in decision making, which helps them feel invested in new policies, he says. In addition, he helps associates stay attentive to their performance by having them set and work systematically on clearly defined goals, for both their business and their life. And he responds quickly to the smallest request, including pleas to deal with copy machine problems.

Once Morelli got his relationship troubles under control, increased sales followed. Within a year, he had almost doubled productivity in the office, from about a dozen deals per associate per year to just under 21.

The new management approach wouldn't have taken root if it hadn't been for Morelli's willingness to look deeply into his own behavior and make drastic changes, he says.

"The consultant asked me, 'Who's responsible for what's happening in your office?" and I saw that I was," says Morelli. "By permitting the negative environment to persist for even a short time, I was promoting it."

Case #4: Water, Water Everywhere

Early one morning a few years ago, Stephen Summers, regional director of Realty Executives' Mid-America Region, in Leawood, Kansas, arrived at his office to find his desks, cabinets, computers, and chairs sitting in eight inches of water. After the offices had closed, a small fire had triggered the sprinkler system, which had run for much of the night. Office equipment and furniture were ruined.

The damage created more than an inconvenience. Suddenly, several dozen sales associates had nowhere to meet clients, no office phone system, and no access to their computer files. "We were basically out of business," says Summers.

He moved quickly. Within 24 hours, he had rented office space in a nearby building, hired specialists to retrieve data on his computers, and re-established telephone communications. The temporary space, at not quite 1,000 square feet, was a quarter of the size of his damaged offices, but it gave his associates what they needed most: meeting space and phones.

And, just as important, it was close to the damaged space. That gave his associates a psychological boost, because over the next four months, while their old office was restored, the associates could see progress being made daily and could reassure customers that their temporary space was just that—temporary.

It also enabled him to continue recruiting. "The temporary space wasn't glamorous, but by walking people over to the old office while it was being rebuilt, I could demonstrate to them that we were still a viable office," he says.

Indeed, during the rebuilding process, Summers says he increased the number of associates at his office by 15 percent.

As Summers discovered, even if you can't foresee a disaster, you can generally ride it out with a strong contingency plan and a fast, flexible response. With decisive action on your part, potential disasters can have a happy ending.

> —*Robert Freedman. This article originally appeared in the February 2003 issue of REALTOR® Magazine.*

MORE ONLINE

Brokerage Insurance Providers

Several REALTOR VIP® Alliance Program partners offer insurance for real estate brokerages. The REALTOR VIP® Alliance Program is operated by the National Association of REALTORS® to link services to NAR members at a discounted group rate. Information on the insurance providers is at www.realtor.org under "REALTOR VIP®."

Dealing with a New Competitor

QUICK TIPS

Redouble recruiting efforts.

Emphasize community roots in branding.

Maintain quality service as bedrock.

Joseph A. Horning, president of Shorewest, REALTORS®, in Brookfield, Wisconsin, is striving to maintain his company's 27 percent market share in the southeastern part of the state.

With 850 associates in 16 offices in the region, the company is a formidable player. But the character of its playing field changed dramatically in the past couple of years when industry giant NRT of Parsippany, New Jersey, acquired six local companies.

Not long afterward, First Weber Group of Madison, Wisconsin, entered the market with the acquisition of Prudential Preferred Properties, a 10-office company.

"It's more of a realignment than an increase in competition when a new company comes in," says Horning.

That's because new companies recruit local practitioners to build their sales force. So their entrance amounts to a reshuffling of the market deck among established associates, he says.

Little Rock, Arkansas, broker-owner Roddy McCaskill, of Roddy McCaskill Realty, witnessed a similar reshuffling when a regional powerhouse moved into his market and made a big media push to gain name recognition. Because the new company recruited local practitioners to fill out its sales ranks, its arrival in the market has had virtually no impact on the market share of McCaskill's nine-person office, which relies mainly on referrals and repeat customers for business, he says.

"As long as we work even harder to keep our clients happy, they'll continue to use us no matter what other companies come to the area," says McCaskill.

Horning has challenged his competitors head on: He's grown his sales force by 27 percent in the past year or so. Many of his new associates are veterans of the companies swallowed by mergers. They wanted to be part of an independently owned, family company again, he says.

The new associates have helped Shorewest boost its performance. For the first five months of 2003, the company's dollar volumes in sales and units closed were up 20 percent and 11 percent, respectively, from 2002, Horning says.

With the stakes up for everyone in Horning's market, it's no surprise that the intensity of brand marketing and battle for consumers' attention has increased. "In the last year we've had a mixture of companies claiming they're No. 1 in some respect," says Horning. "It hasn't been that way in the past."

Even so, Horning's confident Shorewest's branding is sticking. The company's been a fixture in the local media, continues to refine its message, which touts the benefits of working with a locally owned and operated company that's also one of the largest independent brokerages in the country, and spends about $1 million a year on radio, TV, and billboard ads reinforcing its name.

Meanwhile, the other companies must explain who they are. "There's always some confusion as they tell their story and get their name known," he says.

That confusion doesn't automatically give the advantage to the long-time local company. But, with redoubled effort and a focus on what brought customers to the company to begin with, an old, familiar name can continue to make good.

Countering Discounters

With their strong spheres of influence, longtime local brokers have a built-in defense against newcomers, say brokers who've had to defend their market share from new players. But the field changes when new players deploy heavy commission discounts to gain market share.

"Discount commissions are my main concern, since I don't have the volume to compete with them," says Henry Bland III, broker-owner of H.C. Bland Realty Co., a small company in Columbus, Ohio.

Bland has a core clientele he considers safe from most newcomers, but someone offering deep discounts could pull some clients away, he says. Which is not to say the clients won't come back if they're dissatisfied with the discounter's service.

A big discounter came into his market a few years ago and made modest inroads into local companies' market share, says Roddy McCaskill of Roddy McCaskill Realty in Little Rock, Arkansas. But after the newcomer became embroiled in some lawsuits, McCaskill says, the company lost some of its luster.

"Heavy advertising and cheap commissions enabled the company to stack up impressive sales numbers quickly, but it's impossible to provide service both cheaply and well, because you don't have the sales support," says McCaskill. "Eventually the lack of service catches up with you."

—Robert Freedman. This article originally appeared in the August 2003 issue of REALTOR® Magazine.

Go Commercial—and Help Your Residential Business

> ### QUICK TIPS
>
> Look for home buyers seeking other real estate investments.
>
> Keep identities of commercial and residential divisions distinct while sharing costs.
>
> Recruit sales pros seeking autonomy unavailable at big commercial firms.

When Mike Colohan and his wife, Sandy Murphy-Colohan, launched a Keller Williams residential brokerage in downtown Denver in July 2002, they couldn't help but notice the number of commercial real estate offices around them.

Commercial transaction volume in the area was strong, thanks to high interest by investors spooked by the stock market. And both Colohans had commercial experience, Mike as a developer and Sandy as an associate with a big commercial company.

So within four months of opening their office, they launched a commercial division, Keller Williams Downtown Commercial, recruiting experienced associates from some of the nearby commercial brokerages and attracting several residential associates from within their own office who had some commercial experience.

By July of 2003, with about 14 of its 149 associates operating principally in commercial sales, the company was generating close to 25 percent of its revenue through the new division. "We were fortunate to take on some terrific associates," says Mike Colohan, who, along with his wife, is no longer affiliated with the company.

Launching a commercial division can be a smart move for a residential brokerage whose associates are already generating commercial leads.

"If you're selling a house to someone, there's a chance the buyer is also looking for other investment opportunities," says Ryan Mowery, office manager and commercial division manager at John L. Scott Real Estate, Tacoma North in Tacoma, Washington.

This ready-made source of business can help you establish success in the commercial arena. And your residential associates can generate referral fees, passing the leads along to their colleagues a few desks away. "If you have a big residential office, you could almost live off the commercial leads you generate in-house," Colohan says.

But what does it take to launch a commercial division? Success starts with determination.

You need to convince other commercial brokers of your competence and get the word out to potential investors to whom you've sold homes that their residential company is also a commercial player.

Identity Matters

To overcome the perception that you're a residential company in commercial clothing, it's imperative to launch a commercial division with a distinct identity.

"Commercial brokers protect their listings from residential brokers, because they're afraid if you bring in a buyer you'll muck up the deal," says Colohan. Forging a separate identity signals that you have professional commercial associates.

A separate identity is also critical in persuading commercial associates to leave their brokerages and join yours. They probably won't make the move to a brokerage with primarily a residential identity. "You need to have commercial signs and separate phone numbers," says Colohan. "You can't operate from the back of a residential office if you're going to attract anyone from outside."

It's not necessary to make the division operationally distinct, though. In fact, by sharing costs for office space, administrative services, MLS and association dues, and so on, you enhance your bottom line, say brokers.

Nor is it necessary to make the division legally distinct, as a separate LLC for instance. But if you keep the two under one legal structure, you have to be careful about the extent to which you separate the identities. Among other things, you have to keep the name of the residential brokerage somewhere in the name of your commercial arm. Otherwise, federal regulators might challenge whether your commercial division is really part of the larger operation and make you submit separate filings—for a new LLC, say—to create a distinct entity. Thus, the commercial division at John L. Scott Real Estate, Tacoma North is known as John L. Scott TCN. (TCN stands for Tacoma Commercial Network.)

Attracting Outside Expertise

You can ramp up the expertise of your commercial division in two ways: Help residential associates who want to move into commercial get the experience and training they need, or recruit experienced associates with established practices. You're likely to do a little bit of both, brokers say.

Attracting experienced associates is the fastest way to build your commercial business. Experienced associates bring their clients and listings, which gets your signs out into the community. And as more associates see your signs, they see you as a growing player and may consider joining you.

But, before you get to that point, why would they want to join you? For one thing, they might believe they can write themselves a better deal. "Associates are attracted to us because of the opportunity to make more money," says Colohan. "At our office they can create their own business, and we're very flexible on commission splits—up to 90 percent in some cases."

That's quite different from moving up the ladder in the big commercial operations, brokers say. At those established operations, an associate may work for years helping veteran associates while developing clientele. The commission splits are typically in the 50–50 range for newer associates, and at some companies, less experienced associates have limited flexibility in what market sector—multifamily, office, retail, or industrial—they concentrate on. "If the company already has associates in apartment brokerage, you won't be able to do apartments," says Colohan.

John L. Scott TCN recruited its first outside associate in mid-2003, and it's hoping to add another three or four before the year is out, says Mowery. A move into new office space and the launch of a commercial web site will play a big role in its recruiting strategy, says Mowery.

Building from Within

If you have residential specialists who are ready to transition into commercial sales (see "Spot Commercial Potential"), encourage them to identify a market niche, such as apartment sales.

It's important to them and you that any early leads they uncover not be mishandled. A deal gone bad can give the brokerage a black eye and inhibit recruiting. Associates in transition should consult with you about whether to take or refer these early leads that come their way.

If you don't think they're ready to professionally represent the client and do the due diligence, Mowery says, ask them to refer the lead to a commercial colleague in-house, collect a referral fee, and shadow the colleague to learn how the deal's done.

What else can you do to help associates make the change? Training is essential. Particularly beneficial are programs offering specialist designations, such as the certified commercial investment member (CCIM). The designations can help boost your credibility as much as that of your associates. "The right credentials help dispel the idea that, as primarily a residential brokerage, we're not competent in commercial," says Mowery.

However you go about launching your commercial division, the goal is the same: to stop those commercial leads from walking out the door.

"A lot of residential associates run into deals under \$1 million," says Colohan. "If you have 100 associates, you find a few deals a month." Most associates just tell those leads to call a commercial broker, he says. Instead, why not be that commercial broker?

Spot Commercial Potential

You can't build a commercial division on dabblers, says Harold (Hal) Kahn, CRB, CRS®, broker-owner of Kahn Inc., REALTORS®, in Newburgh, New York.

Commercial deals can become complicated quickly. To put together an industrial project, for example, you need to handle zoning, engineering, development, and marketing issues, among others. That said, it's possible to identify residential associates with the potential to handle some commercial.

Kahn's commercial division is small—three associates—but generates about 15 percent of revenue for a company of 25 associates. In part that's because about a dozen of his residential associates take on relatively simple commercial transactions, such as residential development or small investment properties.

If you have residential associates who want to move into commercial sales, Kahn says, be realistic about whether it's the right move for them.

Are they good with numbers? Commercial sales are more math intensive than residential sales.

Can they detach from the emotional side of sales? If making home buyers smile is a key reason they like real estate, they may not enjoy the more businesslike culture of commercial sales. "If you don't like dealing with engineers, you wouldn't like it," Kahn says.

Are they aggressive negotiators? The back-and-forth in putting together a deal is more intensive on the commercial side.

Can they go six to nine months without a paycheck? Commercial deals typically take a long time, so the payoffs tend to be fewer and further between than in residential. When they do happen, however, the commission is typically bigger than in a residential deal.

—*Robert Freedman. This article originally appeared in the November 2003 issue of REALTOR® Magazine.*

MORE ONLINE

Where Commercial Practitioners Get Their Information

Information on a commercial real estate fundamentals class developed by The REALTORS® Commercial Alliance is online at www.realtors.org under "Commercial." The site also includes resources on commercial real estate law, commercial Internet exchanges (online property databases maintained by local commercial associations of REALTORS®), advanced commercial real estate education, and links to the principal commercial real estate information web sites.

3

Marketing

Increasing Foot Traffic through Your Door

When Nicholas Lagos renovated his 1,800-square-foot residential brokerage office in mid-2002, he had more in mind than just making the space look good.

To be sure, new recessed lighting and an etched-glass sign in the reception area showcasing the name of his Arlington, Virginia, company, Century 21 Gawen Realty, were attractive additions. But they were designed to do something more: attract weekend strollers who may not have thought about shopping for real estate when they went out for the day.

"Everything we've done to the office is intended to make it look warm and inviting—more like home than an office," says Lagos, the broker-owner.

His office location helps, too. For the past 34 years, long before Lagos joined the company in the mid-1980s, the office has been well-positioned in the middle of an old-fashioned, Main Street-like retail strip, which is becoming increasingly dynamic. Today, a variety of nearby restaurants and other businesses attract weekend crowds.

The office has always generated solid foot traffic. But thanks to the renovations, Lagos expects to generate up to 7 percent of his business from foot traffic—up from about 4 percent before the renovations. "What we get from foot traffic isn't that much of a share of our overall business, but it's enough to make the investment in the added touches worth it," he says.

Among other things, he's made the office far more visible in the evening, when dinner crowds are thickest. To do that, he directed the recessed lighting in the lobby onto a wall lined with art that's clearly visible from the street. And he installed lighting to illuminate from behind the etched glass sign above the receptionist's desk. "It's very classy," he says.

For the day crowd, Lagos maintains seasonal flowers in rustic planters on either side of the door and keeps a sign advertising his office's notary services on prominent display. The notary services attract a surprising number of people, he says. He also hangs in the front window the company's quality service plaques, which Century 21 awards each year.

Each of the displays in its own small way invites strollers into the office, but his ace in the hole is a large dollhouse he keeps in the lobby, in view of passersby. The dollhouse, surrounded by a couch and comfortable chairs for visitors, isn't for show. It's meant for children to play with—and they do. "It's the thing that catches the most traffic," he says. "A lot of people with kids walk in."

Taken together, the renovations and other small touches add up to a welcoming storefront that encourages people to come inside—and that's all he's hoping for.

"It just makes our customers and our associates feel good about coming here," he says. "It's a family operation, and our office reflects that."

Make Sure You're on Display

If your office is on a high-traffic street that's popular with local civic organizations for hosting parades or crafts fairs, you can boost your business by giving your office a place in the festivities.

Each year, Charles Fishback makes sure his company, Olde Loudoun Realty in Leesburg, Virginia, is part of his town's August Court Days, a colonial-themed antiques and crafts fair that raises money for historic preservation. Fishback and his associates man a table outside his office, located on the town's main strip, to publicize his specialty selling country estates.

During the 2001 fair, a person relocating from Ohio visited his table and ended up buying an old schoolhouse that had been converted into a house. "The buyer and her sister were having lunch in a nearby restaurant and saw our display," he says.

—*Robert Freedman. This article originally appeared in the June 2003 issue of REALTOR® Magazine.*

Winning the Publicity Game

When Chicago's WGN-TV aired a segment in February about young adults taking advantage of record low interest rates to buy their first home, the station turned to Thaddeus Wong, broker of @properties, for commentary on the trend.

Wong, co-founder of the Chicago-area brokerage, had the fortune of speaking to 213,000 households that were watching that weekday evening news program.

Wong's placement on the show was no accident. The segment had been conceived and pitched to a WGN news producer by a public relations agency hired by @properties in September 2002 to help the relatively new brokerage increase its profile in the Chicago area. So when the segment was shot, Wong got the call to make an appearance.

The Public Relations Approach

Without a doubt, such publicity has marketing value that advertising dollars can't buy. Consumers attach credibility to an appearance in a news piece that they won't always attach to paid advertising.

What's more, an appearance in a news program is positioned to cut through the busy media environment and attract consumers to a degree that paid advertising can't be expected to match.

To be sure, brand marketing and listing advertisements are part of real estate brokerages' stock in trade. Many companies get by without the help of a professional public relations company. But when you seek to supplement paid marketing with a systematic approach to media coverage, the services of a PR company might make sense.

A comprehensive media strategy integrates PR into your conventional marketing. So in addition to the weekly newspaper ad, marketing brochures, web site, and yard signs, you strive to achieve targeted news coverage of your company in local publications and appearances on television and radio.

The value of the whole becomes greater than the sum of its parts as the various publicity elements complement each other to deliver a consistent message to consumers.

Find Your Message

The first step in developing a comprehensive strategy that includes PR is determining what you want to achieve through your media outreach efforts.

@properties, launched in March 2000, was making a name for itself working with new-home developers. Its marketing plan relied on a weekly one-page listing ad in the *Chicago Tribune*, direct-mail postcards sent by its associates, a web site, and yard signage. Its principals and associates were rarely quoted in the media.

But the company wanted to expand beyond new-home sales, so Wong and his partners set some PR goals: to convey an image as an energetic, professional, and knowledgeable organization with a high level of customer service; to increase the visibility of the @properties brand; to grow the existing-home sales business; and to project the image of a top-tier company.

The company looked at several PR agencies and entered into a contract with our agency, Taylor Johnson Associates, in part because of its experience working with other real estate clients, including builders and lenders. (See "Finding a PR Agency.")

In the early stages of the relationship, our associates met with @properties executives to identify its marketing needs and develop story ideas, such as the WGN piece on young home buyers, that could showcase the company's expertise.

There's no hard and fast way to work with a PR agency. The agency should educate itself on your business and identify story opportunities; brainstorming sessions with clients to identify story ideas are often part of the mix.

If you're seeking TV and radio coverage, the PR company can typically provide you and other spokespersons you select with media training. Such training can help clients who are uncertain about their presentation skills become more comfortable with the camera.

With the @properties media program now beyond its second year, Wong and others at his 110-plus associate company have become visible spokespersons on real estate matters, even though the company isn't yet half a dozen years old.

Financial gain is difficult to quantify when it comes to PR. @properties closed $272 million in sales in 2002. By the third quarter of 2003, one year after contracting with our agency, it expected to exceed $440 million in sales volume by the end of the year. The company's increase in closed volume can't be directly attributed to increased media exposure. But the figures suggest that media exposure can help a company as it matures and seeks new business.

What are some of the ways you can expect an agency to help you? There are several.

1. *Establish your reputation as an expert.* The next time a TV, radio, or print reporter interviews a real estate broker in your market about home sales trends or other industry matters, ask yourself why that broker got the call. There's a good chance the broker had an agency to broach the contact with the reporter.

   It's the job of a PR professional to maintain contact with editors and reporters in the various media and to help position the client as an articulate source of story ideas and industry information.

   Business editors and reporters need seasoned industry professionals to help them identify, understand, and communicate business trends impacting their community. As a broker, no one knows what's going on in real estate better than you, and that puts you in a good position to help media professionals do their jobs.

   Companies that provide timely and objective market information to editors and reporters obtain regular publicity and acquire the reputation of experts in their fields.

   "The increased visibility we've achieved through our media appearances has attracted customers," says Wong. "Plus, it's improved our recruitment of associates and our reputation among our developer clients."

2. *Build your relationships with media contacts.* Since reporters often return to the same sources, it's key for brokers to nurture media rela-

tionships with calls and letters. You can do that by regularly sharing news tips and article suggestions or even just complimenting a reporter on a story.

The strategy has worked well for @properties. In July 2003 Wong provided commentary on third-quarter national housing figures for WBBM-AM's *Noon Business Hour* broadcast; since then, he has received a steady stream of invitations to appear on the program.

3. *Reach diverse media.* A well-rounded publicity program includes both print and broadcast media (television and radio). As a rule of thumb, consumers turn to newspapers to learn about what's going on in and outside their community and to broadcast media to be entertained.

When it comes to print publicity, the real estate section in your local papers provides a way to reach a targeted audience of people who are interested in the industry and its services. But your options for coverage in print extend beyond the real estate section to the news, lifestyle, and business sections of your local paper, as well as to local and national trade and consumer magazines.

Practitioners also can be good sources for lifestyle articles, such as stories on home renovation trends and hot new neighborhoods, and for business articles that touch on real estate, such as property price trends. (See "Generating Story Ideas" for more topics you can pitch to reporters.)

TV and radio have the potential to reach tens of thousands of consumers. The entertainment focus of broadcast media makes it possible for brokers to use radio and TV to help put a human face on their company and convey a personality that appeals to consumers.

@properties has tapped broadcast media to convey a reputation for professional, knowledgeable, articulate, and charismatic brokers and sales associates. The lively dialogue of TV and radio has helped promote this image by showcasing the personalities, not just the expertise, of the @properties representatives.

4. *Establish a crisis communications plan.* Difficult issues arise in even the most solidly run brokerages: You may be hit with a mold-related lawsuit or someone may be injured at a development you're involved in.

When a crane at one of our builder clients' construction sites fell onto a nearby structure, we provided the media with timely, accurate information and quotes from the builder. We believe this quick response, coupled with the builder's candidness, helped preempt negative coverage that would have resulted had reporters confronted a wall of silence from the builder. Such an outcome wouldn't have been possible without a crisis communications plan.

Your PR agency can help you prepare a set of procedures to follow in a crisis and can help you identify a spokesperson. The spokesperson should be someone in a senior position at the brokerage, not a PR rep. A rep won't know as much about the company or industry as you. And, in a crisis, the company should speak for itself.

In your plan, aim for containment of information, not suppression. Be truthful, and choose words carefully. Look to your PR agency to provide strategic crisis counseling that clearly communicates a company's position and to field media inquiries.

With well thought out procedures, your crisis might be contained to one story, instead of several over a few days.

Plus, with an integrated marketing plan that includes PR, you'll get coverage about the things you do want people to know about.

—*Emily Johnson. This article originally appeared in the December 2003 issue of REALTOR® Magazine.*

TAKING CONTROL OF YOUR OWN PR

A strong public relations effort begins and ends with knowing what editors and reporters need and how to work with them. Here are a few trade tips.

Read the newspaper section you're targeting for coverage carefully to know what the editors cover and how they cover it. You can identify editors' names through the publication's masthead or at the publication's companion web sites, generally in the "Contact Us" section.

Reporters receive a lot of mail. Be sure your releases have news value. Although a new deal may be important to you, be sure it fits into a genuine news story before sending it.

When meeting with a reporter, offer several story ideas to increase your value as a source.

Follow up. If you commit to providing an answer to a reporter by a certain time, do so.

Many reporters work odd hours; provide your home, cell, or pager number.

Avoid using industry jargon for a consumer-oriented article.

If you're not the best source to address a topic, refer the reporter to someone who is.

Buying an ad in a publication doesn't mean you should expect story placement.

Never double-place exclusives (never give the same story to competing publications).

Think of yourself as a source of a story, not as its subject. Single-source stories (about one real estate broker) are rare. It's more reasonable to suggest broad stories with several sources.

When calling reporters, ask if they're on deadline before launching into a conversation. You want to show that you appreciate their schedules and ensure that you have their full attention.

FINDING A PR AGENCY

There are several ways to identify public relations agencies to interview.

1. Ask local real estate editors whose work they value.
2. Track which real estate companies obtain regular publicity and find out the name of their agency, if they have one.
3. Identify agencies with a client base that includes other real estate brokerages and real estate–related companies, such as builders and lenders.

PR SERVICES IN A NUTSHELL

In general, what services can you expect a public relations agency to provide you?

Guidance developing a comprehensive communications strategy that matches your strengths and goals to different media.

A list of press contacts.

A reputation with journalists for providing timely, factual, objective information on your behalf.

Professionally written materials tailored to the style and content needs of particular publications.

Opportunities for exposure in a wide range of media outlets.

Help preparing for interviews.

Help controlling potentially negative publicity to head off lasting damage to your company's reputation.

How much can you expect to spend for PR services? Costs can vary dramatically depending on the level of service you're looking for. You should have a contract with the PR agency that spells out what services you'll receive for what price. Each contract is negotiated on a case-by-case basis, and there's no standard pricing, even within a market.

GENERATING STORY IDEAS

Being quoted in the real estate section of your local newspaper is a surefire way to boost your visibility as a sales pro. But real estate brokers also can position themselves as good sources for articles in other sections of the newspaper, or in national business or trade magazines. Here are some questions to ask yourself as you brainstorm pitches for the media.

Community Lifestyles

Are you seeing more single buyers in your market? That information could fit into a story on changes in the household.

Are second-home purchases increasing in your area? That trend could play into a story on changing recreational tastes.

Are more home owners remodeling? What are the latest tastes in kitchens, backyard decks, landscaping?

Business Trends

Is an old business district on the rebound? If so, what does that mean for surrounding property values?

Are properties sitting on the market longer than before? That slowdown might relate to recent changes in broader economic events.

Handling Negative PR

One of your sales associates is arrested for criminal activity or a fire destroys client records at your office, and reporters are calling you to learn more. The last thing you want is negative publicity. But beware the no-comment approach: That'll only focus laser beamlike attention on your situation.

"You have to proactively manage your reputation in a crisis or else others, including your competitors, will do it for you," says Reed Byrum, an expert in crisis communications, a past president of the Public Relations Society of America, and principal of Strategic Communications in Austin, Texas.

To prepare your company, he says:

1. *Make a plan.* Even the most experienced and articulate broker or office manager can become rattled in a crisis, potentially mishandling press inquiries. That makes a written plan key. Yours should outline what kind of crises you could face:

   Criminal activity. A company broker or sales manager faces damaging allegations, affecting the reputation of the entire organization.

   Statutory and regulatory initiatives. Your efforts to push for zoning changes that would benefit your company attract critical media coverage. Or residents at a public hearing oppose development of affordable housing you're involved in.

   Workplace violence. An associate or staff member is involved in an on-site altercation.

   Environmental disaster (manmade). You represent a developer alleged to have disregarded toxic chemicals buried on a site.

   Product disaster. A vendor to whom you refer clients begins providing substandard service, or one of your associates is alleged to be receiving kickbacks for sending business to certain vendors.

   Terrorism. Since the September 11, 2001, terrorist attacks, political violence is something you can't ignore, even in your own city. In Northern Virginia, home of the Pentagon, which is less than a mile from residential neighborhoods, brokers were quick to speak to the media after the attacks, local practitioners told

REALTOR® Magazine. Their message: The market remained strong.

2. *Develop a process.* Have a game plan for each potential crisis. Who's the designated person who should gather facts? When do you go public with what you know? How often do you update known facts about the situation? In what way can the public have access to factual information?

3. *Appoint a spokesperson.* The person should be a broker or office manager with decision-making authority and, if possible, visibility both inside and outside the company. Media training can help prepare that person to remain levelheaded. (See "Should I Hire a PR Adviser?")

4. *Execute the plan.* Rules of thumb:

> *Employees first.* Before you talk to the media, communicate the situation to your associates and employees. Tell them what happened, what you plan to do, how you'll communicate to the media, and who your spokesperson is. Although you don't want them taking it upon themselves to communicate with media, you do want them on the same page to squelch internal rumor.
>
> *Be proactive.* Make contact with the media before they contact you. That way, you can frame the situation as you see it, get out the facts, and explain what's being done.
>
> *Stick to the facts.* If there was a gas leak in an apartment you manage, provide the media with information such as who's been affected, what you've done to help them, who's been taken to the hospital, if anyone, and whom to contact at the hospital for more information.
>
> *Quash rumors.* Set up a web page or dedicated phone number where you post the latest facts.

Above all, be honest. Not only is it the right thing to do, but it keeps the focus where it belongs: on solving the problem, rather than on your company's character. Says Byrum: "If you stop being honest, candid, and factual, you'll just increase media scrutiny on your company."

—Robert Freedman. This article originally appeared in the April 2004 issue of REALTOR® Magazine.

SHOULD I HIRE A PR ADVISER?

You can develop a crisis communications plan on your own, but unless you have an experienced communicator look it over, you won't know you've missed something until you're deep into a crisis, says Reed Byrum, principal of Strategic Communications in Austin, Texas.

Costs for hiring a public relations firm will vary greatly, depending on the size of your company, the scope of your plan, and your market area. To find a firm, Byrum suggests you start with a local chapter of the Public Relations Society of America, which are listed at PRSA's web site, www.prsa.org. He recommends PRSA members with an Accredited in Public Relations (APR) designation.

MORE ONLINE

Tips and Techniques: Crisis Management

The Public Relations Society of America offers materials on crisis management, including self-study materials to acquaint you with setting up a crisis public relations plan, at its web site at www.prsa.org under the self-study section "Resources." PRSA charges a fee for the program.

Getting the Most Bang for Your Ad Buck

QUICK TIPS

Track where callers heard about your company.

Shift print ads from listings to brand building.

Rely on Web for marketing listing inventory.

This summer marks a sea change in how Reece & Nichols, REALTORS®, the regional residential real estate powerhouse in Leawood, Kansas, spends its advertising budget.

The 2,300-associate company is spending $400,000 in 2005—two-thirds of its annual marketing budget—on Web advertising. The goal: Drive traffic to its web site, www.reeceandnichols.com. The shift marks the first time its Web marketing spending will exceed what it spends on local newspapers and home magazines, which have traditionally consumed two-thirds of its marketing budget.

"It's a big switch for us," says Vicki Riffle, the company's director of marketing. "Over the last year, we've seen a 300 percent increase in people choosing us as their real estate company after finding us online. The Internet is now the buyer's first resource."

Reece & Nichols' new ads—including for the first time on web sites run by local radio, TV, and newspaper outlets—limit company contact info to its Web address. Phone number and mailing address aren't given. "This would have been unthinkable just a few years ago," Riffle says.

The company isn't alone in its shift to the Internet.

With the typical consumer now conducting much of the home search on the Internet, brokers are leading the real estate industry away from traditional media marketing, particularly newspaper classified advertising, to the Internet.

In 1997, brokers and their sales associates spent $755 on newspaper advertising for each home sold, according to media researchers Borrell Associates. In 2004, that figure was down to $605 and Internet ad spending per listing grew from $16 to $148.

What's behind consumers' love affair with web sites?

Efficiency, says Emily Johnson, president of Taylor Johnson Real Estate Marketing, in Chicago. With customized searching by location, price, and product, the Web "is so much more efficient than looking at 15 ads with hundreds of listings and trying to make sense of it all," she says.

And now that they're getting more information online, consumers won't settle for anything less, says Greg Herb, CRB, CRS®, broker-owner of Herb Real Estate, Inc. in Boyertown and Pottstown, Pennsylvania, rural markets near Philadelphia. Herb is also president of NAR affiliated Council of Residential Brokerage Managers.

"The consumer's need for information is different from ten years ago," says Herb. All consumers needed then was the office phone number. But the "Internet-enabled consumer" of today demands more, starting with the price and location—and lots of photos or streaming video, he says.

The Web isn't just making consumer searches more efficient; it's making broker ad spending more efficient, too, brokers say, because it enables them to track what consumers are looking for, how many times they visit a site, how they got there, how many forms they filled out, and how much time they spent there. Such data enables brokers to adjust their product and service mix to reflect what consumers want.

"The accountability of the Web is a big plus," says Riffle.

That's not to say brokers can track only customers on the Web. Like many brokerages, Reece & Nichols surveys customers to find out how they learned about the company—over the Web, by referral, from a yard sign—and gets a solid 20 percent response rate, enough to give it a credible data source for tracking where their customers are coming from, says Riffle. But surveys are costly and labor intensive compared to the automated tracking you can do on the Web.

Other Media Still Relevant

The trend to the Web doesn't mean brokers are forsaking other media. Brokers continue to put money into newspapers, magazines, television, billboards, and marketing events such as home buying seminars, but the nature of those marketing efforts is now principally brand building and to drive people to the Web.

Brand building has always been part of print marketing, but it was never the main focus as it is now, say brokers. What's more, even inventory ads in newspapers today are equally about brand building and getting people to the Web, where they get complete listing information. "Listing ads have gone the way of branding ads," says Johnson. "Typically, listing ads will also have a strong call to action to visit the company's web site for listing information."

What's the latest thinking on how to dole out brokerage ad spending? Here are some thoughts from brokers and marketing specialists.

PRINT

@properties, a residential brokerage launched in Chicago in 2000 and now with 250 sales associates, devotes most of its ad budget to print but it's not to advertise listings in classified ads; it's to build its brand and get people to the Web. "We need print ads to maintain exposure to the market," says Thaddeus Wong, company co-founder.

The high cost of newspaper advertising, which Wong calls "grossly expensive," doesn't help. Wong couldn't share the amount it spends annually on its various forms of advertising, but print ads consume about three-quarters of its annual marketing budget, which is in the millions.

Limiting newspaper advertising to brand-building print ads is also the strategy of Herb. Classifieds, "with their crazy hieroglyphics we use as practitioners," don't fit the new information-rich paradigm of the Web, he says.

Herb devotes about 8 percent of his marketing budget to newspaper display ads, which he estimates generates 1 percent of the calls to his company. (For breakdown on his ad spending to consumer inquiries, see "Worth the Ad Cost?") The ads drive a much higher percentage to his web site, he thinks, although he doesn't have numbers to show that.

CABLE TV

Herb thinks that cable TV, while expensive, remains a strong medium given the number of leads it generates in his market. He typically attracts about 12 percent of his calls from cable TV, but to get that he spends close to 38 percent of his marketing dollar.

Herb divides his cable TV spending between a local channel, where he can reach about 100,000 people with a daily half-hour real estate program, and a regional cable channel, where he buys a daily 30-second spot that can reach a far greater number of people but at a far higher cost than the local channel. Given its limitations, the 30-second spot is only about brand building; the 30-minute program showcases his inventory.

BILLBOARDS

Herb also likes company branding on sport stadium billboards, a nice fit with his company's sponsorship of youth soccer. Plus, it's an economical buy. For about 3.5 percent of his marketing costs, which includes all types of outdoor marketing, including his yard signs, he generates more than a third of his calls.

EVENTS

First-time home buyer seminars and condo opening parties, among other events, are a good brand builder. "People feed off the energy," says Johnson about the parties. "It creates a sense of urgency: 'I better buy now before it's too late.'"

Events are a key part of @properties "cross branding" strategy of getting the company name into different media to tap the strength of each type, says Wong. An example: The company hosts an annual running race, called the @properties Bucktown Run, which associates the company with the young, upwardly mobile clientele it targets.

FREE PRESS

Mentions in key local publications, including the *Chicago Tribune* and *Crain's Chicago Business*, has been a huge brand-building avenue for @properties, says Wong.

Although the mentions are free, since they're editorial coverage, they're not without cost. Wong pays a professional public relations company to help get his company name into reporters' Rolodexes. Costs of PR consultants vary widely based on the level of services you want. And it's hard to measure how much you spend against the number of calls it attracts, but there's no doubt a prominent mention in an authoritative article or TV or radio show can give a company credibility that ads can't buy, says Wong.

Your Message Here

You've laid out your budget and figured out where you want to advertise. How do you go about deciding what message to put across? The main rule to follow: Keep it simple.

"A message is more memorable if the consumer can get it quickly," says Wong. @properties eschews sloganeering but tries to drive home the idea that its sales associates are forward-thinking, in tune with the marketplace, and tech-savvy—just like the hip, urban professionals that the company targets.

How it does that without having a tag is by the look and feel of its marketing. "The type, tone, design, photography—everything about their collateral—is young, edgy, urban," says Johnson, whose company consults on marketing for @properties. "There is energy in everything they do."

Reece & Nichols' top-of-mind message is "Where sold means more," and is meant to convey a value proposition to the 35–55 age group and, secondarily, to women, because they typically drive the buying decision in the family. Using the slogan as a starting point, print and other ads all steer customers to the company's web site where information on the range of company services, including mortgage, title, and homeowners insurance, is available.

"Years ago, the image was all about the company and the associate," says Riffle. "Today, it's just as important to ask, 'How can I help you, Mr. and Mrs. Buyer or Seller?' Service is the name of the game. 'Where sold means more' is meant to convey that."

The quick message for Herb is, "The tradition of excellence continues," adopted about four years ago when the company turned its focus to its brokerage activities after a stint emphasizing one-stop shopping. "We felt we needed to revert back to a focus on brokerage and customer service from one-stop shopping," says Herb.

Whatever aspect of your business you showcase in a simple message, be consistent, says Johnson. That itself can be beneficial in keeping your company differentiated from others. "The public gets confused," she says, "and starts asking, 'Who are you today?'"

Given the shift in where brokers are directing company ad dollars, it's clear consumers will increasingly discover who you are by exploring your company on the Internet—but not without learning about your company first in print, on billboards, and on TV.

—*Christopher Wright. This article originally appeared in the July 2005 issue of REALTOR® Magazine.*

WORTH THE AD COST?

How many phone calls, visits, or online inquiries to your business does it take to make your ad spending worthwhile? That's a number brokers can differ widely on depending on how much marketing money they're willing to spend to get results, among other things.

But before you can get to that question, you must measure where your customers are coming from. That's easier to do online—where you can track your visitors as they click around your site—than it is offline.

Reece & Nichols, a regional brokerage with 2,300 sales associates headquartered in Leawood, Kansas, surveys its clients after their transaction closes. The company gets about a 20 percent response rate, a figure

Vicki Riffle, company marketing director, believes is large enough to make it a valid source of information as the company plans its marketing budget. Survey response in 2004 indicated a 300-percent jump in company Web traffic last year, spurring the company to up its Web advertising significantly for this year.

Greg Herb, CRB, CRS®, broker-owner of Herb Real Estate, Inc., in Boyertown and Pottstown, Pennsylvania, rural markets near Philadelphia, employs a full-time call coordinator, one of whose main jobs is to find out how a caller learned about the company. The coordinator maintains that information in a database. "I would have predicted that the people who call us after watching us on cable TV would have dropped dramatically after our presence on the Web grew, but that's not what we learned from tracking our calls," says Herb. As a result, Herb continues to make cable TV a big part of his marketing budget.

As a case study, here's a look at the percentage of calls Herb received from selected media in 2004 and how much his company spent that year on marketing in each of the media. Not all media are included, so percent of budget figures doesn't total 100.

Adding Up Ad Spending

	Calls	Budget Spending
Signs	36%	3.5%
Internet	20	20.6
Books, magazines	13	15.3
Cable TV	12	37.6
Events	3	8.7
Newspapers	1	7.9

Source: Herb Real Estate, Inc.

MORE ONLINE

Real Estate Ad Spending Trends

Borrell Associates tracks local real estate and other ad spending trends. It charges for reports but offers free report summaries from its web site at www.borrellassociates.com under "Reports."

Planning

Growing Your Business

Grow or die. That's the survival-of-the-fittest philosophy many company owners hold. If you're eager to grow your business, you need to know how to expand smartly, without flaming out. One of your first tasks? Deciding whether to acquire another company and consolidate back-office services or grow organically by opening another office from scratch. The strategy you choose will depend on your objectives and organizational structure.

Generally speaking, if you want to increase revenue quickly, acquisition is your best bet. You can accomplish this in one of two ways:

1. If you're acquiring an office that's geographically close to an existing office, and company cultures are similar, you can consolidate.
2. If you're trying to gain a foothold in an entirely new market, then acquisition without consolidation makes sense.

When speed is less of an issue, organic growth—that is, opening offices from the ground up—is often the better option. It's a realistic approach for your company if you're finding brokers and associates, in an area where you're not represented, actively seeking to affiliate under your banner.

My company, Alain Pinel Inc., REALTORS®, based in Saratoga, California, has gone the organic route. We've grown to more than 1,000 sales associates in 20 offices, up from one office in 1990, largely by launching new offices at the rate of at least one per year. In 2003, the company ranked seventh in sales volume and forty-second in transaction sides in the United States, according to REALTOR® Magazine's Top 100 Companies survey.

What's more, the company has executed this strategy in Northern California, the heart of where residential real estate giant, NRT Inc. of Parsippany, New Jersey, has made some of its biggest acquisitions. Full disclosure: I served as senior vice president of NRT for the Western region through the late 1990s and early 2000s.

How has Alain Pinel added an office a year? Part of our appeal has been that the company offers brokers and salespeople an independent alternative in the rapidly consolidating market.

Of course, you can't grow your company just by being an alternative for salespeople looking to make a change. Your company must be a place associates want to join on its own merits. As a homegrown independent with solid name recognition, Alain Pinel was poised to leverage its brand with associates in new markets.

Finding the right site for a new office is a key consideration. Our most recent launch, in late 2003 in Burlingame, a high-end San Francisco submarket, is a good example of how to do it.

We sited the office adjacent to our office in San Mateo, enabling us to buy advertising for both areas through one media market. The location also capitalized on the fact that our listing signs already dot the neighboring market.

As a result, we found acceptance in the marketplace more quickly than we would have had we not started with some local recognition of our company image and reputation. (For more detail, see "Fast Push into Burlingame.")

If you choose your location well, profitability will follow—but generally not right away. The cost to launch an office from scratch is significant. Although expenses will vary by market, you can expect your rent, tenant improvements, and equipment to easily total $250,000 for an office that's about 5,000 square feet. You also need to factor in your probable operating loss for the first year or two, which might total as much as $250,000 to $500,000. Further, expect it to be at least 120 days before any revenue comes in by way of closed sales.

If planned well, your new office could be profitable within a year. But be financially prepared to wait two or three years.

Acquiring Heft

Acquisition is a faster process. By purchasing an established office, you instantly add associates to your organization and, by consolidating functions, you can lower your operating and marketing costs. Assuming you buy a company that has offices in the same area as yours, you could house managers and associates in fewer offices and locate back-office operations at a single site.

In one case, when I was with NRT, we acquired a company with $4 million in annual administrative costs, an amount almost identical to the costs of our existing overhead in the market. By combining the two companies' operational functions, we were able to reduce overall costs by $3.5 million with no adverse impact to our branches or sales associates. To do that, however, we did have to reduce some of the support staff made redundant through the merger.

We were also able to merge 10 of the acquired company's offices with our established offices. The hard cost of operating each one of those offices was about $500,000 per year. By merging, we reduced our costs by $5 million annually.

We saved on marketing, too. Where each company might have spent $2 million annually in marketing, the combined operation reduced total spending to $3 million, for $1 million in savings. Thus, the combined cost–benefit of the acquisition was $9.5 million, and the merged operations were, I believe, stronger than when we started.

Assimilation Is Key

For such savings to take root, the mergers must be effective. And that requires the people at the acquired company to adopt the vision of the acquiring company, or at least feel that the merger will ultimately be to their benefit.

If associates and brokers don't adopt the new culture or otherwise feel hopeful about their future, they'll look for other affiliation opportunities. How can you help your associates feel they'll be successful in the merged company?

Be open. Sales associates and brokers at the acquired company didn't choose to work with you, and there's little to keep them on board if they feel their needs won't be met in this new environment. So, you should strive to earn their respect.

Maintain continuity. Keep managers of the acquired company in place if you can. Otherwise the merger can feel like a takeover to associates.

Minimize disruption. Show that everything at the office isn't going to change overnight and that only necessary changes will be made.

It's trite but true: People are the key to a successful expansion. Make sure your staff and sales force are ready to go as you piece together your growth strategy.

—Larry Knapp, CRB, e-PRO. This article originally appeared in the June 2004 issue of REALTOR® Magazine.

BEFORE YOU START

Whatever your expansion strategy, be sure you have a strong operational foundation in place. Otherwise, you'll lack the means to sustain your operations as demands on them increase. You need:

A solid game plan. This is an absolute must. Know why you want to grow. Your goal may be to:

Realize greater revenues and profits while keeping your cost and income structure in balance.

Make your company more attractive to future buyers when you're ready to sell it.

Lower per-unit expenses through the efficiencies of back-office and other fixed costs.

In addition, know how you'll grow. You can follow a specific strategy, such as organic growth, or you can mix and match growth plans depending on the situation. For instance, you might expand organically to the next town where you already have market recognition but buy a company that has a strong presence in an area where your company isn't known.

Systems. Do you have strong systems for accounting and financial management, human resources, marketing, training, and information technology (IT)?

Your IT systems are especially important because the real estate industry is seeing an influx of people from other professions who are trained to work with, and expect to have, state-of-the-art technology. These recruits are your top salespeople of the future. Keep them happy.

Financial resources. However you do it, expansion isn't cheap. Acquisition requires significant upfront resources. And organic growth means outputting significant dollars to get a new office up and running before any revenue starts flowing. As a rule of thumb, hold back on organic expansion until you have a financial cushion that can tide you over for at least the first four months of operation.

The right leadership. Your line and branch managers, those directly responsible for the sales- and revenue-generating side of the business, are a critical conduit to the source of your production—your sales professionals. Make sure managers are strong recruiters and provide solid oversight of associates' transactions.

Fast Push into Burlingame

If you plan to grow organically, first decide where you want to expand based on your company strengths. Then cultivate the brokers and sales associates who'll affiliate with your company in the new market.

Alain Pinel, REALTORS®, in Saratoga, California, has developed a reputation as a high-end specialist in Northern California, home to some of the country's most affluent markets. Thus, it was natural for the company to target Burlingame, California, as a key new submarket.

With a current median home price of $1.1 million, according to data from the San Mateo County Association of REALTORS®, the Burlingame area fits our profile. It's also a short commute to San Francisco and Silicon Valley, both of which are established markets for us, and it's adjacent to our office in San Mateo, allowing us to take advantage of our name recognition and existing operations.

We were fortunate in our expansion to this area because a team of top professionals, ready to hit the ground running, came to us last year. But that also meant we had to move fast.

To bring the new team on board quickly, we secured a one-year lease on a space, an office building that had been vacated by a defunct high-tech company. The building is poorly suited for long-term operations. It's off a main road and not large enough for the planned sales force. But it's a space; we installed phones and equipment, which we'll take with us to our permanent location.

I initiated plans for the Burlingame office shortly after I came on board in June 2003, and by November we had 32 associates operating out of the temporary quarters. The number quickly grew to 40, and by early this year, we had nailed down a long-term lease arrangement on a 60-desk permanent office, which will be ready for occupancy this summer.

On tap: A bigger presence in San Francisco and offices in Marin County and the Oakland Hills.

MORE ONLINE

Opening a Real Estate Brokerage Office: The Basics

The National Association of REALTORS®' Information Central maintains a field guide on opening a real estate brokerage. Contents include creating a business plan, exploring business models, and staffing the office. Access to some material requires a fee or a site user name and password, available only to NAR members. The field guides are at www.realtor.org, under "Library."

Scenario Planning: Take Your Future in Hand

Your previously working-class neighborhood gains such cachet that only high-income households can now think of buying there. A major employer in your area folds, throwing hundreds of workers out of work and chilling household confidence throughout the area.

An article on toxic mold in your local newspaper prompts a lawsuit against your company by recent buyers who claim to have found mold in their home.

How well you respond to such scenarios depends on how well you've planned for "what ifs." That's why some brokers are turning to a strategic planning process called scenario planning. Its aim: to ensure your business decisions hold up well in a changing environment.

The classic example of scenario planning is Royal Dutch/Shell Group's anticipation of the oil crisis in the 1970s. As part of a range of scenarios for which it planned, Shell contemplated what was then unthinkable: that oil-producing countries might band together and demand higher oil prices. When members of the Organization of Petroleum Exporting

Countries (OPEC) did just that in 1973, Shell was prepared; it had the jump on its competition because it had already secured long-term oil supply contracts.

Businesses and other major organizations, such as the military, now use scenario planning regularly. The military uses it, among other things, to decide how many troops it needs to fight two regional wars simultaneously.

It makes sense for real estate brokers to use it, too, according to strategic planning consultants. Take the scenario in which your market is appreciating beyond the reach of working-class prospects. A scenario plan, anticipating such an imbalance, might explore moving into different markets that fit your traditional base, getting involved in starter-priced condo development, or targeting your marketing and services toward a higher-end customer. In anticipation of a major area employer folding, a scenario plan might look at opening an office in a part of your market less dependent on a single company or industry. Recognizing the country's mold frenzy, a scenario plan might outline procedures to reduce your company's risk—before a mold article hits the local paper.

"You should spend some time thinking about what isn't right in front of you," says Harold (Hal) Kahn, CRB, CRS®, broker-owner of Kahn Inc., REALTORS®, in Newburgh, New York, and chair of NAR's Research Committee in 2002. "Timing is the critical component in executing any business plan, so forecasting a change in the marketplace is crucial."

The Basics of Creating a Plan

What does it take to embark on scenario planning? Here are a few essential steps:

1. *Analyze.* Start by identifying your company's areas of strength and vulnerability, says David Doeleman, CRB, CRS®, a senior vice president of Bend, Oregon-based Real Estate Champions, a management and sales coaching company. He recommends organizing your evaluation around four basic elements in what's called a SWOT analysis.

Strengths. For example, do you have strong name recognition? Do your management practices help you retain top talent?

Weaknesses. Perhaps you haven't invested as much as your competition in technology. Are you lagging on the Internet compared with others in your market?

Opportunities. Are you well positioned to tap into a new market opportunity? For example, is a strong condo market emerging in your area, with no one company yet establishing itself as a condo specialist?

Threats. Has a deep-pocketed broker entered your market, with plans to launch a media campaign to boost its name recognition?

2. *Identify probable future events.* Look at what may happen over a specified time frame through different perspectives—economic, social, legal, and political—and try to assign some rough probability to each scenario.

   There's no rule for determining a level of probability, says Kenneth P. Riggs Jr., CEO of Real Estate Research Corporation in Chicago.

   Make your best guess on the basis of your knowledge of the market and historic trends in your area. "The assigned level of probability is subjective," he says.

   Here are hypothetical examples of economic, social, legal, and political scenarios affecting real estate practitioners, with assignments of probability.

Economic

Scenario 1: Your area is heavily dependent on warehousing, and, thanks to stagnant retail growth, warehouses are closing or scaling back operations. *Probability: 50 percent*

Scenario 2: Retail growth recovers somewhat, strengthening the warehouse market slightly. *Probability: 25 percent*

Scenario 3: Strong economic growth fuels retail sales, including over the Internet; warehousing sees strong growth, with new facilities coming on line. *Probability: 25 percent*

Social

Scenario 1: Your market is seeing an influx of immigrant households, fueling rental growth but not yet translating into home sale opportunities. *Probability: 85 percent*

Scenario 2: Homebuyer programs with strong outreach spur stronger-than-expected home ownership demand among immigrant buyers. *Probability: 5 percent*

Scenario 3: Business closings and job losses mount. As a result, growth in immigrant households slows, driving rental vacancies, lowering rental rates, and dampening entry-level home sales. *Probability: 10 percent*

Legal

Scenario 1: Your company is hit with several lawsuits when recent home buyers, sensitized by mold stories in the media, seek compensation after discovering mold. *Probability: 5 percent*

Scenario 2: Your company is hit with a single mold-related lawsuit, which gets dismissed as having no merit. *Probability: 65 percent*

Scenario 3: No mold-related lawsuits are filed against your company. *Probability: 30 percent*

Political

Scenario 1: A new mayor is elected to office on a strong smart-growth platform that seeks to channel new residential and commercial development into older developed areas and to curb growth in the suburbs. *Probability: 30 percent*

Scenario 2: Smart-growth candidates fare poorly in elections, and developers discuss plans to build in former pasture area. *Probability: 30 percent*

Scenario 3: Election results deliver mixed representation on the city council with both pro-development and smart-growth lawmakers. *Probability: 40 percent*

3. *Plan your response.* Once you've sketched out scenarios, develop a course of action that aims to address each possible future event. Shoot for plans that address events in multiple scenarios. For example, implementing a plan to curb liability against your company for mold-related claims would be helpful across several scenarios, because it could help keep your E&O premiums down and potentially result in fewer mold-related lawsuits against your associates.

In the case of a new competitor in your market, implementing a plan that boosts your bottom line—internal cost cutting, for example—would benefit you whether or not a deep-pocketed brokerage actually enters your market.

As you get into the planning process, you'll come to realize that scenario planning isn't about predicting the future. It's about extending control over it. As events change, you can change your scenarios and adjust your plans accordingly, and in that way, keep unpleasant surprises at bay.

—*Christopher Wright. This article originally appeared in the March 2004 issue of REALTOR® Magazine.*

SHOULD YOU HIRE A SCRIPTWRITER?

In developing your scenarios and your plans, you need to decide whether to bring in a consultant or do it yourself. "You should strongly consider engaging a consultant when you can't see any plausible scenario other than business as usual," says Harold (Hal) Kahn, CRB, CRS®, broker-owner of Kahn Inc., REALTORS®, in Newburgh, New York.

You can hire a consultant for the entire process or just for specific assignments. Costs will differ by region and level of expertise, but it would be reasonable to pay about $5,000 for a few days of a consultant's time, says Kahn.

Also, be prepared to approach planning regularly. "Planning is a process, not an event," says David Doeleman, CRB, CRS®, a senior vice president with Real Estate Champions in Bend, Oregon. He advises clients to review scenarios every year to see whether conditions remain in line with expectations and to adjust their planning accordingly.

How do you identify consultants? Contact an association of scenario planners, such as the Association for Strategic Planning (www.strategyplus.org)

or the Association of Professional Futurists (www.profuturists.com). Ask staff there about resources for finding planners with relevant business experience. Or ask business-planning instructors with the NAR-affiliated Council of Real Estate Brokerage Managers (www.crb.com) for leads.

MORE ONLINE

Help with Strategic Planning

The National Association of REALTORS®' Information Central maintains a field guide on strategic planning for associations, which includes materials of interest to brokers, including resources on strategic planning for beginners. Access to some material requires a fee or a site user name and password, available only to NAR members. The field guides are at www.realtor.org, under "Library."

Business Models:
New Approaches to Profitability

Larry Whited, CRB, CRS®, believes the big players in residential real estate, wrestling with profitability pressure, will one day soon adopt a business model similar to his: sales associates working out of home offices, accessing documents by computer, conducting their transactions by exchanging electronic files—and offering prospects flexible commission options.

"Big real estate companies five years from now will be virtual offices," says Whited, a 31-year real estate veteran who launched his Cincinnati-area company, Webmls.net, in November 2002. "Big, beautiful offices are history."

That's a bold claim, one that's not shared widely by real estate professionals. But Whited's model and other nontraditional business models have gained currency as brokers wrestle with profitability challenges. Rising costs—driven in part by commission splits to associates now routinely as high as 70 percent to 80 percent—are eating up the company dollar, say brokers. So are higher costs for technology, training, advertising, and office space.

Given these pressures, brokers earn smaller per-transaction margins than they did five years ago—by some estimates, as little as $150 per deal, say brokers.

But brokers who've adopted alternative models say they've found a better way to drive profitability. Here are examples of three alternative models and how they're faring.

Internet Brokerage

Profitability solution: Strong client volume.

Who's doing it: Larry Whited, broker-owner, Webmls.net, West Chester, Ohio.

VIRTUALLY ZERO COST

Larry Whited launched his virtual real estate brokerage, Webmls.net, in November 2002 and within one year affiliated 20 sales associates—and it cost him virtually nothing to do so.

That's because his associates came in with their own clientele, work out of their homes, and cover their own costs. They also pay him $200 to sign on with the company, $50 for each listing they post, and $300 for each closing. There's no commission split.

The main benefit he provides is flexibility on what associates charge and the opportunity to conduct transactions using e-mail and Adobe portable document format (PDF) files.

Of course, Whited's associates still attend meetings and fill out paperwork. But Whited thinks his process reduces much of the back-and-forth of deal making.

How? Here's an example: Cooperating agents are asked to fax offers on Webmls listings. Whited's proprietary system automatically converts each offer to a PDF file, and the associate with the listing e-mails the offer to Whited, who forwards it to the sellers. They counteroffer by e-mail. Once the parties reach e-mail agreement, the associate working with the buyers obtains their signatures on the original contract and faxes the contract to the sellers, who sign it and fax it to their associate. The contract is converted to a new PDF.

"We now have a clean copy of the contract in PDF format, and we have a sale," says Whited. "And no one needed to leave the office."

Whited says he's devised electronic procedures for every facet of the business, including those that are typically done in the office, such as collecting and disbursing commission payments and storing records. As a result, his company maintains neither storefront nor staff.

That low overhead doesn't benefit just him, he says. Because his associates pay him only the flat fees, they have flexibility to attract customers with a range of commission structures. "Brokers with high overhead can't afford to let their associates offer anything but the full commission," says Whited.

Commissions at his company range from 2 percent to 5 percent:

2 percent plus $500 listing fee with 1 percent cooperative split, limited to homes starting at $750,000.

3 percent plus $500 listing fee with 2 percent cooperative split.

4 percent plus $500 listing fee with 3 percent cooperative split.

5 percent with 3 percent cooperative split.

Ninety percent of sellers opt for the 4 percent option, says Whited, leaving associates with a 1 percent commission if there's a cooperating agent. On a $300,000 co-op sale, which Whited calls typical, his associate would receive $3,000 plus $500, minus $350 in fees.

The listing fee is an important part of the mix, because it ensures associates get paid for filling out paperwork regardless of whether the deal closes. "I've earned $25,000 so far this year just in filling out paperwork for my own listings," says Whited. By his count, Whited has listed 50 properties in 2003 through late July.

Whited and his associates tap contractors to manage administrative tasks. They pay a listing coordinator $200 per listing to input data and photos into the MLS and online listing sites; they pay a closing coordinator the greater of $250 or 10 percent of the commission to manage transactions.

Webmls.net is too new to have a track record, but Whited expects to grow his associate roster to 50 by the end of 2004. "Because I have no overhead, I can have an infinite number of associates," he says.

Annuity Brokerage

Profitability solution: Low overhead; high transaction volume, driven by strong recruitment incentive.

Who's doing it: Shaun Rawls, broker-owner, Keller Williams Realty First Atlanta.

GOING FOR THE GOLDEN YEARS

Veteran sales associates have retirement on their minds. As independent contractors, they're responsible for amassing their own nest egg, hence the attraction of a company such as Keller Williams that offers profit-sharing to its associates and carries that profit-sharing through retirement.

That financial lifeline is one of the incentives Shaun Rawls holds out to recruit associates to his office, which launched in 1999 and now has 150 salespeople.

But the benefit is a two-way street. Since the company needs to earn a profit before it can spread the wealth, associates are motivated to help keep costs down. "We keep our books open, so everyone can see where the money is being spent," says Rawls. "This openness makes better businesspeople out of our associates. There's not a lot of waste."

Profit-sharing is based on recruitment: Associates recruit other associates and receive a cut of the profits their recruits generate.

The incentive is seven generations deep, so as one's recruits in turn recruit other associates, the original recruiter continues to receive a portion of the wealth, although in diminishing percentage amounts.

"Some associates make $30 a month, some $100 a month, some several thousand dollars a month" in residual income, says Rawls. In the first six months of 2003, his office shared $211,000, he says.

Rawls builds economy into the administrative structure. The office maintains a closing department and administrative staff, but other services such as marketing and listing input are associates' responsibilities. The company offers a comprehensive tech package, but associates cover the cost of options that go beyond the package.

Rawls caps at $18,000 the amount of annual commission each associate splits with the office. Once associates reach that cap, they keep 100 percent of their commission income, giving them flexibility to plow money into their retirement.

For high-producing associates, the split may be tens of thousands of dollars less than what they'd share with a traditional commission-split company. But it's also largely guaranteed income for the company. Associates who choose a split higher than 70–30 guarantee they'll meet the $18,000 cap.

Many associates reach the cap, Rawls says, because it's set on the basis of market-specific factors, including the competitiveness of the market. It also factors in the cost of running the office to ensure Rawls' expenses are covered.

Rawls believes the formula is working. In addition to his office, he has an ownership interest in two other Keller Williams offices and is set to open another office in Atlanta later this year.

Menu of Services

Profitability solution: High volume; low overhead; fee income.

Who's doing it: Thomas Russell, broker-owner, Help-U-Save, Louisville, Kentucky.

FOR THE DO-IT-YOURSELFER

When consumers call Thomas Russell for help in selling their house, they don't want to see a fancy listing presentation. In many cases they expect to do much of the work themselves, so they like to cut to the chase.

Russell, who launched his company in the Louisville, Kentucky, area some 18 years ago as a self-described discount brokerage, knows how to oblige them.

He offers them a few options:

1. List the house in the local MLS. Cost: $495.
2. Rent a lockbox. Cost: $100.

3. Find the buyer yourself. He negotiates the purchase agreement, writes the contract, helps the buyer find a lender, and closes the deal. Cost: half a percent of the sale amount, plus a $250 transaction fee, plus 3 percent to any cooperating sales-person.

4. Let Russell find the buyer and handle the transaction. Cost: 3.5 percent of the sales price plus $250 transaction fee.

What Help-U-Save receives in exchange for parceling out services in this way is healthy traffic and a way to appeal to high-end sellers, says Russell.

He and another associate, working with two assistants, generate half a dozen listings a week through most of the year. At an average of $300,000, the listings are twice the typical area price, Russell says. That's because his model attracts move-up households who've bought and sold several times and are comfortable taking on a portion of the transaction.

What's more, a sizable portion of sellers opt for full service. In about a third of the listings, he or the other associate will handle the sale, generating the higher commission rate. And on a third of those listings Russell's company helps sellers buy their replacement house, generating another commission. The brokerage claims a 50–50 split on the associate's commission.

Russell maintains an office in central Louisville and keeps the office outfitted with computers using proprietary software to qualify buyers, assess home values, and estimate the seller's net and buyer's expenses. The brokerage also picks up the tab for marketing and signs, which Russell says is minimal.

The model is built around relatively low margins, but with him and the other associate generating some 300 listings a year, the volume keeps income rolling in.

Russell says he'll affiliate a handful of new associates by late fall. "With just the two of us, we're closing one house every 10 days and expect to move that up to one every seven days," Russell says. Why? Because it's a business model that's resonating with customers, he says.

*—Robert Freedman. This article originally appeared in
the October 2003 issue of REALTOR® Magazine.*

Editor's Note: The fees and commissions cited and business models described in this article illustrate only those offered by the practitioners quoted and aren't intended by REALTOR® Magazine or NAR as suggested or recommended business practices for other practitioners. Fees and commissions are established by each brokerage individually and negotiated freely with clients and customers, and each brokerage adopts and establishes its own business practices to best serve its goals and preferences.

MORE ONLINE

The National Association of REALTORS®' Information Central maintains field guides providing insight on alternative business models, including discount and fee-for-service approaches. Look for the field guides on opening a real estate brokerage and fee for service. Access to some material requires a fee or a site user name and password, available only to NAR members. The field guides are at www.realtor.org, under "Library."

Business Models:
Full-Service vs. Limited-Service

With interest rates inching up and price appreciation expected to ease in 2005, will sellers become cost-conscious and assume more transaction work themselves, paying for a few à la carte services? Or will they opt for a salesperson who can deploy the full arsenal of marketing and consulting services to nab them top dollar? In other words, what's the latest word on the full service versus cost savings debate?

For Wes Atiyeh, associate broker at Long & Foster, REALTORS®, in Richmond, Virginia, there's little doubt sellers will call a full-service broker. "In a slower market, sellers have so many more needs than they do in a strong market," he says. "They need different ways to market their house, among other things. That creates a lot of challenges for sellers try-ing to do much of the work themselves."

But Lawrence Bunnell, CEO of InSight Realty, a provider of à la carte selling services also based in Richmond, sees a different reality. "When the market cools, you're not going to get as much for your house," he says. "You're going to have less equity. It makes sense for sellers to go with services that can save them money."

Whether sales slow in the year ahead, there's no doubt that record home sales over the past four years have been good for brokers providing services on an à la carte basis. The reason, says residential brokerage con-sultant John Tuccillo, principal of John Tuccillo and Associates, Arling-ton, Virginia: Listings have been attracting a lot of buyers, making intensive marketing less necessary. "This is the peak [time] for à la carte brokers," he says.

Although no group keeps data on their growth, à la carte brokers are becoming a stronger presence in the industry. The National Association of Real Estate Consultants, launched in 2000 to provide training to prac-titioners offering services on a fee basis, saw its membership leap from about 250 in 2001 to 1,400 at the end of 2004, says Susan Burr, the group's executive vice president. That's a 460 percent increase.

And the number of franchises at Help-U-Sell, the national fee-for-service system based in Syosset, New York, grew from just over 200 at the end of 2002 to 700 at the end of 2004, says Rick O'Neil, company president. That's a 250 percent increase.

There's no one type of à la carte broker. Business models range from providing MLS entry only to full service, but with services ordered indi-vidually. The common thread among à la carte brokers: Each method gives customers a degree of choice.

An analysis of the *2004 NAR Profile of Home Buyers and Sellers* data shows that a small proportion of consumers are making select choices: 7 percent of salesperson-assisted sellers coordinated the appraisal and home inspection, among other third-party services; 6 percent sched-uled showings with buyers; 4 percent held an open house; and 3 per-cent bought newspaper and magazine for-sale ads. The 2004 findings are NAR's first on the issue, so comparisons with previous years aren't possible.

Will the proportion of sellers performing some marketing and sched-uling tasks go up in the years ahead? Long & Foster's Atiyeh doesn't think so. Now that they've tapped à la carte brokers, he says, some younger, often first-time owners will switch to a conventional brokerage when they sell because they realize all of the things that go into the process. "They get tired of limited service," says Atiyeh.

Adds Doug Corbin, GRI, an associate with Exit Real Estate Results, a full-service brokerage in Winter Springs, Florida, "We've had people come to us after a seems-too-good-to-be-true arrangement falls apart," he says.

Proponents counter that there are two trends working in favor of the new à la carte models: the changing face of buyers and the maturity of the Internet.

As younger baby boomers and other Internet-savvy buyers come to dominate the market, they're bringing a hands-on approach that favors the à la carte model, says Daniel Rubén Odio-Paez of Drodio Realty in Falls Church, Virginia. "These consumers want to do things for themselves," he says. "Brokerages need to provide the tools to let them do that. The real value of practitioners is helping consumers negotiate and make sure they're getting the best deal."

Drodio isn't a fee-for-service brokerage but offers incentives for clients to do some of the work themselves under the company's sub-brand Rebate Reps. On the buyer side, Rebate Reps rebates a portion of the commission based on the amount of work—including home searching—the buyers do for themselves.

The Internet also is the key component of InSight Realty's business plan. The company operates in three major metropolitan areas—Washington, D.C., including southern Maryland and northern Virginia; the Research Triangle area of Raleigh, Durham, and Charlotte, North Carolina; and the Atlanta metro area—all home to a tech-savvy clientele.

InSight's Bunnell says his aim is to get in front of the Internet-savvy seller who either is reluctant to pay a commission or, because little equity has been accumulated in the house, can't afford to pay a commission without bringing a checkbook to the closing table.

"Our model has so far stood up well in both up and down markets," says Bunnell. "In strong markets, such as northern Virginia and the D.C. suburbs, we've been able to increase market share by offering sellers a way to increase their marketing exposure and at the same time maximize their net equity. In areas such as Atlanta, Charlotte, and Raleigh, which have been relatively slow over the past few years compared with the hottest markets, our model has allowed sellers to compete at an advantage by lowering their list price by the amount of savings we provide over traditional brokerages. In many cases, these home owners would be unable to sell without a service like InSight."

Bunnell wouldn't disclose his company's sales volume but says his listings have grown by more than 60 percent from 2002 to 2004 and that part of that increase is fueled by sellers who would otherwise tap traditional brokerage services. "Historically, most of our clients were FSBOs. But now we're seeing an increase in customers who would typically tend toward traditional services," he says.

Your Most Lucrative Role?

For brokers who are unsure how to position their company, the answer might be somewhere in the middle. That's what Elizabeth Newbury, ABR®, GRI, broker-owner of Newbury Realty in Dallas, is doing. Newbury launched her company in March 2004 as a hybrid, offering clients a choice from full service for a commission to various limited-service tiers, including an MLS-entry-only tier. At this lowest tier, Newbury requires sellers to sign a disclosure acknowledging that the company isn't responsible for the transaction.

"We want our associates to have the flexibility they need to work with the client the way the client wants," she says. "If the market slows, clients can negotiate what they want from our associates and at what commission level. That works for all markets."

Newbury's philosophy is that you build credibility by counseling clients to take a less-expensive approach when it's clear full service isn't warranted. "My first listing sold under the new brokerage was a property in an area undergoing urban renewal," she says. "The house was going to be torn down. So the key to selling the property was to offer it to builders. We offered the sellers a reduced-service listing and built a level of trust by doing so," she says. The house sold within 24 hours of being listed, says Newbury, who then represented the sellers in the purchase of their next home.

To date, about three-quarters of her company's listings are full service, a ratio Newbury doesn't expect to change in a slower market. She believes sellers' increased marketing needs will offset the attraction of spending less for à la carte services.

Still, that tension—the increased need for marketing and the attraction of spending less for services—will be at the heart of the drama as full-service and à la carte brokers continue to battle it out for market share.

> —*Robert Freedman. This article originally appeared in the February 2005 issue of REALTOR® Magazine.*

MORE ONLINE

How Real Estate Models Are Changing

Resources available online at www.realtor.org look into changing real estate business models. Enter the term "the future of real estate brokerage" in the search bar to bring up a summary of a report by the research division of the National Association of REALTORS® on that topic along with other resources, from NAR and others.

Technology

Helping Associates Work Better, Faster, Smarter

You've got technology performing all kinds of feats of wizardry for you—tracking prospects, creating virtual tours—but are these functions adding to your company's bottom line? It isn't always easy to answer that question.

With some technology, such as lead-generation solutions, you can easily measure the success of your investment with hard numbers. Just add up the number of leads you're getting and compare that with the number you were getting before.

Other tech products, such as marketing analysis tools, don't produce easily measurable gains or losses. But they still can help you realize important results: sales associates who work better, faster, and smarter.

"I'll invest in technology if I know it'll help my associates save time or money or make money," says Michael Johnston, ABR®, CRB, broker-owner and manager of The Home Specialists Real Estate Co. in Pocatello, Idaho.

With technology's payoff notoriously difficult to calculate, a few rules of thumb from brokers and managers may be your best gauge as you weigh your investments.

Look at what you gain, not just what it costs. "If all you're going to do is worry about cost, technology might never make sense," says Daniel

Mancuso, CRB, GRI, executive vice president of Murphy Realty Pre-ferred Homes in Rumson, New Jersey. "We look at how an investment will help us make money [by being more productive] and whether it has a 'wow' factor," he says. "If there's something we can do to impress potential clients and demonstrate our expertise, we consider that a good investment."

Buy the provider's reputation, not just its product. Past experience taught Johnston to consider the company behind the tool when evaluating the worth of hardware and software. With hardware, for example, he tries to stick with a proven, big-name vendor such as Hewlett-Packard.

"You need to know that the company has a support system in place to help if you have a problem," he says. "With technology, inevitably you'll have questions and require assistance. If it's not there, the tool could be worthless to you."

A tech adviser can help identify benefits. "If you don't understand tech-nology and how it can serve your company, find someone with the right background and credentials to investigate and explain it to you," says Michael Polly, e-PRO®, GRI, vice president of Denny Grimes and Company in Fort Myers, Florida.

For companies with resources, tech expertise can be brought on staff or hired on a consulting basis. At smaller brokerages, it's often the broker-owner or a team member who must take the lead.

Johnston fulfills that role for the 17 associates who work at his com-pany. "I'm a noncompetitive broker, so I look for tools that will help the associates," he says.

The Right Stuff

Like Johnston, many brokers have spent time scouting the right tools. Here several share insights on their best investments.

Lead generation leads the way. Real Estate One in Southfield, Michi-gan, with 1,800 associates in 48 offices, uses a custom-built applica-tion, Buyer Trend Analysis, which enables associates to enter the ZIP code for the location of a new listing, says Stuart Elsea, the company's president of financial services. The program sorts through information on past sales in the state to prepare a report profiling the most likely buyers of the home and where they live. "It saves our associates time by telling them exactly where they should focus their marketing effort," says Dan Elsea, Real Estate One's president of broker services. It also lets them count the number of leads they're getting and whether those are heading up or down.

The company spent about $8,000 to hire the programmer to develop the software and another $2,000 to buy the property records, Stuart Elsea says.

Printing outputs results. Bringing print jobs in-house reduced per-copy printing costs by 50 percent or more, speeding printing times and reducing errors, says Mancuso at Murphy Realty.

The company signed a three-year lease on a professional-quality color copier for about $500 a month and now does most of its printing in-house, he says. Per-copy costs have been cut in half, but, just as important, turnaround is faster and staff can check for errors after a single test copy rather than wait until the whole print job comes back from the printer as is often the case with small print jobs. "That alone produces big savings," says Mancuso.

Sales associates work with an in-house specialist to create flyers, he says. "When they make their presentation to the seller with first-class marketing materials, it's always impressive."

Tracking software gives associates a marketing edge. Like many brokers, Anthony Marguleas, president of A.M. Realty in Pacific Palisades, California, relies heavily on the Internet as a source of listings. To this end, his company operates, or has exclusive rights as the real estate provider on, a number of web sites. For example, his company bought rights to be the exclusive real estate provider on LosAngeles.com.

To capitalize on that, he hired a programmer to write software that automatically deposits leads from the different sites into a single database and sends out an automated response acknowledging receipt. Then a virtual assistant follows up on the leads, verifying information and sending viable leads to associates. "The full-time virtual assistant screens each lead within 30 minutes after it arrives," he says. "We've also set up spreadsheets to track each lead and monitor closing ratios."

Through this system Marguleas generates about 6,000 Internet leads a year, of which about 5 percent end up as leads worthy of follow-up for his 15 associates, he says.

Development of the integration software cost him several thousand dollars, and the programmer charges a fee each time the system needs to be changed to integrate a new site. Factoring in the virtual assistant, who receives a salary plus a bonus for each lead that closes, and costs to operate sites and gain rights on third-party sites, the company pays tens of thousands of dollars per year. He recoups some of that with a 20 percent referral fee to associates who take the viable leads.

Open-platform solution increases sales insight. One of the critical technology decisions Michael Polly of Danny Grimes and Co. made a few years ago was to switch from a specialized real estate contact management solution to the open platform of GoldMine, which he says allows for more customization.

"Our real estate program didn't have the flexibility we needed," says Polly. "With the open format, we can create custom reports that calculate commission splits; show where our business is coming from geographically; and provide insight into the status of transactions." Polly says the switch to the open system reduced costs while sales increased.

The price of GoldMine (www.frontrange.com) varies based on the number of users. Polly's company paid about $110 per user, he says. A single-user system would cost about $180. There are no recurring costs, but if you want to add applications to the system and you don't have in-house tech support, you'll have to pay a tech consultant, says Polly.

Customized listing presentations impress customers. A.M. Realty's Marguleas deploys technology to help his associates impress customers with their marketing tech savvy. "As soon as we get a call for a listing appointment, we take a picture of the home and create a domain name for that property based on its address," he says. "When sellers see we already have a picture of their home with its own URL in the brochures and flyers at the presentation, they're amazed we've already gone that far for them."

In a perfect world, looking at concrete gains stemming from your tech investment would be the rule rather than the exception. But for now, if you see your associates working better, smarter, and faster, that might be all the measurement you need.

WINNERS, NOW AND TOMORROW

So many tech tools, so little time to investigate them. Which show the most promise? Here are a few technology categories that brokers say are worth investing in. In some cases, brokers defray their costs by charging associates a fee; in others, they negotiate bulk-buying discounts for associates.

The Web. Anything done to enhance the company's Internet presence, capture leads, and secure solid search engine placement is considered money well spent.

Color printers. As prices drop on color laser printers, companies that bring printing in-house can realize cost savings and maintain consistent quality in all print promotions.

Digital cameras. These are among those rare tools that pay for themselves, in this case in savings on film, processing, and time spent traveling to and from the photofinishing center.

Smartphones. The convenience and reach of an always-on e-mail/phone/personal digital assistant (PDA) solution can help boost productivity without burdening associates with more equipment.

Global Positioning System (GPS). If you equate time with money, the time regained daily by a navigation system that efficiently routes associates from point to point, and around gridlock, can quickly justify the expense.

Transaction management. This is a great idea that needs further refinement before all parties to a transaction, regardless of tech proficiency, will embrace it. NAR is helping bring the technology along; the association has partnered with Real Estate Business Systems LLC, a subsidiary of the CALIFORNIA ASSOCIATION OF REALTORS® to create a transaction management system due this summer.

Custom-built database applications. Brokers who have a clear idea of how to build their database, what they want from it, and how to use the information will reap rewards for years.

Flexible, simple software. Whether generic or real estate specific, the best software allows users to easily manipulate and repurpose data.

Turnkey virtual tours. Frustrated with early experiments to create their own virtual tours, some brokers find it more cost-effective to let outside vendors handle the chore.

—*Michael Antoniak. This article originally appeared in the May 2005 issue of REALTOR® Magazine.*

MORE ONLINE

Technology That Makes Sense for You

Technology columnist Michael Antoniak looks at a range of technology targeted to real estate brokers and their sales associates at REALTOR® Magazine Online under "Tech Watch" in the Technology section at www.realtor.org/realtormag.

Spinning Returns from Your Investment

QUICK TIPS

Give associates everything they need on your network—then charge access fee.

Channel Web inquiries to relocation department until they ripen into leads.

Add virtual tours to reduce time associates spend showing homes.

If there's one mantra on brokers' minds today, it's that technology has to start paying for itself. Spending on technology differs widely among brokers. But David Cocks, managing partner of CompensationMaster, a compensation consulting company in Charlotte, North Carolina, estimates most brokers spend between $420 to $660 per associate per year, depending on market and brokerage size.

That spending is typically something that brokers shoulder by themselves. Two-thirds of brokerages don't share their technology costs with their sales associates, NAR figures show.

Naturally, brokers want to know what they're getting for their investment—and they're getting better at figuring that out. More than a decade into the revolution that swept technology into the real estate industry, many brokers are finding efficiencies and managing costs in a way that ensures a better return on their tech spending.

Service with a Smile—and a Fee

In 2001, when Mark T. Eibner, CRS®, GRI, launched MB Realty Oasis, a 100 percent commission company, outside Denver, he had little interest in taking a business-as-usual approach. He built his company with technology at the foundation.

Through a Web-based transaction management system called the Oasis Platform, his associates interact with their customers, coordinate transactions, and access the company's affiliated services—mortgage lending, title insurance, home inspections, and homeowners insurance—without having to be physically present in the office.

All of his professional support staff, including the heads of his Web, office services, and marketing operations, are accessible via the transaction platform. That enables associates to work out of their home offices; so far, 80 percent of his 50 associates have chosen that route. The online system allows Eibner to build his business without having to grow his office space to match. In fact, he's looking at years of growth before his office space, which can accommodate 250 sales associates, fills up.

Eibner's office space is substantial—6,400 square feet in suburban Denver in the Oasis Building. Much of that space accommodates his ancillary operations and in-house services, including a marketing department, and provides meeting space for his associates and their customers.

To recover his technology costs, Eibner charges associates a monthly Web platform access fee of $295 and a per-transaction fee of $295. For associates who tap his in-house marketing department for brochures, virtual tours, closing gifts, and other services, he charges a per-transaction fee of $375. Up to 90 percent of his associates use the marketing services.

Internet Leads (and Followers)

Tonda Burr and Katy Boles can't estimate the amount of business they've lost because of it. The culprit? Web site leads that aren't tied to a listing or addressed to a specific sales associate.

Getting sales associates to follow up on these leads, called general web site leads, is a major task and has led Burr and Boles—chief operating officer and CEO, respectively, of Graham & Boles Properties in Winston-Salem, North Carolina, in 2003, but now retired—to institute a two-channel policy designed to help them recover these lost revenue opportunities.

When these general leads come in, they're channeled to the relocation department. Relocation staff work with consumers until they're committed to the home buying process. Then the leads are passed along to sales associates, who pay the company a referral fee.

The policy doesn't apply to Internet leads that are tied to a particular listing or directed to a particular sales associate. These leads go directly to the sales associate.

Burr says the sales associates accept the Internet referral fee as money well spent, given the amount of processing the broker does before the lead gets to the person. "In our experience, general leads from our web site need anywhere from two to nine months of hand-holding before these consumers are ready to look seriously at properties," says Burr. "We make a significant investment in developing these leads and our associates understand that. I really feel that acceptance of Internet referrals is a communications issue."

Saul Klein, CRB, president of Internet Crusade, a real estate sales and technology consulting company, sees Internet leads as an untapped source of profit for both brokers and sales associates. "It's no accident that there are companies such as HomeGain, HouseValues.com, and now LendingTree that have business models focusing on lead generation," says Klein.

Nor does Klein think associates will hold it against brokers who try to make a profit off improved Internet lead management. When done right, he says, Internet leads enable sales associates to spend less time and money on prospecting. In the future, generating high-quality Internet leads may be seen as a major draw for soliciting top sales associates to join brokerages.

"Sales associates have been paying referral fees to other practitioners sight unseen for years," Klein says. "Why wouldn't they want to cut their prospecting time and dollars for warm leads from their broker?"

Burr's success in managing Internet leads owes much to her openness with the company's sales associates, she believes. Burr says, generally, salespeople are unaware of the high cost of operating a brokerage. But sales associates at Graham & Boles know that the company spends more than 1 percent of gross revenues on technology and about half a million dollars on advertising each year.

"The competition is trying to recruit your associates," Burr says.

"That's why you must remind sales associates what you do for them—how you free them up to focus on selling. Brokers have a strong value proposition for sales associates; they're just not doing a good job of communicating it."

Say Good-bye to Ink?

As more buyers migrate to the Internet, brokers may finally start to realize reduced print advertising costs, one of the early promises the Internet held out. Brokers are unlikely to jettison newspaper advertising entirely, but many brokers have spoken publicly about decreasing newspaper ad budgets.

At Graham & Boles, the approach has been to refocus print advertising from selling listings to selling the broker's web site, then letting the web site sell the listings.

Burr believes the two-pronged approach gives the company more advertising bang for its buck and puts the company in a position to start trimming its $500,000 print advertising budget.

Spending less on print ads is something Prudential Fox & Roach has already begun doing, according to Chip Roach, CEO and vice chairman of Prudential Fox & Roach, REALTORS®, with dozens of offices in Delaware, New Jersey, and Pennsylvania.

The company still advertises in major metro papers, but it stopped advertising in 40 local newspapers and funneled that money, in an almost dollar-for-dollar shift, into providing virtual tours on every company listing. It's too early to quantify the benefits of this approach, but the company is happy with the feedback it's getting from its sales associates.

"Consumers are telling our salespeople they love the virtual tours," says Roach, "and our sales associates are telling me the tours shorten the home search process."

As many brokers are finding, Web-based technology is a great tool for increasing the efficiency and productivity of your sales associates and boosting your ability to generate company leads. The cost of staying up to date can be steep, but savvy brokers are discovering ways to bring bottom-line balance to their tech investment.

—*Matthew McDermott. This article originally appeared
in the January 2003 issue of REALTOR® Magazine.*

MORE ONLINE

Starting Point for Investigating Tech Products

Start your search for information on the right products for you and your associates at the "Technology" section of REALTOR® Magazine Online at www.realtor.org/realtormag.

Supporting Your Systems without Spending a Lot

Keeping up with technology is expensive—but so is servicing it. For many real estate companies, hiring in-house tech support staff doesn't make economic sense. In fact, outsourcing your tech needs to an information technology specialist can be more cost-effective.

Not to mention time efficient. Naturally, you and your associates want to focus on sales and marketing, not on downed servers, corrupt files, and e-mail glitches. "Technology has become a real hassle for brokers and has to be rationalized so we can refocus on our core business," says Paul Turcotte, owner of RE/MAX Destiny, a one-office company with 16 associates in Cambridge, Massachusetts.

Turcotte and another RE/MAX broker in his area, Steve Koss, use Corporate IT Solutions in Boston for their tech support. The arrangement has not only enabled them to focus on their core business goals, it also has given them the chance to cast a fresh eye on their tech systems.

Koss, of RE/MAX Landmark, REALTORS®, a brokerage with more than 100 associates in Boston, Milton, Sharon, Stoughton, Taunton, and Westwood, Massachusetts, worked with Corporate IT to unify five offices through one back-end database. In one fell swoop, he standardized equipment, software, internal communications, schedules, paperwork, and forms, leading to fewer tech glitches and easier associate training.

If you have tech setup or support issues that you think may be best handled by a consultant, you need to identify the consultancy that's right for your job. Here's how:

1. *Articulate your goals as a brokerage.* Do you want to create an intranet for posting your company policy and standard real estate forms? Enable wireless networking? Set up spam-busting software? Consultants can help you implement, streamline, maintain, or standardize technology solutions, including

   Back-office software.

   Data backup.

   Office Internet access.

   E-mail.

   Web site design and hosting.

   Desktop and laptop support.

   Real estate–specific software.

   Mobile devices (PDAs).

   Office computers and software.

   They can also set up and maintain your company-wide network. Depending on your needs and the capability of the consultant, your platform can be housed on your own servers or hosted by the consultant. Turcotte has plans to house his system with Corporate IT Solutions. Koss owns and houses servers himself, but Corporate IT maintains his network.

2. *Develop and present a request for proposal to IT companies.* Describe your business goals, your current infrastructure, and your technology needs. Respondents will give you pricing information and a list of their services.

   Turcotte received quotes as high as $200 per hour for network engineer services. In the end, he selected Corporate IT, which offers him a price break if he purchases network engineer time in blocks. A block of 40 hours costs him $90 per hour.

   When you review proposals, be sure the fee structure is clear and you understand what your monthly bottom line will be.

3. *Make sure your contract includes a service-level agreement,* recommends Aubrey Jackson, a strategic architect at the National

Association of REALTORS® Center for REALTOR® Technology, a tech information resource for NAR members. Such an agreement stipulates performance standards for the consulting company. At the least, your agreement should include a satisfaction guarantee, indicate the minimum response time to your calls, impose billing penalties on the IT company for poor service (usually in the form of credits toward future services), and include a termination clause that you can invoke, says Jackson.

The termination clause is key, given the uncertain staying power of some tech companies. Should you have any concerns about the viability of your IT company, Jackson says, you want to have the power to act on it before you have a bona fide IT emergency, like a network shutdown.

The bottom line, say brokers and IT consultants, is to consider your cost in associate productivity every time a computer fails or your network crashes. You won't have to operate reactively if you find the right pros to keep your systems humming.

A Consultant for You

Information technology consultants range from international corporations to one-person operations. So there's help out there for any budget.

If funds are tight, consider tapping computer whizzes at community colleges and technical schools. They often moonlight for local businesses, says Saul Klein, CRB, president of Internet Crusade in San Diego.

Another good source of referrals is your local board. Robert Sadler, when he was association executive of the Reno/Sparks Association of REALTORS® in Nevada, saw a need for low-priced tech support among his smaller brokers. So the association arranged for a network administrator from a local university to support interested brokers, who benefit from a group discount.

—Matthew McDermott. This article originally appeared
in the July 2003 issue of REALTOR® Magazine.

MORE ONLINE

Finding IT Companies

Directories of IT companies that offer support on an outsourced basis are available online. These online directories include the Outsourcing Center, at www.outsourcing-center.com, Outsourcing Central, at www.outsourcingcentral.com, and the Outsourcing Institute, at www.outsourcing.com.

Unplugging Your Associates

In real estate, sales associates who are faster than their competitors at meeting prospects' needs are the ones who get the business. That makes it attractive for your associates to carry wireless devices that link them to resources at your office—MLS listings, e-mail, documents, property photos, their calendar.

But figuring out which devices to recommend to your associates is a challenge. To avoid costly mistakes, real estate technology specialists say you should:

Assess what functions your associates need in a cell phone, notebook, or personal digital assistant (PDA).

Research which products to recommend to your associates. Talk with colleagues at companies who've already made the move to wireless, and run your plans by tech professionals.

Test for usability.

The Right Devices

If you're helping your associates choose the wireless devices they'll carry, one maxim to follow is: "Buy for where your business is today. Don't try to predict your technology needs three years from now, because the devices change every two years anyway," says Mark Lesswing, vice president of the National Association of REALTORS®' Center for REALTOR® Technology. CRT offers IT professionals at REALTOR® organizations free advice on technology selection and implementation.

Lesswing and Bill Hartung, former director of technology for John L. Scott Real Estate in Bellevue, Washington, which made wireless devices available to its associates beginning in 2001, recently shared their collective wisdom on choosing products.

Cell phones. Look for products that accept both analog- and digital-transmission signals. These are known as dual-mode phones. Analog lets you send and receive voice transmissions; digital lets you send and receive data or text transmissions. It's important to have analog capability in your phone so that you can take calls in areas that are difficult for digital signals to reach, says Hartung. Check with cellular service providers in your area to identify which offer both analog and digital coverage.

Notebooks. Look for a notebook with either wireless networking (Wi-Fi) capability or a wireless modem built in, or make sure these are available options. If your notebook doesn't come with built-in Wi-Fi capability, it should come with a PCMCIA expansion slot to accommodate a wireless adapter. The next level of wireless technology is already rolling out in some parts of the country. This third-generation (3G) technology will enable always-on access to the Internet and e-mail from your notebook using a special card. The technology also promises to extend the reach of other wireless devices.

Wireless-enabled PDAs and smartphones. These devices can provide your associates access to voice, e-mail, Web, task list, calendar, and contact-management functions. Among the products that offer these capabilities: Samsung's i500 and PalmOne's Treo 600. If you live in an area that offers live MLS access, check with your local MLS provider to see which hardware platforms it supports for wireless access.

A Palm or Pocket PC or any multifunction handheld device with the right software allows associates to edit, compose, and send documents from the field. "It's really impressive for an associate on the road to be able to send a document or call up a spreadsheet while simultaneously talking to a customer," says Hartung.

Synchronization. If associates will be using a PDA as an extension of their primary computer system, they'll need to understand the importance of data synchronization. It allows them to update information between PDA and computer so that they'll have access to the same data.

Ramp Up with Research

Once you outline your basic needs, how do you winnow your choices?

Reviews. For free reviews or discussion-board postings, type the name of the product or product category ("PDA comparison") into an Internet search engine such as Google. But make sure you check several reviews on the same product. "Never rely on any one opinion, because it could be biased," says Hartung.

Peer groups. Hartung's company belongs to an alliance of real estate companies. He surveys members of the alliance regularly with regard to his options for technology implementation and troubleshooting. Experts also recommend that you ask vendors for customer referrals and talk to those customers about the process and results.

NAR's Center for REALTOR® Technology. CRT's Outreach Initiative provides advice on technology selection and implementation. Learn more at www.realtor.org/CRT.

Does It Work for You?

After you've narrowed your equipment choices, it's time to test the alternatives. Whenever possible, use demo models at the store. Vendor-owned stores—such as Sprint and Cingular outlets—sometimes allow you to use a phone for a trial period. During that time, if you're not satisfied, you can return the phone and service and pay only for service charges.

If a consultant is helping you select technology products, ask for a demo model so that you can "beat up" the system, says Hartung. That is, take the phone or PDA to the outer reaches of your service area to see how well it works, test its synchronization with your primary PC, assess

Javascript support. Also view associates' most frequently visited Web pages to see whether the pages format correctly for the small screen. Test the ability of the device to access the Web, not simply by accessing Google or some other common site, says Lesswing, but by trying the sites that are key to you, including your local MLS.

"If you demo it, you'll be assured of getting a device that works in your business," Lesswing says.

Smart Shopping

Hartung's associates usually buy equipment from the vendor who provides the company's test equipment. "Vendors are eager to do corporate programs and give group discounts," he says.

But he also looks at comparison-shopping web sites, such as www.Froogle.com, a Google site, and www.PriceWatch.com. This research gives him and his associates a good idea of what devices should cost, he says.

Part of the trick in buying is knowing your suppliers' product-introduction cycle, Lesswing says. "The best time to buy is late summer or March," he says, because vendors clear out the previous year's models in August and get rid of remaining holiday inventory in March. "You'll pay a huge premium if you try to buy next year's model in the holiday season," he says.

Pitfalls to Avoid

Coverage gaps. Thirty percent to 40 percent of the country still doesn't have 3G digital-wireless coverage, but this is changing. Lesswing expects national 3G networks to be completed by 2006. For now, buy a dual-mode phone that flips between analog and digital coverage. As 3G technology rolls out, wireless access by phone, PDA, and notebook will become more ubiquitous and reliable.

E-mail access issues. Don't set up mobile e-mail on a post office protocol (POP) basis, Lesswing says. If associates access e-mail from a handheld device (BlackBerry, PDA, smartphone, notebook), the e-mail disappears from the primary PC, so they'll have no backup copies.

Instead, use an IMAP server in your office, which keeps associates' mail in a central place until they're ready to download it to their primary PC.

Lost data. Getting synchronization to work is the No. 1 problem with wireless technology, Lesswing says. It's not uncommon for a contact list to be lost from both a PDA and a PC if both pieces of equipment become infected with a virus. To protect yourself, at least once a week back up your PC's hard drive to a CD-ROM. That way, if your data gets zapped from both the PC and the PDA, you have up-to-date information from the PC.

Faulty equipment. Wireless technology is less than perfect, say Hartung and Lesswing. Cell phone coverage gets dropped when there are sunspots or you drive through a tunnel. One out of every five devices doesn't work properly, Hartung estimates. Battery life is a constant irritant. "Some of the technology still has flaws. It's not all tried and true," he says. On top of all that, obsolescence is a fact of life.

Despite potential drawbacks, Hartung says, if you close just one deal with the help of your PDA, it's paid for itself.

Setting Up a Wireless Office

Are you planning to set up or upgrade your office network? Thinking of recommending wireless devices to your associates? Both occasions are good times to consider installing a wireless network.

With wireless, you eliminate the cables that connect the computer server with your associates' workstations, making it easy to rearrange your office, add new associates, or move to a new location. Thanks to growing demand for wireless networks, costs for equipment won't break the bank, and much of the latest equipment can now be purchased with built-in wireless functionality.

If you're starting from scratch, you can figure your equipment and setup costs will at least be comparable to that of a wired system—you won't have cabling costs but you'll need to invest in other wireless equipment. If you already have a wired system, the cost of conversion to wireless will depend on whether you buy all new wireless equipment or adapt your existing equipment to wireless use.

That's the main downside to going wireless: The equipment you've been using for a couple of years probably isn't equipped with wireless capabilities. Many vendors offer upgrade kits to retrofit older equipment but not for all versions of their products.

Here's a basic wireless network setup estimate for an office with eight associates:

Wireless router (a switch to control data flow from the Internet to the network): $120

Wireless card ($90 for each computer to talk to the router): $720. A wireless card isn't needed if you buy a wireless-ready notebook or desktop.

Extension antenna (to expand the range of your Wi-Fi signal and get around impediments, such as a steel wall): around $100

Server with networking software (the designated computer for storing documents and backup data): $1,400

Setup labor (assuming four hours at $80 per hour): approximately $320

Total: $2,660

WHAT ASSOCIATES PAY

Instead of buying wireless devices in bulk to get discounts for your associates, try using your bulk-buying power with vendors to negotiate discounts that your associates can tap when they visit a vendor to buy their devices. (NAR has negotiated a variety of such discounts for its members. Visit REALTOR® VIP home page for more information.)

At John L. Scott Real Estate in Bellevue, Washington, associates are free to use the cell phone of their choice, but they receive a 12 percent discount off the standard price on company-recommended phones, according to Bill Hartung, director of technology. For PDAs, associates receive a 12 percent discount through John L. Scott's supplier, plus $100 off from the company itself, and another $50 incentive from the network provider. Those discounts are in addition to any special promotion the vendor is offering to the general public.

—Christopher Wright. This article originally appeared in the November 2004 issue of REALTOR® Magazine.

MORE ONLINE

Wireless Networking Q&A

Get a sense of what's involved in converting to a wireless system for your office from a Q&A on the topic at REALTOR® Magazine Online at www.realtor.org/realtormag, under "Wireless communication Q&A" in the Technology section.

Wireless Services

REALTOR VIP® Alliance Program partner Nextel Communications offers monthly voice, GPS, and phone plans. The REALTOR VIP® Alliance Program is operated by the National Association of REALTORS® to link services to NAR members at a discounted group rate. Information on Nextel Communications is at www.realtor.org under "REALTOR VIP®."

6

Ideas for You
(A Look at What Your
Competition Is Doing)

Starting Up in a Big Rival's Backyard

Intero Real Estate Services
San Jose, California
www.interorealestate.com

Nowhere has consolidation in residential real estate been more pronounced than in Northern California. A half-dozen years ago, the area was flush with strong, independent brokerages—Cornish & Carey, Contempo Realty, and Jon Douglas Co., to name a few. But one by one, these companies joined NRT, the Cendant-owned brokerage company that sits astride residential real estate like a colossus.

Now, with a five-year noncompetition contract clause expired, Gino Blefari, a former senior vice president with NRT, is challenging his former company in its Northern California stronghold with the launch late last year of Intero Real Estate Services.

In very short order, the company has grown into a big player in its market. Its first office, in the Silicon Valley community of Morgan Hill, 12 miles southeast of San Jose, topped the local sales charts just three months after opening its doors. It generated about $250 million in sales volume in more than 400 transaction sides for the fourth quarter of 2002, according to MLS information provided by Intero. In the same time period, the nearest competing office closed about $150 million in about 275 transaction sides, Intero says.

"I know it sounds ambitious, but I want to create the greatest residential real estate company ever," says Blefari.

The former partner of Contempo Realty is off to a strong start. Since opening Intero's Morgan Hill office in October 2002, with more than 40 associates drawn from his former brokerage, Blefari has grown the company to more than 160 associates in 6 offices throughout Silicon Valley. Blefari's goal is to make Intero 400-strong before the end of 2003. Interesting aside: The Morgan Hill office is managed by Kevin Moles, brother of Cendant Real Estate Franchise Group CEO Bob Moles.

What's behind the growth? The key, Blefari believes, is embedded in the name Intero, which means "whole" in Italian. His holistic approach means making associates' personal growth one of the company's top goals. "For associates to serve their customers well, they need to have a broker who helps them keep their lives in balance," he says.

They also need a strong sense of ethics. "Early on we had an associate who tried to steal a customer from an associate with another company," Blefari says. "Once we learned about the incident and confirmed it with the customer, we let the person go."

To help associates keep their financial lives in balance, the company is setting up a system to help them pay their taxes and save for retirement. "Real estate people have a hard time planning for their taxes and their retirement, so we'll deposit a portion of their commissions into accounts that take care of these things for them."

Backed by startup capital from the Mercury Companies in Lakewood, Colorado, Intero has built a 39-person executive suite that includes an education manager, who's putting into place an accredited licensing curriculum.

This isn't the executive suite of a company that plans to stay small for long. Says Blefari: "We've set up the infrastructure we need to handle growth into the long term."

*—Robert Freedman. This article originally appeared in
the April 2003 issue of REALTOR® Magazine.*

Providing Liquidity to Net Customers

Flaherty Group
Kensington, Maryland
www.flahertygroup.com

Ready cash is something even households in a healthy financial position often have trouble finding these days, thanks to a tendency for people to sock away funds in stocks and other less-than-liquid investments rather than low-interest savings accounts.

But the cash-strapped home buyer isn't a challenge for residential brokerage Flaherty Group Inc., REALTORS®, in Kensington, Maryland. Stepping in with financing to help its clients close or make post-purchase renovations has been a hallmark of the company since it launched in 1972.

And that positions Flaherty to excel in its southern Maryland market even if home sales flatten out as interest rates rise, say company executives.

"When the bottom fell out of home sales in the late 1980s, our financial tools were extremely valuable in keeping business flowing," says broker Cynthia Davis. "Should the market slow again, all of our tools—equity advances, guaranteed sales—will be more important than ever."

In a typical equity advance, the company provides cash for an earnest money deposit or down payment so that the buyer doesn't have to draw down on, say, a line of credit, which could hurt the buyer's FICO credit score, says Davis. Today about 2 of every 10 Flaherty Group transactions involve an equity advance, she says.

The company's guaranteed sales program, launched in 1973, was the first in its market, says Paul V. Flaherty Jr., the founder. The guarantee enables new- and resale-home buyers to submit an offer without making it contingent on the sale of their current house. Flaherty will buy their house if it hasn't sold before closing. That can give buyers a leg up on other offers, says Davis.

The guarantee became a defining feature of the company's success in the tough 1980s, he says. Thanks to the strong market in the past few years, the company uses the program infrequently now, but in anticipation of cooler sales ahead it's reacquainting new-home builders with it, says Davis.

The company also steps in with financial assistance to home owners—those referred by people the company has a relationship with—confronting foreclosure. "People facing a hard time because of illness, divorce, or job loss call us rather than go through a lender because we can make a decision immediately," says Davis. "Paul and I are the loan committee."

To run its lending programs, Flaherty taps lines of credit and pools of investor money, says Davis. The pool is accumulated from investments and investment property the company's acquired and sold and from clients and friends who've invested with the company.

For all its emphasis on financing, the company doesn't see itself as a lender; the programs are in the service of its brokerage business. "We use them to attract buyers and sellers," says Davis.

With 15 full- and part-time associates, the company closed $52 million in residential business in 2003 and was on track to grow that by 15 percent by the end of 2004, says Davis.

"We've been stepping in with financing for a long time," says Flaherty. "People in our market know this, and it's given us great credibility."

—Robert Freedman. This article originally appeared in the February 2005 issue of REALTOR® Magazine.

Adding Home Styling to Your Services

Creative Image Interiors/Swanson Realty
Palatine, Illinois
www.lifestyledhomes.com

A picture is worth a thousand words, but when you set it against a mauve wall, it might be worth a thousand dollars in what it can help a house command on the market. That's the thinking behind the services of home stylists, in some cases known as stagers, the design consultants whom sales associates employ, particularly in the high-end market, to make a house look as attractive as possible for sale.

But to Bobbi Hauser, GRI, styling is too useful to be limited to upscale homes and too important to be left to designers outside real estate. That's because styling can help salespeople reposition a house on the market in terms of price and, in some cases, add to the overall value of the neighborhood—pluses for almost any listing.

Styling—Hauser calls it "lifestyling"—can include permanent changes to a house, such as interior painting, new carpeting, and new windows, not just those for marketing purposes.

Because changes such as these can increase a home's value, they're a strategic consideration best managed by a licensed practitioner, says Hauser. To put her styling ideas into practice, she operates Creative Image Interiors/Swanson Realty.

Hauser's company is too new to have much of a track record, but she's working with half a dozen brokers to provide styling services to their associates. Styling costs vary greatly, but a typical project might cost $2,000, she says.

By having licensees take these projects on, sellers can factor the cost of styling into the commission. That can take the sting out of the costs and extend the affordability of styling to houses in mid-range markets. Remember: Commissions can be split only between licensees.

"I provide a contract rider to the sellers' associates that delineates everything I'll do to improve the value of the house," says Hauser. "They factor those services into the commissions they negotiate. When the sale closes, I receive a cut of the commission in the same way that a buyer's rep would."

Styling works well for older houses on large lots that builders like to buy and replace with high-end homes, she says. Builders say the existing houses have little value outside the land they sit on. But by adding styling changes, sellers can attract owner–occupant buyers, who can challenge builders' ability to keep their offer low, she says.

The technique also can give a competitive edge to sellers who list their home while new models in the community are still being built. And exterior styling, such as landscaping, can encourage buyers to look at a house with a shopworn appearance.

For 2004, Hauser's goal is to roll out presentations to educate brokers to the benefits of styling, and to train associates to build styling into their services. "When practitioners see what I can do to a house, they know their clients will want that," she says. "They see the sense in using commission money to increase the overall value of the home and—over time—market values in the area."

—*Joseph Haas. This article originally appeared in the February 2004 issue of REALTOR® Magazine.*

Catering to City Dwellers on a Country Purchase

Living Structures
Cairo, New York
www.livingstructures.com

With its picturesque dairy farms, Greene County in the Northern Catskills has long been a secret retreat for second-home buyers from New York City with big dreams and a limited budget. And now that the area's secret is getting out, Hal and Claudia Zucker believe their experience selling real estate to New Yorkers will position their small brokerage to capitalize on the influx of city folk to this still rural area.

"We're trying to bring a range of services—instant access to associates, online resources—that you don't always find in rural areas," says Claudia Zucker, broker-owner of Living Structures in Cairo, New York, about two hours outside midtown Manhattan.

The Zuckers cut their teeth on New York City real estate in the 1980s—Claudia as a sales associate and Hal as a developer specializing in loft conversions. They opened their own brokerage in Albany in the early 1990s, and in early 2004 shifted their main office to Cairo. With eight sales associates, the company sells throughout Greene County.

The company is on track to close $15 million in sales this year, in a market with a median home price of about $110,000, says Claudia. That volume includes some small commercial sales. In 2003 the company closed about $12 million.

"New Yorkers have discovered that Greene County prices can't be beat, and they're really driving the market. Plus they expect to work with brokers who offer the same level of service they receive in the city," says Claudia.

At Living Structures, associates wear pagers; all calls on their listings go directly to them, not to the broker; and, in one of the company's signature services, associates are required to return all calls the same day, ideally within the hour.

In other ways, though, associates are given wide latitude. They're encouraged to work from home, there's no floor-time requirement, and part-time associates are welcomed.

In their training, associates are prepped to help big-city clients avoid the kind of surprises that come with buying in a rural area where, among other things, a quarter of the houses still use a septic system. "We're not creating home inspectors," says Hal. "We're trying to make our clients' lives easier. If the house was built in 1986, for example, we know the original roof is nearing the end of its life, and we know the hot-air heating system, even if it passed inspection, will need to be replaced soon."

The company offers associates a graduating commission split, reviewed quarterly, starting at 50 percent and ending at 70 percent. In a twist from the typical compensation plan, in which the split reverts to the starting level every 12 months, associates maintain their ending split into the next year. The split is adjusted downward only after a drop in volume of 5 percent or more from the previous quarter.

To manage its growth and for investment, the company bought a parcel of land near Windham, another small Greene County village, on which it could build stand-alone office space if needed. "We want to see how we do where we are now," says Claudia. "I'd love to have associates in different parts of the county. There's so much going on here now because of the growth: theater, new restaurants."

And that spells opportunity for a company that's already poised to serve big-city buyers.

—*Robert Freedman. This article originally appeared in the December 2004 issue of REALTOR® Magazine.*

Making Downtown Revitalization a Niche

Progressive Urban Real Estate
Cleveland, Ohio
www.progressiveurban.com

Keith Brown and David Sharkey have grown their company's gross commission income 130 percent over the past five years in some downtown Cleveland areas that some residents and property developers had written off as dead.

Progressive Urban Real Estate's 40 licensees closed $50 million in gross sales in 471 transaction sides last year for $1.9 million in income, up from $830,000 in income in 1999.

Business has become so active in Brown and Sharkey's downtown markets that other brokerages are, for the first time in years, eyeing their turf. "Other companies have started looking around, but I'm not sure they have the same urban philosophy we have, and it's that philosophy that sets us apart," says Brown, who launched the company in 1986, specifically to help drive a renaissance in Cleveland's urban neighborhoods.

Thanks in large part to efforts by the city and nonprofit community development corporations working the downtown neighborhoods, that renaissance started taking root in the late 1980s and now growth is firmly implanted.

All but a handful of Progressive Urban's sales associates live in the neighborhoods they sell and come to their job with a belief that a thriving urban center is vital to community health. "If they didn't share that belief system, they wouldn't be with us," says Brown.

A large portion of company sales comes from some two dozen condo and single-family housing developments the brokerage markets as the exclusive agent. Progressive Urban's relationships with the developments are longstanding. On many of the projects, Brown came in early as a predevelopment consultant, recommending unit count, size, and amenities, among other things. Then, after completion, the developer would turn project marketing and sales back over to Brown.

Progressive Urban has been a developer in its own right, too, cobbling together financing for several projects in the mid-1990s with the help of local community development agencies, private foundations, and banks looking to score points under the federal Community Redevelopment Act. The act requires banks to make credit available in all areas where they collect deposits.

The company's involvement in development started about a dozen years ago when Brown and Sharkey took over marketing of a new downtown apartment project on behalf of the bank that owned it after the developer went bankrupt. They successfully converted the project into condos.

The company's business isn't all in new development. A handful of

Progressive Urban's associates concentrate on their own listings, in the downtown or in close-in suburbs, such as Cleveland Heights and Shaker Heights.

Brown is expecting another big jump in sales for this year—his goal is $2.4 million in gross commission income for 2004—thanks to renewed interest in downtown living. "Before, people thought there was no urban market here," he says. "Now they're finding us."

> —*Robert Freedman. This article originally appeared in the July 2004 issue of REALTOR® Magazine.*

Tapping Technology for That Whizbang Effect

HomeSmart Real Estate
Mesa, Arizona
www.homesmartinternational.com

When you walk into HomeSmart Real Estate's office on South Alma School Road in Mesa, Arizona, just outside Phoenix, the receptionist greets you cheerfully, as she would at any other brokerage. But there's a logistical oddity: She's actually several miles away at the company's headquarters, and she talks to you via a wall-mounted plasma screen. Still, she can see, via camera, if the salesperson you're visiting is there and can announce your arrival.

Once you're inside, the technology at this fast-growth brokerage really gets exciting. In the glass-encased conference room, the associate shows you a "mini movie" of homes for sale—virtual tours that include aerial shots of neighborhoods transmitted via satellite technology. The movie's projected onto a plasma screen, and the associate can choose to display the MLS or neighborhood information, an online contract, or a web site.

"Technology sets us apart," says Matthew Widdows, broker-owner, who launched his company in 2000 and grew it from one office to four by 2004. He has two more Phoenix offices and one in Southern California slated to open this year. He's also fixed his sights on Las Vegas for the near future.

Tech wizardry has enabled him to expand rapidly without adding office space, he says. He's been able to nearly triple his roster of associates from 250 in 2003 to 600 in 2004 and grow his transaction sides from 700 to 2,200 in the same period—all with about a dozen support staff.

The cost to outfit each office with virtual technology was about $25,000. "You're going to spend [significantly] upfront for something like the virtual receptionist. But the savings from not having to hire people for each office, train and manage them, and provide benefits offset that," he says.

Souped-up conference rooms and virtual greeters aren't the end of the company's commitment to technology. Most associates operate remotely, from either home or car. To reduce their need to come into the office, the company posts documents online, and contracts are automatically converted to electronic TIF graphics files when they're faxed to the office. When someone calls an associate's work number, the associate is alerted by e-mail that there's a message.

Key cards enable associates to access all the offices so that they can work wherever it's most convenient. And the offices are designed with open workstations and equipment that are identical across branches, simplifying use.

HomeSmart operates as a 100 percent commission company. Associates pay $25 a month plus a $250 per-transaction fee as well as a $50 per-transaction fee for errors and omissions insurance. Alternatively, they can opt to pay $75 a month and a $250 fee only on the first transaction each month. Those who want more services, such as marketing assistance or a dedicated desk, pay additional fees. The company also operates an in-house mortgage operation.

The advantage of technology over hiring a lot of support staff: "Tech is a highly controllable variable," says Widdows. "We're counting on that to make us efficient and let us grow quickly."

—Robert Freedman. This article originally appeared in the May 2005 issue of REALTOR® Magazine.

Attracting Clients through a Blend of Business and Art

French & French Fine Properties Inc.
Sante Fe, New Mexico
www.french-french.com

Founded by missionaries and embraced by artists, Santa Fe, New Mexico, is a magnet for retiring, art-loving baby boomers seeking to treat life's bumps with the healing properties of turquoise cabochon gems and yoga. They appreciate a good real estate deal, too.

French & French Fine Properties Inc. has been tapping into high-end consumers' business and art sensibilities since its launch in 1983. The company says it holds a 50 percent share of well-to-do buyers in a market that saw a 62 percent increase in high-end home sales in 2003. Indeed, the company's 110 associates in four offices closed some 1,050 transactions in 2003, about half of the 2,291 closings in the area, according to figures provided by the Santa Fe Association of REALTORS® Inc.

"Many of the people who live here are relatively well-off retirees and second-home buyers," says Pat French, cobroker-owner, who founded the company with her husband Michael. "They have a different approach to life. They're serious, but they're fun-loving and creative, too, and in a way very European—like you'd find on Paris' Left Bank. They respond to our company because our associates very much reflect those attributes themselves."

When they're not selling real estate, the company's associates are often writing, painting, or sculpting—and sometimes mixing those creative pursuits with their business. A few years ago the company hosted an art show at the city's Center for Contemporary Arts featuring the work of 35 of its associates.

For a company of artists, French & French has its feet planted firmly on the bottom line with a mix of technology, alliance, and marketing initiatives.

Technology

Metro e-Guide, with information on the city, is e-mailed or sent on CD on request.

Online and CD listing presentations enable associates to market to out-of-town and busy in-town customers.

Virtual tours at a local theater have replaced new-listing caravans.

Alliances

French & French is allied with 10 regional and national relocation companies, including Cendant Mobility.

The company sells luxury homes through Christie's Great Estates, whose international headquarters is in Santa Fe.

Forty local vendors, including hotels, spas, and other providers, offer discounts to out-of-town buyers.

Marketing

Shoppers buy knickknacks and browse homes using Internet kiosks at the company's real estate store. Wells Fargo Home Mortgage and First American Title Insurance rent space in the store.

The company publishes SantaFe.com, an online magazine, which features city event and community information, and channels visitors to the company's site.

In all its marketing, the company makes sure people know what a gem Santa Fe is, says Pat French. "It's a small city, so we must sing our song loudly."

> —*Robert Freedman. This article originally appeared in the April 2004 issue of REALTOR® Magazine.*

Learning from the "Fixer-Upper" Franchise

HomeVestors of America
Lighthouse Point, Florida
www.homevestors.com

Jodi Turbyfill, broker-owner of Moreau Realty Inc., leaves most of her company's business these days to the two associates who work with her at her Lighthouse Point, Florida, office, near Ft. Lauderdale. That's because

Turbyfill and her husband, Terry, have their hands full buying homes that have seen better days, fixing them up, and selling them for as close to market price as possible. And it's all for their own investment.

Buying homes for their own portfolio and selling them is common among practitioners, but Turbyfill is getting help—and visibility—as a franchise affiliate of HomeVestors of America. *Entrepreneur* magazine, in its January 2003 issue, ranked HomeVestors, an eight-year-old Dallas-based franchisor, the 156th hottest franchise for 2003.

Not all HomeVestors franchisees are real estate licensees, but having a franchise in a market can mean more business for local practitioners. Sales associates from other companies have shown Turbyfill's listings to buyers and, within the past year, have started referring potential sellers to her, she says. By her estimate, she typically sells a property within a week of putting it on the market.

The HomeVestors brand has grown from a handful of affiliates, mainly in the South, to about 180 in almost 20 states, largely on the back of a marketing campaign built around the slogan, "We buy ugly houses," and proprietary software that lets affiliates quickly zero in on the economics of a deal. The company also provides affiliates a source for financing property acquisition and rehab, and helps them offer seller financing. First-year costs—including franchise fees, training expenses, and operating reserves—range from $136,150 to $219,450, according to HomeVestors.

HomeVestors' visibility is based on an aggressive billboard, TV, radio, and telephone directory campaign in franchisees' markets. "Our goal is to train the market so that when someone needs to sell a home quickly, they call us," says Bob Rometo, HomeVestors' director of franchise development.

Its franchisees generally buy homes at roughly 65 percent of fixed-up market value, using the discount to make rehab cost-effective.

Many of the sellers from whom Turbyfill buys are looking for a quick sale, often because they inherited the property and lack the resources to fix it up, or because they've lived in the house for years, in many cases with pets, and are overwhelmed by the thought of investing the resources to make the house presentable to buyers.

Turbyfill, who has owned her franchise since June 2001, says she averages about 20 transactions a year. She and her husband are the only full-time staff, although they have construction crews and contractors who work with them on a regular basis. They're turning a profit, she says, though she won't reveal her bottom line.

Companywide, HomeVestors is selling about eight franchises a month, Rometo says. The company expects to have 300 franchises by the end of 2004, and eventually 700 offices nationwide, he says.

"The houses are great for neighborhoods and for the buyers," Turbyfill says. "Plus, my husband and I are doing what we like to do."

—Joseph Haas. This article originally appeared in the January 2004 issue of REALTOR® Magazine.

Building a Big Following in a Small Town

Century 21 Home Team Realty
Scotts Bluff, Nebraska
www.c21hometeam.net

Serving Scotts Bluff and Gering, Nebraska, twin towns separated by the Platte River, Century 21 Home Team Realty's 14 associates closed 490 sides in 2002, an average of 35 per associate. That's well ahead of the average 13.2 transactions per associate for the country's top 100 companies, as tracked by REALTOR® Magazine in its 2003 "Top 100 Companies" (July, page 32).

To boot, the company, which today affiliates 16 associates, says it controls about 40 percent of its market. As of October, it had earned $1.1 million in gross commissions for 2003 on sales volume of $33 million. The company projects it'll close on 475 home sales for 2003.

How does Home Team, which serves a market of 23,000 people, do it? Through aggressive brand marketing, a strong referral business, and teamwork, say company owners Linda Dedic, CRS®, GRI, and Darlene Kovarik, CRS®, GRI.

With roots that go back more than 50 years, Home Team is the old-timer in the area, leaving other companies to play catch-up with its brand marketing, says Dedic. "When other companies try to do what we're doing, we change our style and do something else," she says.

Take Cable TV. Dedic says Home Team was the first to heavily advertise on a local TV shopping program. When other brokers started advertising on the program, the company enhanced its ads with interior shots and photos of the sales associates. To get more attention for open houses,

Home Team scheduled many on Saturdays, rather than Sundays, the prevailing practice in the area.

The company's affiliation with a national brand also helps, both in available referral and technology resources and in marketing. In fact, about 15 percent of its business is by referral through various national franchises, since there are few other national franchise affiliates in the area, Dedic says. The company's longtime local roots are behind many local referrals, she says.

The company is big on marketing, keeping its brand in front of people in large weekend ads in the newspaper and on cable. It's been aggressive on the Web, too. Until the past year, the company was the only real estate office in the area offering virtual tours of its listings on its web site. With other companies following suit, Home Team is adding animation and planning a redesign.

It hasn't hurt that the Scotts Bluff area, about 150 miles northeast of Denver, is attracting people from that metro area in search of less traffic and smaller schools. In addition, an expanding regional trauma center is a major attraction for professionals, who in turn are helping to kindle investment in the area. It's also attracting seniors moving to the area to be closer to medical care.

Behind the marketing and referral network, though, is a strong team ethic. "If a return customer comes to our office, whichever associate is there will assist the person and pass the information along to the associate who worked with the consumer previously," Dedic says. "We all lean on each other. It's not like some offices in larger cities where you might never see your colleagues."

—Joseph Haas. This article originally appeared in the December 2003 issue of REALTOR® Magazine.

Serving the Hispanic Investor

Ruano Brokers Inc.
Hialeah, Florida
www.ruanobrokers.com

A surging Hispanic population has helped make Hialeah, Florida, which borders Miami, the fifth largest city in the state and helped secure a unique niche for the Ruano family's two generations of real estate professionals.

It's not home ownership the Ruanos are focused on, even though residential sales are integral for some of the associates at their company, Ruano Brokers Inc. Instead, the Ruanos are reaching out to the growing Hispanic investor community that's hungry for small income-producing properties. That strategy helped the company increase gross sales income 36 percent from June 2002 to June 2003, says Anel Ruano, 33, broker.

"Many of our clients, whether they've come from other countries or been here a while, know what they want in properties and are knowledgeable business people," says Ruano. "But they often need us to fill in certain blanks for them about how the commercial investment process works."

It doesn't hurt that Ruano is a family business—a strong plus among its family-oriented Hispanic customer base. Anel Ruano's father, Jose A. (Tony) Ruano, CIPS, is company president and a widely known local real estate veteran who writes a column for *El Nuevo Heraldo*, the Spanish version of the *Miami Herald*, and hosts a Spanish-language real estate TV show.

Jose opened the company as Ruano Realty in 1989 but closed it in 1999 to make time for other commitments. Anel relaunched it in 2000 as Ruano Brokers. His mother, Adria, and brother, Adelkys, are sales associates. And a handful of associates from the original company still work with the family.

The company acts as a bridge for clients who, although business savvy, have little experience with real estate–related tax matters or with the protocols and rules of commercial real estate sales.

With 1031 exchanges, for example, investors new to the United States or just starting out in property investment are unlikely to be aware of the exchange procedures. Although Ruano Brokers isn't an exchange intermediary—the special-purpose entity the IRS requires to conduct trades—the company guides investors to the intermediaries and consults on the transactions.

The company's typical client—many are repeat customers who first started working with the company when it was Ruano Realty—is a buyer or seller of a $500,000 to $4 million shopping center, apartment building, or warehouse.

For Anel Ruano, the company's future is in reaching out to larger property owners and investors, including in the non-Hispanic community, and creating a conduit between them and the company's Hispanic investor base. To get there, he has put the company on the Internet and plans to open three more offices.

"We're ready to take our business to the next level," he says, "to bring together the best of our strong Hispanic business culture with the investment opportunities that exist."

—Robert Freedman. This article originally appeared in the August 2003 issue of REALTOR® Magazine.

What the Timeshare Niche Is All About

Stroman Realty Inc.
Conroe, Texas
www.stroman.com

He has 70 associates affiliated with his brokerage. So you'd expect that Wayne Stroman, president of Stroman Realty, would be moving a lot of houses. Actually, few of his associates sell homes. Instead, they sell timeshare intervals in resorts around the world. Stroman says he's hoping to broaden people's interest in timeshares at a time when the vacation home market is growing by leaps and bounds.

With baby boomers deep into their peak earning years at the same time that their aging parents are turning over much of their assets to their children, the market for timeshares is huge, says Stroman, who chairs the National Association of REALTORS® Resort Real Estate Forum, a panel launched last year to help REALTORS® stay on top of resort trends.

Last year, about 2.7 million U.S. households owned a U.S. timeshare interval, up from 155,000 in 1980, according to the American Resort Development Association (ARDA). That growth trend is likely to continue with the entrance in the past few years of major resort developers, including Cendant Corp., Disney, Hilton, Hyatt, Marriott, Sheraton, and Westin.

In addition, improved resort construction and increased professionalism of salespeople have moved the industry away from its hard-sell tactics of the past, Stroman says.

Given differences in unit quality and market areas, timeshare prices vary widely. In general, though, buyers of new timeshares today can expect to pay an average of $12,500 retail, plus annual maintenance fees, for a two-bedroom unit that they can use one week a year, Stroman says.

He believes his company's 20-plus years of timeshare experience leaves him well-positioned to maintain a strong presence in the resale niche. But he also believes he can build on that position—to the tune of 20 percent revenue growth in 2003—with his launch in January of Resort Interval Interchange. The launch marks Stroman's entrance into timeshare exchanges, a fast-growing part of the industry. Last year, the industry posted about three million exchanges worldwide, an all-time high, according to ARDA.

In an exchange, timeshare owners trade units with one another, enabling households to occupy a unit in a different resort or a unit in the same resort but at a different time.

Stroman's company can now help clients buy, sell, rent, or exchange existing units. The only aspect of the industry his company isn't involved in is new-unit (or retail) sales, which are dominated by resort developers. But he shows little interest in moving in that direction. "It's more practical for households to buy a timeshare on the resale market," he says. "First-time resale units can sell for 20 percent to 40 percent below the original price, making them a popular value with a lot of households."

Besides posting little appreciation, timeshares can be difficult to resell. But Stroman says his team of salespeople improves owners' prospects for a sale. The company doesn't release sales figures, but it maintains one of the largest sales operations of its kind, says a spokesperson. "The fact that we're successful in a difficult business says something about the quality of our people," Stroman says.

—Robert Freedman. This article originally appeared in
the July 2003 issue of REALTOR® Magazine.

Working with Others to Leverage Buying Power

Realty Guild
Haverhill, Massachusetts
www.realtyguild.com

From its roots as a networking club of four companies in the mid-1980s, this 65-company-strong band of small, independent Massachusetts residential real estate brokerages has grown up. And its members are profiting as they tap their collective buying strength.

With between 3 and 45 sales associates each, the member companies of the Realty Guild could hardly hope to reap the economies of scale in vendor purchases, such as ad buying, that the big players in their markets enjoy.

But thanks to the bargaining power they gain through their affiliation with the Guild, the little guys have grown big muscles. Large buys for each small member company in key media outlets, including the *Wall Street Journal*, the *New York Times*, the *Boston Globe*, and REALTOR.com, are routine. Even expensive TV advertising is within their reach.

The experience of the James L. Cooney Agencies, in Lowell, Massachusetts, is a case in point. Last year the 56-year-old company, with half a dozen sales associates, landed a showcase residential listing. The company piggybacked on a group buy in the *Wall Street Journal* and the *New York Times* to reach affluent buyers outside its normal channels, and that reach was pivotal in getting the word out on the listing.

Member growth has brought other changes, too. The group just launched New England Home Mortgage Corp., a joint venture with American Home Mortgage, giving its members their own mortgage arm. And, in a move toward concierge-type services, the Guild inked an affiliation with a national moving company.

Core competency: Despite its expansion, the Guild has retained its two core characteristics. Networking remains a key focus, and indeed its members stay in touch through monthly meetings.

In addition, Guild services remain voluntary. Members sign up—or not—for big media buys or special vendor offers as they see fit. "Our members are fiercely independent," says Inez Steele, the Guild's executive director. "That's their strength. So nothing we do is dependent on everyone signing up to do it."

To keep the Guild manageable and create value for its members, membership is by invitation only and limited to one company per community. In Boston and other bigger metro areas, membership is limited to one company per neighborhood. The annual fee is about $2,500, an amount that the members quickly get back through their discounted media and other buys, Steele says.

"We want to keep the Guild relatively small so its members stand out in consumers' minds," says Ralph Miller, CRB, CRS®, broker-owner of Hughes & Hughes Real Estate Co. Inc. in Natick, Massachusetts, and 2002 president of the Guild.

What's next: The Guild is now looking outside Massachusetts to explore opportunities with similar organizations in other states. Among the groups it has shared advertising and ideas with is System 1 Real Estate Network, in Norwalk, Connecticut, whose members operate about 50 offices of independents in Connecticut and New York. "We'd like to see models like ours in other parts of the country," says Miller. "The more there are, the more independent companies like ours can benefit in a business where size often has the advantage in buying power."

—Robert Freedman. This article originally appeared in the February 2003 issue of REALTOR® Magazine.

Making Your Storefront Interactive

Hammond GMAC Real Estate
Cambridge, Massachusetts
www.hammondre.com

Tod Beaty in late May launched what he and technology developer Stephen Randall say is the first interactive window display for property listings in the world.

Thanks to the same technology that lets you control your TV from your recliner, shoppers strolling outside Beaty's Hammond GMAC Real Estate office on Brattle Square in Cambridge, Massachusetts, can use their cell phone to scroll through property listings displayed on a large flat-screened monitor in the office window and order up property details, obtain travel directions, and leave a message for the listing associate to get back to them. All without setting foot in the store.

"It's a tremendous bridge for people who want to browse homes without having to take the big step of going inside the office to speak with a sales associate," says Beaty, broker-owner of the Cambridge and Belmont offices of Hammond GMAC.

Sellers love it, too. "They can't wait to have their properties in it," he says.

And well they might. With his Cambridge office located just off Harvard Square, popular for dining, shopping, and entertainment, hundreds of strollers walk by Beaty's storefront each day and night, promising the kind of exposure that sellers dream of. "We generate about 10 percent of our customers through foot traffic," says Beaty, whose two offices closed 403 transactions in 2004. "The interactive storefront is a natural for capturing that traffic."

Now all that's needed are some early adopters. In the first three weeks after launch, a handful of shoppers used their cell phone to interact with the display, and two sent word to Beaty to have the listing associates follow up. But by early June, Beaty couldn't tie any sales directly to the display. Even so, there's little doubt he sees a future in this kind of interactivity.

"Once people realize the display is interactive, they smile and get out their cell phone and try it out," he says. "But there's a familiarity hurdle to get over. Many people have been walking by our office for years and are used to seeing our listings on monitors in our storefront window. Even though we tried to make it pretty obvious that this screen is interactive—the instructions are displayed right by the listings—many people continue to look at the display the way they always have."

Beaty and Randall, whose Somerville, Massachusetts-based company LocaModa developed the system, are exploring ways to beef up response. Among the ideas:

- Offering a prize to shoppers who try out the interactivity and leave a message with the company.
- Moving the monitor to a side window where shoppers aren't used to seeing a display, and where the daytime sun doesn't bleach out the screen.

- Limiting operation to night. Screen visibility is better and night operation would give people the opportunity to shop after office hours.

- Install monitors off-site in a kiosk, possibly in a supermarket, where some people might be more inclined to interact. A kiosk would also extend the company's reach without having to open a new office.

For Beaty, the system is relatively user friendly. LocaModa hosts the service on its computer, manages the listing content, and generates traffic reports. Beaty pays a single monthly subscription charge of $1,000. That amount is based on the number of listings he has showcased (nine) and the amount of detail he makes available to those who click through the main picture. LocaModa doesn't charge a setup fee.

"It's just another arrow in our quiver," says Beaty. "And once it gets going, we'll know immediately when buyers come through the system and how to contact them, because we'll have their phone numbers. We just need people to cross that threshold of interactivity."

*—Robert Freedman. This article was
written for REALTOR® Magazine.*

The Next Level for
Apartment Locator Services

Chicago Apartment Finders
Chicago, Illinois
www.chicagoapartmentfinders.com

If your experience with rental locator services dates back to when you were entering college, you probably remember being offered instant coffee out of Styrofoam cups while waiting for a leasing associate and filling out your search form sitting in a wobbly, second-hand chair. If that's the case, you won't be prepared for Chicago Apartment Finders.

The coffee comes premium, not instant, with fresh-baked cookies, and you can forget about the wobbly chair. Sack out on overstuffed sofas if a leasing associate isn't available or play computer games, check your e-mail, shoot baskets—anything you can do in your apartment. That's because the waiting room is designed like an apartment, so you feel right at home.

And also impressed.

"When customers come through our doors, we want them to see immediately that they're in a successful company," says Justin Elliott, ABR, 29, who founded the company with his college buddy, Andrew Ahitow.

Since its launch in late 2002, the locator company has grown to be Chicago's second largest with 40 leasing associates working out of 2 offices and projected to generate $6.5 million in gross commission income in 2005 on 6,600 rental transactions. And Elliott says his company is poised to jump ahead of the city's largest locator service before the end of 2006.

The company's rise is built on two foundations:

1. Ending the cycle of transience among leasing agents that's typically plagued locator services by offering them high commission splits up front and giving them immediate direction through intensive, week-long orientation.

2. Becoming a resource beyond finding apartments by offering customers information on everything they need once they move in: finding a bank, getting the cable turned on, renting furniture, obtaining a gym membership. "For our typical customer—18–30 years old—renting marks a big point of churn in their life and often this is the first time they need to think of these things," says Elliott.

To keep its leasing associates on board beyond the 4–6 months that's typical in the industry, the company offers a 30–70 leasing commission split to start (with the associate getting the 30 percent), up from a typical starting rate of 25 percent, and ratchets that up to 45 percent as associates meet performance milestones. Commissions are typically equivalent to the first month's rent, which landlords pay to the locator service.

The company seeks to make its new associates comfortable from the start with a six-day mandatory orientation that's provided to groups of five to six new associates. The orientation includes tours of rentals to help them start with an understanding of the market.

The strategy shows signs of working. Of its eight original leasing associates when they launched, six are still with them, and the average tenure among their associates is almost two years. "The client is so much better served with an experienced leasing associate and it saves us huge costs in turnover," Elliott says.

The company's top associate is 24 and earned $115,000 in commissions in 2004 and is on track to come close to doubling that in 2005. It has five associates earning more than $80,000 in 2004, and Elliott expects almost a dozen associates to earn more than $100,000 in 2005.

—Robert Freedman. This article was
written for REALTOR® Magazine.

SECTION

II

Managing People

The Art and Science of Working Together

Andrew Fletcher knows something about motivating people. The broker-owner of Impact Real Estate in Niles, Michigan, pumps in high-energy music over his office sound system and rings a bell whenever an associate gets a listing or sale. With only a handful of sales associates in 2004, he had almost doubled his sales volume from his company's first full year, in 2002, and was making similar gains in 2005. To be sure, Fletcher's high-energy approach might not work in every real estate brokerage office, but it shows there are few techniques brokers won't try when it comes to keeping their sales force in high gear. That's because people issues are number one on managers' minds, brokers say. Everything flows from sales performance, so knowing the latest thinking on recruitment and retention can be instrumental in keeping your company's growth potential on track.

Here you'll find a roundup of ideas from brokers and managers on recruiting and retention, and you'll hear from sales associates on what they look for in a company and why they like where they are. We also look at behavioral testing, something more brokers are doing today. And we touch on health and safety issues, which are key to keeping your sales force on the move and motivated to take their sales to the next level.

119

Recruiting and Retention

Shrink Your Washout Rate

Talk to brokers across the country and most will tell you they have a low washout rate—the rate at which new associates leave within the first year. But is that really the case? Studies say about 50 percent of new associates don't make it to their first anniversary, and there's agreement with that statistic among brokers—when they're not talking about their own company.

Whatever the magnitude of the washout rate, there are steps you can take to keep it from getting too high. Veteran brokers share their ideas.

The Money Hurdle

Bar none, the biggest pitfall for new associates is that they don't have enough savings to maintain themselves financially for as long as it takes to build their business, say brokers.

One way to address this is to affiliate people right out of high school or college who are living with their parents and have few expenses, or try affiliating retired teachers or county employees.

Retirees from the public sector typically have a pension that can keep them financially afloat while they build their business, says Scott Bloom, a salesperson and mentor to new associates at Coldwell Banker Residential Real Estate Inc. in Boca Raton, Florida.

"In real estate, you can't appear to be hungry," says Bloom, and that's something that new graduates and retired persons are positioned to avoid.

Once you affiliate new recruits, let them know upfront what it takes to get established and then give them the tools to get them through that first year. That means a frank discussion of money matters and plenty of training. At RealtySouth, the big regional brokerage based in Birmingham, Alabama, new associates must attend extensive training once they affiliate with the company, and "they might spend their first month in class getting post-license state training," says Jim Dye, regional vice president.

Planning and Prospecting

Another big first-year hurdle is drift, the lack of steady progress toward a sales goal. To address this, you must give new recruits challenging but achievable prospecting goals and hold them accountable for meeting those goals. "Associates fail because they simply don't prospect," says Rick Murry, regional sales manager of Shorewest, REALTORS®, and sales director of the company's Brookfield/Waukesha, Wisconsin, office.

A reluctance to prospect may stem from not understanding its importance, wanting to avoid rejection, or preferring to work on the sexier parts of the business like deal making, say brokers. Requiring associates to craft and maintain a business plan can be a key to keeping them in the hunt for customers. "Right from the get-go, we establish daily contact goals," says Bob Welsh, branch broker at Prudential Utah Real Estate in Midvale, Utah.

Accountability in meeting goals is as essential as the goals themselves. "I touch base with them every day about their daily goals," says Welsh. "I'm not as concerned with how many listings or sales they had this month as I am with, 'Have you met your goal today?' I try to know that number for each associate because it's very powerful as a manager to go up to an associate and say, 'Have you talked to your 10 people today?'"

Stay Alert to Trouble Signs

You've told them about money issues they can expect their first year. You've given them training and helped them set prospecting goals. And you're holding them to their plan. And yet something's not clicking.

Be aware when your new associates are struggling. Aside from the obvious—they're not making money—Welsh looks for signs that associates' enthusiasm and involvement are waning. "You don't see them coming into the office as much, and when they're in, they don't have a game plan for the day," says Welsh.

You want to catch trouble early, before their enthusiasm for the industry gets irreparably harmed by the slow pace of success. "If I see associates who are obviously trying, whose motors are running, then they might just need a tune-up," says Dye. "I have more patience, and I give them more time."

A helpful strategy for brokers in these instances is to assume the perspective of a business counselor and probe for areas of improvement. "Are you not talking to enough people?" Welsh asks his recruits. "Are you not getting enough appointments? Are you not converting enough appointments? What part of the process is breaking down?"

Analyze Performance Data

You need hands-on data before you can tell whether associates aren't going to succeed, says Bernice Ross, chief executive officer of Realestatecoach.com, a virtual training and coaching company in Austin, Texas. "Go out in the field with them or have an experienced associate go out with them to see what they're doing," she says. "Or have your new associates do a sample listing presentation in front of you."

Observing their performance gives you data to help you determine where they're going wrong, if they are.

"If you've got associates who are not performing, put them on a three-month up-and-out program," says Ross. "You say, 'I can see you're struggling. I'd like to meet with you once a week for the next 12 weeks. We're going to outline what you're going to do each week so that we can get you where you need to be.' By the end of the 12 weeks, either they'll decide they don't want to be there, and they'll elect out, or you'll have created a situation in which they can win."

Peaceful Partings

When you know associates won't succeed, how do you let them down easy? "I'm getting better at that," says Murry, "getting better at recognizing that the sooner the person moves on, the better for both of us."

In fact, Murry says, "Most people know. Often, people come to me with the idea themselves. It's a face-saving thing. They say, 'I've come to the conclusion this just isn't for me.' I was on the verge of telling them the same thing, but I appreciate that they've come to me."

Pam Bessette, GRI, co-owner of All Florida Realty Services Inc. in Port St. Lucie, Florida, tries to prepare associates when she meets with them each week so that when an associate's production becomes an issue, it's less surprising. "Then we make it a mutual decision. It's not, 'You're not making enough money; you've got to go.' Instead, we talk about how this business is supposed to be putting food on the table and it's not. Maybe they'll do better at something else, and they'll be happier. And we encourage them to do business on a referral basis."

"Try to make it a win," says Dye. "Help associates find what's best for them. Offer alternatives, like going back to class or doing a coaching or contact management program. If that doesn't work, show them that they're spending money, but to what end? It's not about me, it's about what's in their best interest."

Once in a while, associates just won't let go. "Sometimes you have associates who don't want to leave, and you have to tell them, 'You need another broker, because you're not succeeding like I think you can. Maybe somebody else can help you get out what I think is inside you,'" says Dye. "You're firing yourself."

Being willing to "fire yourself" and thereby open up the door for other new associates might be just the ticket for getting a start on curbing your company washout rate.

> —*Gabriella Filisko. This article originally appeared in the*
> *September 2005 issue of REALTOR® Magazine.*

THE BENEFITS OF FREE MENTORING

When Coldwell Banker Residential Real Estate Inc. was introducing a coaching program for its brokers two years ago, an associate in its Boca Raton, Florida, office, Scott Bloom, asked if he could take it a step further.

Bloom acts as a mentor and coach to all new associates, an average of two to five each month, with no charge to the associates.

Bloom is paid only out of the company portion of new associates' first three commissions. "In the past," says Gus Rubio, senior vice president and manager of the company's 19 offices in Dade County, Florida, "we would take the mentor's share out of both the associate's and company's dollar, so associates were hesitant to ask for advice because it was money out of their pocket. Now, why wouldn't associates use Scott's expertise? It doesn't cost them anything."

Bloom also gets a portion of the company's take on all rentals that associates fill before their third sale closes, in addition to a bonus based on company sales, among other things. "It's not a get-rich-quick job," Bloom says. "It's about $1,000 per month. But it's nice to train people and see them become successful."

Bloom's guidance seems to be sound. Of the 13 Dade County Coldwell Banker rookies of the year last year (new associates who earned $50,000 in closed gross commission income during the first 12 months with the company), 4 were associates Bloom mentored.

AVOIDING EXIT CONFLICT

There are a few steps you can take to minimize the potential for legal conflict should an unhappy sales associate file a lawsuit upon departure.

Most brokers have independent contractor agreements with their associates, so be sure to check—and follow—the terms in that agreement. "If there are obligations in your agreement, you've got to follow the agreement," says Ralph Holmen, associate general counsel at the National Association of REALTORS®.

If you feel your standard agreement isn't clear or needs strengthening, don't hesitate to make changes. "Think about the issues or questions raised when an associate leaves and how you'd like to have those matters resolved," Holmen says, "and revise the agreement to be sure it clearly reflects how you'd like to handle the situation." For example, be sure to address what happens to departing associates' active listing as well as their pending sales. You want to be sure you're covered on both counts.

Also, be clear how your state law applies. Even though most associates are independent contractors, they might still fall within the scope of some states' employment anti-discrimination laws. Holmen says to be sure you have a record of a legal reason for termination—such as lack of production—and that there's no basis for the associate to claim a potentially illegal termination on the basis of such factors as gender or race.

MORE ONLINE

Recruiting and Retaining Salespeople

The National Association of REALTORS®' Information Central maintains a field guide on recruitment and retention. Contents include ideas on attracting the best salespeople, recognizing people with great sales potential, and sharpening hiring practices. Access to some material requires a fee or a site user name and password, available only to NAR members. The field guides are at www.realtor.org, under "Library."

Attracting and Keeping the Best

There are more people trying to make it in real estate than ever before—NAR membership now stands at more than 1.1 million. The sheer volume can make it difficult to find the most promising recruits and keep your sales force happy. REALTOR® Magazine asked eight residential real estate brokers how they're filling their ranks and keeping good associates in the fold.

What can I do to recruit rookies?

Give them the chance to earn licenses quickly. We offer new recruits courses that prepare them to take the state licensing test in 18 days. Getting into the field quickly is attractive to downsized professionals looking for a second career, new college grads, and others hoping to jump into real estate while it's hot.
> Larry A. Matos, president and broker, Century 21
> M&M and Associates, Modesto, California

Tell them what to ask. When they're starting out, they don't know what questions to ask brokers during an interview. When they come to us, we provide them with a booklet of questions—What is E&O insurance and how does it work? What is relocation and how does it work?—they should ask us. When they're finished with our interview, I feel we've educated them and I encourage them to use the questions if they interview with other companies. They appreciate that.

> Jacqi Giordano, director of recruiting and
> career development, Star Real Estate,
> Fountain Valley, California

Try the Real Estate Simulator. Use this online test to attract pre-license candidates, get a sense of what personality traits and skill sets prospects would bring to the table, and whether people will fit in. It's found on many company web sites and can be used to document the type of recruit who does best at your company. For pricing and a demo, visit www.realestatesimulator.com.

> Carol Johnson, president, The Recruiting
> Network Inc., Schaumburg, Illinois

Target direct mail to a neighborhood where you don't have an associate working. Announce that you're looking for someone to represent your company in that neighborhood. The technique has netted both some new and experienced associates.

> Jack O'Connor, CRB, managing partner and broker,
> Prestige Real Estate Group LLC, Englewood, Colorado

Contact new licensees immediately. Send recruitment letters to contacts on your state's list of new licensees as soon as the latest roster is available. Follow up with personal calls, notes, and interviews. Hours can make the competitive difference.

> Johnson

Rely on your associates. Ask them to assist you in recruiting people in their own image. Good people attract good people.

> William (Bill) Baker III, broker-owner, United
> Country Virginia Realty, Clarksville, Virginia

How can I help rookies succeed?

Get them to a closing within 60 days. The longer it takes for that first sale, the more likely they'll drop out of the business. If they can close quickly, their confidence soars. Make it easy for recruits by finding them a neighborhood to work where they're comfortable and are positioned to meet people casually. And make sure you or a sales mentor is ready to help them bring the deal to fruition.

> Richard (Rich) Cosner, CRB, president,
> Prudential California Realty, Anaheim, California

Let them pick their manager. We encourage new recruits to interview the managers of our offices until they find one they click with.

> Giordano

Offer mentoring. New recruits hone their skills with the help of experienced associates. Our veteran associates always include the rookies on their listing appointments.

> Baker

What can I do to recruit experienced associates?

Take away their business. Nothing grabs competing associates' attention faster than losing listings to your company. When our associates' FOR SALE signs start popping up in competing associates' territory, they're very receptive to us when we call to tell them we can help them achieve the same success.

> Cosner

Know more about their performance than they do. Be familiar with competing associates' MLS stats, cooperative transactions, web sites, and market niche when you call to introduce yourself to them. When you know more about their production details than they know themselves, you can bet their managers aren't providing them with the statistical support they need to leverage their marketing strategy.

> Johnson

Make personal contact. Calling great-performing associates to let them know they're the kind of people you want associated with your company is still the best way to make an impression. It's effective even if the timing isn't right for them to leave because when that time comes, they'll call you.

> Steve Brown, ABR®, CRB, vice president and general
> manager, Crye-Leike, REALTORS®, Memphis, Tennessee

Take them to a movie. We asked each of our associates to invite 10 colleagues from other brokerages whom they most like to work with to a movie outing. This gave the other associates a feel for our corporate culture firsthand. It also helped create cooperative relationships.

Jeanine McShea, vice president of sales,
@properties, Chicago, Illinois

Invite them to your productivity seminars. Don't limit your speaker seminars to just your associates. Give other salespeople a chance to meet your team, learn about your company, and improve their business. It's a favor they won't quickly forget.

Giordano

What are experienced associates looking for?

Individualized coaching. They aren't looking for training. There's plenty of that available to them through NAR and other sources. And they're not looking for a few percent more in their split. They're looking for a company to help them build a strategy—based on their skills and knowledge—to take them from 30 to 50 sales a year.

Cosner

Management systems. To get to the next level of productivity, associates are looking for brokers who have the resources to help them root out and manage leads quickly and effectively. Management systems are especially crucial to mid-range producers who lack the skills and resources to handle prospecting and follow up on their own.

Johnson

Ownership opportunity. We were launched in 1999 as an associate-owned company, with 26 partners; today we have more than 100 partners out of 265 associates. Clearly, not all associates seek to become partners, but the option to own is attractive to many veteran associates because it enables them to grow along with the company, helping them build a nest egg for the future. They can also become a partner in our title and escrow businesses.

O'Connor

Technology. Associates with advanced technology skills want to move up the technology ladder, not down. They won't fall for false technology promises made by managers who aren't fully conversant about the specifics of the company's technology support offerings.

Johnson

Why do associates leave?

They're having a bad year. This usually happens when, flush with business, they stop prospecting. Then, when their business ebbs, they have nothing in the pipeline. As their broker, let them know that you know how they're performing relative to last year or to the previous quarter. That way you can intervene before a problem occurs. We brainstorm with them on ways to get them back into prospecting. Don't just give them relocation business or a lead, if they ask. That will only help them for a day.

Brown

They're feeling a sense of isolation. Managers often falsely assume their top performers require little personal attention and instead focus on new recruits. The reality is, even top performers need regular personal attention from their managers to thrive.

Matos

They're up against bad rules. Brokers can put an unreasonable burden on strong-performing associates if they institute a companywide rule, such as mandatory office time, that's really just aimed at dealing with one or a few problem associates.

Brown

They're receiving insufficient support. We work hard to retain, and increase the professionalism of, our support staff so that they, in turn, provide great service to our associates and their clients. Early in 2004, for example, we launched a program in which we've made home ownership more attainable for our company's salaried staff by providing 3 percent of the purchase price, up to $5,000. We also donate 100 percent of any commission we make on the purchase toward the down payment.

McShea

They're opening their own shop. They see their broker making gross commissions on the transactions they produce and think the broker is getting rich. Or their entrepreneurial spirit is growing. Some just want to become the next niche broker or franchisee in the area.

Brown

How can I make associates stay?

Instill a sense of loyalty by treating them well. My biggest challenge is to continually remind myself to focus on what I can do to help those I work with. Our office environment fosters team spirit, cooperation, and mentoring between associates. We work at making the workplace fun. It's not unusual for us to fire up the grill for cookouts. Several of our professional alliance partners (mortgage brokers, computer technicians, soil scientists, surveyors) stop by to join us.

Baker

—Robert Freedman. This piece originally appeared in
the July 2004 issue of REALTOR® Magazine.

TODAY'S NEW RECRUITS: THEIR STRENGTHS AND WEAKNESSES

What value—and challenge—do all the new licensees streaming into the industry bring with them? We asked our panel of industry experts to report on real estate's new entrants.

Strengths

Bilingual communication. To a greater degree than 10 years ago, we're attracting recruits from a rich array of cultures, particularly Asian and Hispanic, and these recruits come with language skills to reach buyers from these cultural backgrounds.

Richard Cosner

Good training from their previous fields. Those with business experience know technology, finance, marketing, sales, and database management.

Carol Johnson

Business organization. Those coming into this business right out of college bring the attitude that this *is* a business and requires a professional approach. That means discipline, organization, and a business plan. They're not coming in to see if they can make some money while they decide what to do with their lives. Plus, their technology skills are sec-ond nature to them.

Cosner

Financial resources. They're coming over from other fields with money to invest in their career. They're writing business plans and purchasing marketing materials, coaching, and mentoring services. They aren't sitting around, waiting to be trained.

Johnson

Strong understanding of law and practice. We've seen a dramatic improve-ment in this area in the past 10 years, thanks to better instruction and more sophisticated recruits from corporate jobs. New recruits are much more aware of what's right and what's wrong when dealing with a spe-cific situation than recruits of the past. It used to be you went to school just to pass the state real estate licensing exam. But now instructors walk you through ways to respond to different situations.

Jack O'Connor

High motivation. They want to be in control of their own business suc-cess and are asking informed questions in interviews with brokers. They no longer see the corporate world as a source of job security.

Johnson

Weaknesses

One-on-one communication skills. We've become such an electronic society that we've lost some face-to-face skills. We try to help new recruits in this area by setting up chances for face-to-face or over-the-phone contact with customers in a nonthreatening environment. For example, we organized a party in one of our offices featuring wines from 14 countries and various cheeses and encouraged new associates to call and invite our past clients—and talk some business.

O'Connor

Marketing and closing skills. New licensees are coming in knowing the rules of the game but with little knowledge of practical skills such as prospecting, negotiating, and getting to closing.

William Baker

Generational sensitivities. Typical sales associates are in their mid-fifties and increasingly buyers are in their twenties. Technology is the biggest barrier between these generations, although that's diminishing. There are also disconnects between young associates and older buyers and sellers, such as downsizing baby boomers. The key here is creating a culture in which associates treat their customers as partners. That means young associates asking their older customers a lot of questions, operating with integrity, and holding each other accountable for honest interaction.

Steve Brown

MORE ONLINE

Latest Thinking on Hiring and Holding Stars

REALTOR® Magazine Online maintains broker toolkits on recruiting and retention. Among the topics: best questions to ask when interviewing, what top performers want from you, and ensuring your training pays off. Access the toolkits at www.realtor.org/realtormag under "Brokerage Management."

Why Associates Work Where They Do

Wouldn't you like to know what sales associates are thinking when they decide to affiliate—or not affiliate—with your brokerage? Here are questions sales pros say they like to get answers to before they decide where to hang their license, followed by their thoughts on why they like working where they do—and why they don't.

Questions for Brokers

1. What's the average associate sales volume?
2. What's the associate turnover rate, especially among experienced ones?
3. How much flexibility is offered on commission splits?
4. Are there sales quotas, and if so what are they?

5. What costs are included in desk fees? Which costs are charged separately?

6. How are broker charges deducted? Are they taken from commissions when received, paid once a month, or some other way?

7. What is the company's market share, and how has that share changed over the past three years?

8. Are there niches or geographic areas the company specializes in?

9. What types of corporate advertising does the company do and what is the response rate from the ads?

10. How profitable is the company, and how has the net return changed over the past three years?

11. Is the brokerage company run in a businesslike manner, with policies to ensure smooth operation?

12. What is the owner's growth strategy? Expansion? Franchise affiliation? Merger?

13. If the owner is over 55, what's the business succession plan?

14. What's the culture of the office, friendly and low-key or aggressive and motivated?

15. How much hands-on associate support and training is there?

16. What's the company's reputation? Have complaints been filed against it in the past five years with the real estate commission?

17. Does the company have strong name recognition?

18. Does the company offer ancillary services?

19. What technology is used?

Why I Work Where I Do

Sales associates share why they made a switch.

A smaller, independent broker was able to implement changes faster, pay commissions on the day of settlement, and keep overhead low. Plus, the broker's a friend, not an enforcer.

Steve Jacobson, CRB, CRS®, Brian Logan
Real Estate, Washington, D.C.

A company that's considering opening a new office in the future provides an opportunity for growth, a sense of a startup with the security of market share.

> Patricia J. Hyland, ABR®, Flemming
> Realty, New Paltz, New York

A bigger office offers more opportunity once you're established. I don't want to be a big fish in a small pond; I'd rather be a little fish and still have room to grow and achieve.

> Joan Cox, GRI, CRS®, Metro Brokers-Priority
> Properties, Inc., Englewood, Colorado

A broker with sales experience and a respect for what it takes to succeed in sales, along with a fierce adherence to the National Association of REALTORS® Code of Ethics and a commitment to superior service.

> Vickie Flowe, Century 21 Hecht Realty,
> Cornelius, North Carolina

The lure of the chance to make more money and to run my own business with limited management interference. Getting past the difficult decision to "upset" a comfortable position was the hardest part of making the change.

> Rayelynn Fagot-Canzoneri, ABR®, CRS®,
> Metrosell Team New Orleans, RE/MAX
> Real Estate Partners, Metairie, Louisiana

A broker who really took the time to answer my ton of questions and really talked to me about the business.

> Susan Crawford, Coldwell Banker Ward &
> Misenheimer, Durham, North Carolina

Access to an attorney for legal advice (free of charge) plus leading edge technologies give me the tools to serve my clients better.

> Kimberly Lester, John L. Scott Real Estate,
> Issaquah, Washington

Honesty and integrity about how the business works. In my years with the company, I've seen my broker lose associates to other companies that promised them a rose garden. Sometimes those associates returned when they found out that their garden had more thorns than ours did.

> Liz Francis, Century 21 North Homes,
> Puget Sound, Washington

Be a part of the decision-making process that shapes our office. I'm treated as a partner.

> Roy Chambers, Keller Williams Realty,
> Everett, Washington

A broker who has a sense of humor and knows how to have fun as well as provide support. She's adamant that we have balance in our lives and helps us see everything in perspective. You've got to love someone who'll jump in the water to help paddle our entry into the local charity race—a floating castle made of milk cartons—to victory.

> Sally Thompson, ABR®, John L. Scott Real Estate,
> North Seattle, Washington

Five Reasons Why They Leave

Too high an overhead.

Too much bureaucracy and company control.

Too small a share of the commission.

Too many meetings.

Too many transaction fees and unnecessary charges.

> —*Mariwyn Evans. This article originally appeared in the January 2003 issue of REALTOR® Magazine Online.*

---

10 REASONS I CHOSE MY BROKERAGE

1. The reputation of the company's associates in the transactions I was involved in.
2. Owners and brokers who were smart businesspeople with several well-managed offices.
3. Geographic proximity to my home.

4. Company's standing among other real estate offices in the area. I wanted to be around other successful associates to inspire myself to reach the next level.

5. Professional office facilities with private offices but enough agents to keep overhead costs down.

6. A company commitment to education.

7. An experienced office manager who could answer questions when needed.

8. A skilled office staff to assist clients and associates.

9. Autonomy—I really feel like I run my own business.

10. Great name recognition—both for the franchise and the company.

Mary Zentz, CRS®, GRI, RE/MAX
Suburban, Arlington Heights, Illinois

Behavioral Testing:
Hire Recruits That Fit In

For many companies, affiliating associates is a stab in the dark. Brokers often rely on their instincts about whether an applicant possesses the traits to hit the ground running and effectively mesh with the rest of the sales force. That's not to disparage gut feelings. Instincts serve hiring managers well.

But today, given escalating broker costs in training and putting out fires set by inexperienced associates, relying on chance isn't good enough anymore. What's more, a new recruit who's good at selling may operate in a style that rubs others in the office the wrong way. That could harm office camaraderie and impact others' productivity.

For these reasons, an increasing number of real estate office managers and brokers are adding analytical behavioral assessments to their hiring processes—not just for sales associates but for office support staff as well. They're also using testing to help associates improve their performance, address potential behavioral conflicts in the office, and identify existing salespeople's traits to match recruits to the office.

"It helps you get a good heads-up on people's personality—whether they're expressive or analytical or amiable—and I really like having that upfront information," says Beckie Hanley, senior vice president at William Raveis International in Greenwich, Connecticut. "If I'm looking for an administrative person, sales manager, or assistant, I want the person to be more analytical or amiable than emotional in order to bring strengths that top salespeople might lack."

Judy LaDeur, president of Forum Recruiting and Management Solutions in Chicago, works with several large regional brokerage clients and tests hundreds of sales professionals a year. LaDeur says she's seeing more real estate offices using some form of behavioral profiling to identify recruits' behavioral traits.

To be sure, behavioral testing in recruiting remains the exception rather than the rule. But it's gaining ground, recruiters say.

Several years ago, few of the country's large independent residential real estate companies had even heard of testing; now many are exploring it, recruiters say. Some national franchise companies, too, including Keller Williams and the California and Hawaii regions of RE/MAX International, are starting to use it.

Given its increasing presence in real estate offices, is there a downside to testing? There could be if brokers and managers think assessing someone's behavioral traits will give them all the answers about someone that they need. It won't. "It would be a mistake to assume you can determine whether to affiliate someone just on the strength of an assessment," says LaDeur. "It's just one tool for you to use."

Different Traits Mean Different Paths to Success

There are a handful of major analytical tests, including Myers-Briggs, which analyzes people's thought processes, and DISC (dominance, influencing, steadiness, and compliance), which focuses on behavioral traits. The DISC test identifies eight behavioral styles:

1. *Analyzers:* Quality performers who can have a hard time closing projects; they're cerebral detail people.
2. *Conductors:* Driven, competitive, focused, sometimes explosive performers. They're weak on detail work.
3. *Coordinators:* Quality performers who have a calming, relationship-oriented touch.
4. *Implementers:* Detail people with a sense of urgency for getting things done. But they're weak on persuading.

5. *Persuaders:* Influential performers who are good at getting people to see things their way.

6. *Promoters:* Enthusiastic performers who are good at getting others excited about a project.

7. *Relaters:* Relationship-focused performers; sociable.

8. *Supporters:* Family-oriented, calming performers.

Each trait in its own way can lead to real estate success. But different traits work better in different environments, depending on the broader characteristics of the office. For example, an implementer could complement an office with a lot of persuaders or conductors.

Find out what style of team you have by testing a sample of people and using the scores to develop a profile. Once you've identified that profile, you can look for recruits who complement the mix. (See "Matchmaker, Matchmaker.")

Finding the Right Tool

Not all behavioral tests will be right for your recruiting efforts. Look for these features in the system you adopt:

Ease of use. In general, testing systems use a series of questions to assess applicants. But the questions must be easy to understand and shouldn't take more than 30 minutes to answer. Any more than that and people will answer hastily just to complete the questionnaire.

Technologically advanced. Many systems are Internet based—a big plus, especially if the testing company can e-mail a report to your office immediately after the candidate completes the test. The online tests should be intuitive and user friendly since you, not a technology person, will administer, interpret, and use them. Keep a paper-and-pencil version on hand in case the technology doesn't cooperate at test time.

Accurate. Make sure the report you get is face valid, which means the people answering the questions agree with the picture the report paints of them. Also make sure that the tool is designed to spot cheating on the test takers' part. Test takers are said to cheat if they answer certain combinations of questions inconsistently, which is seen as indicating that they're trying to answer questions in a way they believe the broker wants.

Performance based. The testing company should help you develop a profile of who would succeed in your company and analyze test results in a way that meets your needs. For instance, if you're looking for support staff to work with conductors, you can use the reports to identify the best people for that.

Multiple uses. These systems cost you money. It's better to get one that is flexible and can be used for various purposes, rather than a system that works just for recruiting new associates. For instance, a system that also helps you communicate more effectively with existing salespeople and staff by helping you identify people's learning styles and preferred methods of communicating is a valuable tool.

Time for Testing

Tests are available for well under $100 per person tested, although total costs would be more if you add consulting services to analyze the results.

But to the extent testing can help you identify the right support staff and salespeople who have the traits to sell well and who'll stick around after you've invested time and money to recruit and train them, the investment may well be worth it. The alternative could be too much reliance on one's instincts.

—Michael Abelson. *This article originally appeared in the June 2003 issue of REALTOR® Magazine.*

MATCHMAKER, MATCHMAKER

In every office you'll find rainmaker types—people who generate the big ideas and pull in the clients—and indispensable detail people who turn rainmaker leadership into results. Who works well with whom, and at what jobs? Here are a few ideas based on the DISC behavioral styles.

The Rainmakers

Look for conductors, promoters, persuaders, and relaters to be your office rainmakers. Generally, they're sociable, enthusiastic, and visionary. Conductors tend to be competitive and not as sociable as the other rainmakers, preferring to get right to the point. Relaters may be the most sociable of all, and sometimes may need help to stay on task. Persuaders and promoters can be thought of as fitting somewhere between the other two. No one type of rainmaker is superior to the others, and any office would likely do well to have a mix of different types.

Since rainmakers often neglect the details, look for support staff who can fill in where these top salespeople are weak. Similarly, if a top performer is looking to hire team members, that person can look for people whose behavioral styles would be complementary. "I've used the DISC to identify the skills missing in my teams and then used the report to make sure the people I'm hiring have those skills," says Dianna Kokoszka, managing broker for Keller Williams Advantage Realty, Lakewood, Colorado, who's had a team of six administrative staff and buyer's agents at previous companies. Kokoszka, who has sold more than 250 properties a year, made her remarks while she was an associate with RE/MAX Affiliates in Golden, Colorado, in 2003.

The Detail People

Implementers, supporters, analyzers, and coordinators are typically detail oriented and focus on objectives. Analyzers are cerebral and do well at structured tasks, making them good choices for back-office functions such as accounting and technology support. They may not make the strongest salespeople, but they could be outstanding in roles demanding strong attention to detail, including personal assistant and office executive. They may not always mix well with conductors.

Supporters are calming and helpful, and can keep sociable people on task without ruffling feathers. Strong supporter types often fill personal assistant positions. Implementers can be thought of as easier-going versions of analyzers, and coordinators as more task-oriented versions of supporters.

MORE ONLINE

Take the Jung Typology Test

Humanmetrics.com offers a sample Jung Typology test (based on Myers-Briggs) at its web site, www.humanmetrics.com.

Simulating the Real Estate Sales Experience

Upward Motion's online program, at www.realestatesimulator.com, walks you through the types of situations sales associates confront daily to help you determine if a real estate career is a good match for you. Brokerages can host the simulator on their company web site as a recruiting aid.

Inclusionary Recruiting:
Brightest under the Rainbow

QUICK TIPS

Get community leaders involved in your recruiting efforts.

Conduct home buying seminars in areas with strong diversity.

Help new immigrants gain English proficiency.

Bill Mathers didn't set out to turn his residential brokerage into a melting pot reflective of the growing cultural diversity in Charlotte, North Carolina. But thanks to a recruiting and management style that's drawn a loyal cadre of sales associates from all walks of life and cultural backgrounds, Mathers has found himself presiding over a microcosm of a changing America. And now he intends to nurture that aspect of his business.

"It never occurred to me that we were creating anything special here, but now I'm starting to think about it," says Mathers, who launched MathersRealty.com in the early 1980s with a handful of associates and has since grown it to about 117 associates, all working out of one office.

Just under half of the company's associates are minority or foreign-born, many having been in the United States for only a few years before earning their real estate license and landing in Mather's company. Some 22 languages are spoken at his office, including Chinese, German, Greek, Italian, Polish, Russian, and Spanish, making the company popular with immigrant customers. "Hearing so many languages spoken here adds to why I love coming into the office every morning," says Mathers.

The Inclusionary Approach

As Mathers' company attests, brokers don't need to make upfront policy declarations to attract and retain associates from a range of cultures. But there are tactics you can use to actively recruit an ethnically diverse sales force, say brokers.

An *open attitude*. Embracing people of different ethnic backgrounds can't be faked, says Gene Simpson, ABR®, broker-owner of Jobin Realty in Fairfax, Virginia. "You must be willing to welcome cultural differences," he says, such as recognizing what other cultures regard as a sign of respect. Simpson owns an office of 80 associates, of whom about 40 percent are minority or foreign-born.

Genuine openness means parking preconceived notions at the door before interviewing candidates from other cultures, says Sharon Taylor, CRB, CRS®, executive vice president of MathersRealty.com. "It's easy to be judgmental based on the way nonnative speakers approach English," she says. But fluency and how English sounds coming out of a foreign-born person's mouth are two different matters—an important distinction.

"I have one associate who is a nonnative speaker and, when she gets excited, she speaks English really fast. Given her accent, it becomes hard to understand what she's saying," says Mathers. "It's appropriate to help people for whom English is a second language address that because it can affect their success. But behind her language challenges, there's no doubt how effective she is."

Encouraging continuing education is a chief way to help with language problems. Taylor encouraged one associate who was self-conscious about her language skills to take English classes at the community college. She did, and it helped her speak more clearly, which bolstered her confidence. Taking classes toward professional designations, such as the ABR®, CRS®, or GRI, also helps nonnative speakers hone their language skills while they develop their industry knowledge, Taylor says.

Inclusive outreach. As communities become diverse, finding a pool of minority and foreign-born licensees to draw from becomes easier, thanks to licensing rolls that increasingly reflect the changing community. "We're finding that the list the state real estate commission publishes twice a month of people scheduled to take the licensing exam is very diverse," says Taylor. "That gives us a great starting point."

But your state commission's pre-license list is only one recruiting avenue. Others include:

Community leaders. Learn who the cultural leaders are in the community you're targeting. "We joined the Latin American Chamber of Commerce and asked the organization's leadership to tell us how to best handle recruiting," says Mathers. "Such involvement can be extremely important to give your efforts credibility, but you have to report back to the leaders on how it's going. That reinforces to them that you're serious. Soon they had people calling me."

Places of worship. These are good sources, especially for finding African American and Hispanic candidates. "It's important for many faith leaders to encourage people in their community to move into these visible positions," says Mathers.

Presentations. Speak at events sponsored by or that attract distinct communities of people. You can kick-start those opportunities by hosting your own career or home ownership events or joining your local or state association's diversity committee.

Mathers, a member of the North Carolina Association of REAL-TORS® Equal Opportunity Cultural Diversity Committee, has touted real estate sales at a Hispanic high school career convention, which has brought exposure to both the industry and his brokerage. "Real estate is one of the few businesses in which people with a lot of initiative can succeed whether or not they choose to pursue higher education," says Mathers. "That's an important message for people to hear."

Regional giant Coldwell Banker Burnet in Edina, Minnesota, sponsors job fairs and other events, including home ownership seminars, which are aimed at home buyer opportunity but can double as recruiting outreach, says Robin Peterson, GRI, company president. Among the events her company has hosted: the 2004 Cross Cultural Home Ownership Alliance Conference, which promoted home ownership among African American, Hispanic, and Asian communities. The company has 3,000 sales associates in 38 offices in Minnesota and western Wisconsin.

Peer recruiting. The best source for diverse recruits by far is your own minority and immigrant sales associates, say brokers. If minority and foreign-born associates are comfortable at your office, they'll pull in others from their community who are interested in a real estate career and "speak positively about the company and the career opportunities we offer them," says Peterson.

In early February, in what he says was a fairly typical week, Danny Brock, ABR®, e-PRO®, broker-owner of Century 21 Brock & Associates in Wilmington, North Carolina, had half a dozen interviews lined up with people interested in affiliating with his company, several of them minorities recruited by his existing associates. Brock, whose brokerage has 32 associates, says about 15 percent are minority or foreign-born.

Like many brokers, Mathers offers his associates a recruitment incentive. If an associate brings in another, the original associate receives 8 percent of what the newbie makes (the company dollar side) up to

$15,000 in a calendar year. The commission incentive continues as long as both remain at the company. If the newest associate then recruits someone else, he gets the same arrangement and the original associate receives 4 percent of the second recruit's commission.

For Mathers, peer recruiting has become so common that it's the main reason for the growth of diversity in his office—and also one of the reasons the recruits fit in fairly quickly. "The beauty is that others [of that cultural background] can help with the recruits' transition," says Mathers.

Mathers has found his diversity efforts are good business. In five of the past seven years, Mathers' top producer has been either a minority or foreign born. Isn't that what the American dream is all about?

—*Robert Freedman. This article appeared in the
April 2005 issue of REALTOR® Magazine.*

RESPECT DIFFERENCES, EMPHASIZE POLICY

Once on board, it's respect for cultural differences that keeps recruits from going elsewhere, say brokers. You show respect by taking seriously the different views recruits bring into the office without changing your standards to accommodate them.

In some cultures, for example, it's not unusual for buyers and sellers to continue negotiating for a better deal right up until the keys change hands—a far cry from the United States, where negotiations end after the purchase agreement is signed.

In cases of cultural differences such as this, brokers should acknowledge the different approach but hold firm on accepted practices in the market. Continuous education is key, says Simpson. "We must educate associates so that they can in turn educate their customers and clients that transactions are conducted a certain way here," he says. Reiterate the company policy to all associates.

Simpson says he pays half the tuition for his new associates to get post-licensing training in the first six months after affiliation, and also covers half their costs if they want to pursue professional designations.

A NOTE ABOUT DISCRIMINATION

As you recruit, be aware that the federal Civil Rights Act prohibits discrimination in hiring, firing, promoting, and other actions affecting employees on the basis of their membership in a protected class: race, color, gender, age, religion, disability, and national origin. State laws may cover additional classes here, too. Although most sales associates are independent contractors for tax purposes, it's sound practice to be aware of the prohibition against discrimination when affiliating new associates with your brokerage.

In addition, don't automatically assign sales associates to work with prospective clients simply because the client and the sales associate are both members of the same protected class under the federal Fair Housing Act (race, color, religion, gender, national origin, disability, and familial status) or their state's fair housing laws (which may also include sexual orientation, marital status, and source of income). Instead, let customers take the lead on whom they want to work with by letting them volunteer their preference, if any.

MORE ONLINE

Diversity Training for Your Associates

Brokers can sponsor the At Home with Diversity training program developed by the National Association of REALTORS® for their sales associates or learn about organizations in their area offering the program. The training introduces sales associates to the ways they can cross cultural bridges to help households from other cultures in the home buying and selling process. Access the At Home with Diversity program under "Diversity" at the Government Affairs section of www.realtor.org. Access an NAR diversity toolkit, with research reports on diversity issues in real estate, at the same section of the site.

Four Steps to Rookie Success

Prelicensing classes are full of students eager to break into real estate, but many won't stay in the field beyond a few months, brokers say. The reason: Rookies become discouraged by the slow pace of ramping up their business. Boost their chances for long-term success by helping them build a customer base even before they earn their real estate license. Once you extend an invitation for them to join your company:

1. Help them select an area they're comfortable with that isn't an obvious farm for another practitioner.

2. Assist them in identifying neighborhood publications, including community group or home owner association newsletters, in which to run personal marketing ads.

3. Work with them to execute a marketing program for the farm area. Execution includes developing a web site and marketing materials that position them as a neighborhood specialist.

4. And once they receive their license, have them start walking the area, attending yard sales, and getting to know the residents. This is how they'll learn helpful tidbits they can share with prospective customers about such things as which pizza parlor offers weekend discounts or which homemaker works as a freelance seamstress. Making themselves visible is more important than cold calling.

Ideas are from Kimberly Dawes-Luther, vice president of career development, RE/MAX Dallas Suburbs, Plano, Texas.

—Robert Freedman. This list originally appeared in the March 2005 issue of REALTOR® Magazine.

Health and Safety

Work-Life Balance: Got Health?

Wally Folks, GRI, has been known to give out vitamins to friends and associates. He's been encouraging his sales associates and staff for years to pay more than lip service to their health.

"In 1989, I learned I had high levels of cholesterol, blood pressure, and triglycerides," says Folks, broker-owner of Century 21 Folks Realty in San Antonio. "They were off the charts. My doctor said he knew four people whose levels were that high, and three of them were dead. From that point on, I knew the importance of taking care of yourself."

When one of Folks' associates finally took himself in for a physical earlier this year, the results brought the same reality home to him: Testing identified several polyps in his colon.

The polyps weren't cancerous, but for a man in his mid-forties, as this associate was, getting at them early meant the difference between a routine procedure and a major operation.

For Folks, success in real estate is as much about taking time out for yourself as it is leaping from the dinner table to meet with a client. "We're on the go all the time, and with all the stress in our business, it doesn't make sense to ignore your health so you can earn $1 million a year," he says. "If you have a stroke, you won't be earning that anyway."

Whether your company is large or small, putting health on associates' radar screen is less about implementing expensive programs than setting the right tone, say brokers.

Several associates at Wilshire, REALTORS®, in Pacific Palisades, California, a new-condo specialist with a few dozen associates, acquired the exercise habit several years ago after watching their two brokers, William (Lynn) Borland and Bill Schwarz, compete in marathons and sailing races, respectively. "We don't have the resources to get a bulk discount at a gym for our associates or bring in speakers for a nutrition seminar, but we can lead by example," says Borland, a veteran of 45 marathons who runs each morning. "All we can say is, 'Here's what we're doing,' and it works. Your associates realize that, with a little effort, they can do it, too."

Put Family First

Just as important as exercise is time spent with family and engaged in activities you find intellectually stimulating. That time helps promote the work-life balance that's essential to staying at your peak, says Marianne Barkman, senior vice president at John L. Scott Real Estate in Bellevue, Washington. "When you promote a balanced lifestyle in the office, you can't measure the effect it has on your associates. But from our experience, they're hungry for the chance to focus on personal growth," she says. "Whenever we offer activities that help them find ways to gain balance, they jump at the opportunity." The company offers work-life balance training for all of its roughly 3,800 sales associates and brokers.

Now, even NAR has gotten into the act of helping members gain balance in their life. The association's FamilyTime Initiative, introduced at the 2004 REALTORS® Conference & Expo in Orlando, is designed to help you carve out quality family time. There are also family-first resources, in DVD format, that you can share with buyers and sellers as client gifts.

"How do you strengthen the time you have for you and your family and make it more meaningful?" says Al Mansell, NAR 2005 president, who spearheaded the initiative. "That's something we're hoping these resources can help you with."

The DVD is produced jointly by NAR and Million Dollar Round Table, an organization of top insurance and financial planning advisers that developed the first FamilyTime program in the 1970s. The program's goal, like that of Folks, is to help you focus more on the quality—rather than the quantity—in your life.

Low-Cost Ways to Promote Health

Ready to get your associates thinking about their health? Start with a few ideas from brokers who are already doing it:

Launch a book club. Start out meeting once a month, then increase the frequency to once every two weeks as demand warrants. Focus on leadership books such as *The 21 Indispensable Qualities of a Leader* by John Maxwell, or keep it broad to include inspirational books such as *The Four Agreements: A Practical Guide to Personal Freedom* by Don Miguel Ruiz. "Associates appreciate the opportunity to get to know their peers on a different level, and it gives them a chance to read thought-provoking books they wouldn't otherwise find the time to read."
Marianne Barkman, senior vice president,
John L. Scott Real Estate, Bellevue, Washington

Hold friendly competitions. Three possibilities: bowling, volleyball, and "wallyball" (volleyball played inside a racquetball court). Start out meeting one weekday evening every two months, then increase the frequency to once a month if demand warrants. If you have two or more offices, have one office play another, or have brokers and managers play associates. "For some of our associates, it's a great release, and more are expressing an interest in joining."
Todd Hetherington, CRS®, GRI, CEO, Century 21
New Millennium, Alexandria, Virginia

Help associates get family support for their work. Since even top associates can fail if family members aren't on board with their hectic schedule, brokers should help associates make planning a family affair. That means encouraging associates to

Involve their family in goal setting. Chasing a sales goal might be gratifying to associates, but it could foster resentment in the family. Family members should have input into associates' goals and work schedules.

Schedule time for family. If associates coach soccer or just like to be there when their children engage in certain activities, make it clear you support their absence from the office at those times.

Schedule time for solo activities. If associates take two afternoons a month to, say, deliver meals to senior citizens, encourage them to build that into their schedule as rigorously as they do sales meetings.

Celebrate their successes with their family. Encourage associates to have pizza night or another regular activity after a closing, anything to make their family feel a part of the success.

Matt Williams, broker-owner, Realty Executives
Williams-Sykes Realty, Wappingers Falls, New York

Encourage tag teams. To give associates with young families flexibility to spend time with their children, create sign-up forms to enable associates to tag team with other associates who can cover for them when they're on a family matter. The sign-up forms can list dates and times when people are available, to help associates match up with tag-team partners.

Hetherington

Encourage health maintenance. At a median 51 years, sales associates are at an age when regular medical attention is crucial for nipping health problems in the bud. Provide them friendly reminders to

Have regular blood, urine, and other diagnostic tests. This helps them get the jump on cancers, diabetes, and other degenerative disorders.

Get plenty of rest. Is five hours a night enough? They should check with a doctor.

Ask about supplements. Is it appropriate to take supplements such as Vitamin C and beta carotene? Encourage them to find out what a doctor thinks.

Wally Folks, GRI, broker-owner, Century 21
Folks Realty, San Antonio, Texas

Offer healthy alternatives to snacking. Replace your soda and other vending machines with fresh fruit delivery and your conventional water cooler with one that filters impurities, such as those using reverse osmosis. And subscribe to a wellness newsletter that you can circulate through your office.

Kim Cipriano Prior, vice president of corporate business and
public relations, Lyon Real Estate, Sacramento, California

Partner with others to leverage resources. Work with other local companies or your local REALTOR® association to bring in speakers or sponsor health and wellness programs you otherwise couldn't afford.

William (Lynn) Borland, broker, Wilshire,
REALTORS®, Pacific Palisades, California

Helping your associates maintain their good health can be as easy and cost-free as offering them a little encouragement. But the benefit to you and to them can be as great as a lifetime of productivity and sound work-life balance.

The Feng Shui Way

Good health isn't just about getting the right mix of vitamins and exercise. So says feng shui consultant Suzee Miller. The former broker-owner of Paradigm Properties in Laguna Hills, California, now teaches clients about arranging their office using feng shui principles, applying the ancient Chinese energy-balance blueprint called *ba-gua.*

If you want your associates, staff, and visitors to experience positive energy in your office (and who wouldn't?), try these feng shui tips from Miller:

Add a welcome doormat. The entrance is where all blessings and abundance enter a business. Try a mat of deep blue, representing water, which increases wealth.

Showcase colorful flowers in pots. They lift the energy in the room. Try flowers or pots of red, representing fire, which increases business.

Ensconce a healthy green plant. A plant adds the wood element, which can lift energy and morale.

Remove clutter. If left to sit, piles of paper and trash will prompt the holographic universe to mirror back to you the same negativity in the form of difficult buyers and sellers or contracts and escrows that fall out.

Keep nonbusiness visuals to a minimum. That means go sparingly on family photos and other personal items. Otherwise the environment could create anxiety and stress.

—*Robert Freedman. This article originally appeared in
the October 2004 issue of REALTOR® Magazine.*

MORE ONLINE

Helping Associates Stay Proactive on Health

REALTOR® Magazine Online maintains a "Your Health" section with resources you can tap to help your associates stay proactive on their physical well-being. "Your Health" is under the site's "Tools" section.

Preempting Stress

An online help center at www.helping.apa.org operated by the American Psychological Association makes resources available to help people cope with stress before it grows into a hard-to-manage problem.

Keeping Associates Attuned to Safety

Thanks to REALTOR® Safety Week, practitioner security is in the spotlight one week every September. But how do you make your sales associates' well-being a year-round concern? Set up an ongoing safety program that associates can't file away and quickly forget.

Start by visiting the Real Estate Safety Council web site (www .warealtor.com/safety), for its *Personal Safety Guide*, and REALTOR® Magazine Online, for its prepackaged Sales Meeting on Safety. Both resources are free.

In 2002, practitioners in Washington D.C., launched the nonprofit Real Estate Safety Council after the murder of one of their colleagues. The Council's guide has been adopted by dozens of state and local associations in the United States and Canada.

What's in the guide: Twelve safety posters, one for each month. Each poster highlights a tried, true, and tested safety tip designed by and for real estate associates with the help of safety experts, crime survivors, and police.

How to use it: Distribute the guide at a sales meeting and walk your associates and office staff through the topics. Your associates will likely come up with their own safety ideas as part of the discussion. Pass those ideas on to the Council. Then put up one poster each month to keep your associates' focus on safety.

Personal Safety Guide at a Glance

Know whom you're dealing with. Encourage associates to meet customers at the office and photocopy customers' driver's license.

Tell someone at the office whom you're going with. Let that person know where you're going and when you should be back.

Keep a cell phone at your side. Keep it charged, program in 911, don't leave it in your purse or car, and make sure the office has the number.

Be safe at open houses. Don't advertise a listing as vacant. Establish escape routes and call a designated friend or colleague hourly.

Have a distress code. If a person makes you uneasy, call your office and speak in a prearranged code—"Bring the red file to 123 Maple St."— to avoid arousing the person's suspicion and to dispatch a colleague or the police to join you.

Don't be overly personal in your marketing. Say no to glamour shots and don't give away revealing personal information.

Heed your gut reaction. If a prospect makes you uneasy, bring a buddy with you on showings.

Dress for safety. Don't wear expensive jewelry, limit the cash and cards you carry, dress for the weather, and wear shoes you can run in.

Keep your car ready. Keep it serviced and park it where you can access it quickly. If you must take one car, never let the prospect drive.

Let customers lead. When showing a house, let the customer enter a room first. Don't turn your back on the person.

Take flight, and sometimes fight. Throw your wallet or purse one way and run the other. Usually, an assailant will go after the money. If you strike back, mean it.

Other Material to Mine

You'll find more resources to share with your associates at REALTOR® Magazine Online:

A link to the REALTOR® Safety Week home page.

The Prepackaged Sales Meeting on Safety, which includes an agenda, talking points, activities, and a 10-second rule for assessing your surroundings. Are you parked in a well-lit, visible location? Is anyone present who shouldn't be?

A link to NAR's Field Guide on Safety, a compendium of safety tips and articles.

With these tools, you'll offer a real service to associates and help them make staying safe second nature.

—*Robert Freedman. This article originally appeared in the September 2004 issue of REALTOR® Magazine.*

MORE ONLINE

Ready-to-Go Safety Programs

No need to reinvent the wheel when it comes to safety. Well-thought-out programs are already in place. Start with the package of materials developed by the Real Estate Safety Council with assistance from the Washington Association of REALTORS® at www.warealtor.com/safety.

Know Sexual Harassment When You See It

Sexual harassment in the workplace is a key safety issue, both for women and men. But what constitutes sexual harassment isn't always clear. Help your sales associates gain a better awareness of what constitutes sexual harassment with this simple test.

Sexual Harassment Quiz

1. Most sexual harassment is based on sexual advances.

True

False

2. Before someone can complain of sexual harassment, he or she must have lost some tangible job benefit.

True

False

3. The company can be held liable for sexual harassment committed by its brokers or sales associates.

True

False

4. A broker can be held liable if a client, customer, contractor, or other nonemployee sexually harasses a sales associate.

True

False

5. If you are talking to a co-worker about sexual fantasies and another sales associate overhears the conversation, that person can't complain of sexual harassment because the comment wasn't directed at him or her.

True

False

6. If a person submits to sexual harassment and engages in a sexual act with someone from the office, he or she can't complain about it afterward.

True

False

Answers

1. False. Sexual harassment can be a power issue and may not involve an actual advance.

2. False. No tangible benefit, such as a promotion or a pay raise, needs to have been lost for sexual harassment to occur. Actions that create a hostile work environment are also illegal.

3. True. The company may be held liable for sexual harassment by the broker and, in some cases, the sales associates during work-related activities.

4. True. The broker may be liable if he or she was notified of the conduct and failed to take immediate corrective action.

5. False. If a conversation interferes with the person's work and creates an offensive, intimidating, or hostile work environment, it may be sexual harassment.

6. False. The issue is whether the advances were welcome, not whether the complainant's participation was voluntary.

> —*From* Sexual Harassment Awareness and Prevention, Facilitator's
> Guide, *National Association of REALTORS®, available*
> *under "Quizzes" at REALTOR® Magazine Online.*

Helping Associates Cope with Personal Crises

One day one of Mark W. Re's sales associates just disappeared. No call. No e-mail. It wasn't until several days later that the associate's wife called and explained the mystery: Her husband had checked himself into an alcohol rehabilitation clinic, which allowed him to make only one call, which he'd made to his wife. Re, CRB, CRS®, is executive vice president and chief operating officer of Gallinger/GMAC Real Estate in Syracuse, New York.

For brokers and managers of real estate offices, it's a rarity to have an associate suddenly drop out of sight like that. Less rare is helping your associates as they navigate a personal crisis, such as an illness or divorce. Indeed, that's part of the daily job description, says Jan Mansfield, CRB, CRS®, broker-owner of Century 21 Country North Inc. in Rockford, Illinois.

With 150 sales associates in five offices, Mansfield says it's typical for her to have three to four coping with a personal crisis at any one time.

Given the likelihood you'll have an associate in crisis at some point, it's imperative you see your role as part counselor and part friend, not just to help maintain associates as a productive part of the office but also to help them as people, says Mansfield. "Because we're independent contractors, we have a different bond with our people than corporate employers do," she says.

To help them weather the storm as quickly as possible so that they can shift their focus back to work, consider these ideas.

- *Launch a support group.* Mansfield started a group that meets regularly to give her associates a comfortable setting to open up with others. Her group is called "Not for Women Only" to make it clear it's open to male associates, too.

- *Show leniency.* In ordinary circumstances, Re expects associates who RSVP for a special training session the brokerage has arranged at some expense to pay their registration fee regardless of whether they attend. But when one of his associates learned she might have cancer (thankfully she didn't) halfway through a multiweek course, he gave her a rain check. "It's obviously just the right thing to do," he says.

- *Help financially.* If you give associates assistance, make it clear whether it's a loan or a gift and be prepared for some people to take advantage of your generosity. "People are very appreciative and, when you've made them a loan, they typically go out of their way to pay it back once they can. But there'll always be a few people who won't," says Mansfield. If the loan is informal, you lack legal recourse to get it paid back, so you absorb the loss. That can create tension between you and the associate. But in many cases the person ends up leaving soon afterward anyway, Mansfield says.

- *Minimize financial loss.* In cases where associates must take a leave of absence for a few months, help them arrange for other associates to cover their transactions, say Mansfield and Re. That does more than keep the pipeline flowing; it takes pressure off the associates so they can concentrate on recovery, the brokers say.

- *Beware of crisis addicts.* Occasionally you'll run into an associate who is always in a crisis. This person may be hiding behind crises as an excuse not to work. Let these associates go. "We had one associate who was going through divorce forever," says Mansfield. "She just wasn't working. We ended up terminating her, but she would have found any excuse not to work."

Above all, be there for your associates in need, even if it just means being a friend. "Write them a note, leave them a voice mail," says Mansfield. "Little gestures help carry people through."

—Robert Freedman. This article originally appeared in the
September 2005 issue of REALTOR® Magazine.

Achieving Work-Life Balance

Editor's note: For many of your sales associates, the pursuit of success often leads them on an exhilarating ride as they develop clients and close tough deals. But that ride can come screeching to a halt if it leads to burnout.

Is there a role for brokers and managers in helping their sales associates maintain a healthy balance between work and home life? Yes, says J. Lennox Scott, chairman and CEO of John L. Scott Real Estate, Seattle, Washington. In the following excerpt from his book, Next Generation Real Estate *(Dageforde Publishing Inc., 2002), co-authored with John L. Scott Real Estate Director of Public Relations Shelley Rossi, Scott shares a plan brokers can use to help associates keep their lives in balance.*

In any profession, it's easy for individuals to become so consumed by their career that perspective is lost, causing life to become unbalanced. Unfortunately, this is all too common in the real estate profession and often results in practitioners becoming burned out.

To be successful in next-generation real estate, it's vitally important for a practitioner to have a business plan, but even more important, the practitioner needs to develop a life plan.

Real estate companies must do their part to support their brokers and sales associates in this process by partnering with them in the development of life plans.

A life plan refers to a person's entire life, of which the professional aspect is only one component. Not to be confused with a business plan, a life plan addresses the different elements of an individual's personal life, such as

Spiritual growth.

Personal growth.

Physical health.

Personal relationships.

Parenting.

Powerful work experience.

Passion in life.

Personal finances.

Philanthropy.

Responsibility to future generations.

Community contributions.

Environmental protection.

What's important to think about when developing a life plan is where the work life should fit in. Work life should be considered the economic engine for a life plan. When work life is fulfilled, the individual is able to make money and build personal confidence, which transfers to the other areas of life. It works in the other direction, too; as one gains confidence in other areas of life, the work life will benefit. Because there are so many different aspects to any one person's life, it is important to organize those areas according to priority, so as to have a healthy balance. By doing so, the individual is better able to gain perspective and create an underlying purpose that provides life with an overall direction.

A life plan encourages people to set goals and develop affirmation. It communicates a sense of purpose and fosters positive thoughts and perspectives.

The motivation comes from looking deeply within to the underlying purpose in life, as opposed to looking to outside factors for motivation. When individuals take the time to organize the vital areas of their life, their focus is clearer and their outlook more positive. People with positive attitudes gravitate toward other people with positive attitudes. Furthermore, it takes less energy to achieve goals and move through life with a positive focus.

So how does this relate to real estate? Having a life plan allows real estate professionals to accomplish more in life, including their work life. It also has the potential to enhance relationships, both personal and professional. Having a life plan creates excitement that is reflected in interactions with business associates and clients. A life plan ultimately provides the tools to accomplish success in next generation real estate and in all areas of life.

Before developing a successful life plan there are several factors to consider. First and foremost, every person needs to ask, "What would I like to accomplish in life?" All your associates should have some idea of what they want to accomplish in life, whether it's personally, professionally, or both. The answer to this question will provide the direction needed to develop the objectives in a life plan.

In beginning the life plan process, the following questions should be considered.

What do I want?

What do I want to see?

What do I want to be?

What kind of person do I want to become?

What is my purpose in life?

What do I want to have?

Where do I want to go?

What would I like to share?

What is working in my life and what isn't?

What gets in my way?

Another way to go about this is to develop a *want list* made up of the eight highest priorities in your life. Making such a list will help uncover the answers to the previous questions.

Life is full of change. Therefore, a life plan should reflect change. The life plan developed at age 25 will probably be different by 40. The fundamental elements stay the same, but priorities shift depending on which stage in the life cycle has been reached. A life plan is best developed when one is young, because it provides strategic planning for the rest of that individual's life.

It's worthwhile to reexamine the life plan every year to keep sight of one's goals. The life plan will evolve a great deal over the years, but it's important to have constant direction and a plan from which to continually work.

Having a life plan is something I believe so strongly in that at John L. Scott Real Estate we are offering seminars to our brokers and sales associates to help them develop their life plans. Unfortunately, very few of us were taught about life plans in school, so it's important for managers and other real estate leaders to teach practitioners about their importance. I am in partnership for success with the professionals in my company; therefore, I make it a priority to provide them with the resources they need to achieve their goals. Developing and sustaining a life plan is a very important element of success and something that all sales associates and their brokers should aspire to achieve together.

> —*J. Lennox Scott and Shelley Rossi. Scott is chairman and CEO of John L. Scott Real Estate in Seattle, Washington. Rossi is director of public relations for the company. The passage is excerpted from* Next Generation Real Estate *(Dageforde Publishing Inc., 2002). Used with permission. Information on ordering the book is available from Rossi at shelleyro@johnlscott.com.*

HELP YOUR ASSOCIATES GET THERE

There are a number of ways you can help your associates develop a life plan to help them achieve a satisfying career and home life and avoid burnout. The approach taken by John L. Scott Real Estate, Seattle, Washington, is built around a day-long seminar offered to its associates. The company contracts with a trainer, Claudia Wicks, to host the seminars at locations around the company's Pacific Northwest operating area.

The first half of the seminar is a personal planning component. The trainer and participants discuss the importance of developing life plans and what the plans should include. Wicks guides participants through the process using a workbook, "Strategic Planning for the Soul." The workbook provides, among other things, guidance on creating "life accounts" for their goals, a personal mission statement, and an implementation plan.

The second half of the seminar concentrates on business-plan development. Wicks guides associates through the process that helps them identify their strengths and build a bottom-line oriented plan around those strengths.

"We've received a lot of positive feedback on the seminars," says Shelley Rossi, director of public relations for John L. Scott Real Estate. "It's making a great deal of difference for many of our associates."

Office Environment and Associate Motivation

Office Design That Keeps Associates on Top

The way your office looks can make a big difference in how well you compete—for customers and for associates.

"It's such a competitive environment that your office has to sell itself," says Michael Nevis, who opened an office in spring 2005 in Almaden Valley, California, for Alain Pinel, REALTORS®, a Northern California brokerage.

When Nevis was working with the architect to design the office, he had three goals in mind:

1. Attracting and keeping the best associates.

2. Making associates as productive as possible.

3. Putting customers at ease.

"This office makes it clear that we see the associates as our clients," says Nevis, who joined Alain Pinel in 1992 and has spent the past year preparing to open the company's first office in this high-end area near San Jose. "Creating nice-looking offices isn't a luxury anymore. The days when real estate offices could make do with plastic chairs are gone."

Even with more sales associates working from home, brokers are paying increasing attention to the look, feel, and flow of their offices, using "backstage" areas to boost associate productivity and "front stage" areas to help make customers feel like pampered guests.

"Associates are looking at the space when they're deciding whether to affiliate with the broker," says Susan Loeschner, district account manager with Denver-based Jordy Carter Furnishings. The company is a RE/MAX approved office designer. "The office environment must be smart and aesthetically pleasing."

To achieve both—and deal with the realities of escalating real estate costs—brokers have evolved their offices in several distinct directions. Today's offices have

- *More associates.* With the exception of boutiques and mom-and-pop brokerages, real estate offices are growing. "It's increasingly common to see offices of 150 associates—and even more than 200," says Nevis, who opened the Almaden Valley office with 40 associates and built space for 150.

  The trend is driven in part by rising real estate prices, which make it advantageous for brokers to concentrate as many associates in one location as possible. But technology also plays a role. With more associates connecting to the office remotely, handling 150 associates in one office is less of a management challenge than in the past, because only a fraction of the associates are in the office at any one time.

  That means more total square footage but less space per associate. "Many associates don't come into the office for more than eight hours in the whole week," says Nevis. "If all 150 associates were in the office at once, we could accommodate them. But the space is designed with the expectation that that doesn't happen often."

- *Flexible space.* Even with space at a premium, hard-walled offices aren't going away; brokers continue to dangle them as an incentive for associates to reach higher productivity. And private offices are increasingly important as more associates work in teams.

But the furniture for private offices is going modular. "Associates are coming and going, adding assistants, or deciding to work from home, so brokers need to change space quickly," says Loeschner. "They need to go in and change a single office to a double office in an hour."

Innovation in design has helped brokers accept modular furniture after years of holding back. "Five years ago brokers were afraid modular furniture was too techie-looking," says Loeschner. "It's more substantial-looking now, which is what brokers tend to prefer. Manufacturers are presenting furniture systems that offer a more sophisticated look, incorporating woods, metals, and detailed trim options."

- *Fewer cubicles.* Brokers continue to offer a gradation in workstations, from desks arranged in clusters to cubicles to semiprivate or shared offices to private offices. But in some companies, brokers are eliminating the cubicles.

  "Most associates, when they move up from open desks, are more productive in semiprivate or shared offices than in cubicles," says Jack Rainey, owner of Rainey Contract Design, a Memphis, Tennessee, company that works on office design for regional brokerage company Crye-Leike. "Brokers started moving away from those five or six years ago."

  The reduction in cubicles isn't creating issues for those seeking private space, since associates are increasingly mobile. They get privacy on the road. When they're in the office, they're looking to plunk their laptop down and start working. Thanks to wireless connectivity and hard-wired connection ports, which more and more offices have, any open desk is sufficient. "They just want to be instantly connected," says Nevis.

- *Separate front and back areas.* The idea that the reception area, conference rooms, and, in some cases, manager's office constitute a front area distinct from the backstage area is gaining currency. "Brokers are trying to get away from open visibility of associates' work spaces," says Loeschner. "They want the reception and conference areas to be visible, but they don't want customers coming back to where associates are working."

  The trend is about privacy and confidentiality as much as aesthetics. "Clients and associates from other companies shouldn't have to walk through the office to converse with associates or to see the manager," says Nevis. "They should be able to go directly to the manager straight from the reception area and conduct business in a way that's confidential and private."

There's also a productivity issue, because when associates see a colleague from another office, it's human nature for them to want to stop and talk. And that can put visiting associates in an awkward position if they're pressed for time, says Nevis.

Aesthetics are a factor, too. Brokers are increasingly seeing the importance of managing customers' experience with the brokerage, and that means creating an environment that's professional yet comfortable rather than clerical or administrative. "Reception areas are seen as a way to showcase the brokerage," says Loeschner (see "First Impression").

All these trends point to the need to create an office that combines functionality with a bit of showmanship. The functionality helps associates serve their customers, even when they're away from the office, and the showmanship gives them a sense of pride. "In a really competitive environment for sales associates," Loeschner says, "having an office that meets those needs can make a difference in hiring and retaining top producers."

—*Robert Freedman. This article originally appeared in the June 2005 issue of REALTOR® Magazine.*

FIRST IMPRESSION

When customers walk into your office, they should gain a sense of confidence in your professionalism. How you carry off that first impression will vary depending on your market. But, for many companies, creating the right first impression translates into lavish appointments:

- *Built-in reception desk.* A desk constructed to be part of the room—not just brought in—indicates permanency. Marble and granite desktops are common choices. Expect to pay $4,000 to $12,000, depending on where you are and the materials you're using. Marble and granite are on the high end, says Susan Loeschner, with Jordy Carter Furnishings in Denver.
- *Fireplace or water feature.* These features are increasingly popular with brokers to convey a homey, relaxed feel. Fireplaces use natural gas, and water features tend to be small waterfalls standing upright, mounted on the wall,

or horizontal on the floor. "They just add to the ambience of the office," says Loeschner. Cost: $1,000 and up, depending on size and material.

- *Seating.* There's a premium on comfort but couches and chairs should still be of commercial, rather than residential, design and quality. Commercial furniture is more durable and stresses ease of access; residential furniture wears out more quickly and can be hard for seniors and persons with a disability to get in and out of. Expect to pay at least $1,200. The sofa should come with at least a 10-year warranty, not including fabric. That typically comes with a two-year warranty.

- *Color.* White walls remain popular, especially with bold patterns in the art and in the carpet, but color palettes are increasingly common. "The last office we did had 10 different paint colors in the palette," says Loeschner.

  The offices of Memphis, Tennessee–based Crye-Leike, REALTORS®, favor burgundy and brass, says Jack Rainey of Rainey Contract Design in Memphis. Adding color typically adds little over the cost of white walls, because the paints usually sell for about the same amount, says Loeschner. But the painter might charge a bit more because switching paints makes the job more labor intensive.

- *Conference rooms.* Larger and more visible than in the past, meeting rooms today typically accommodate 8 to 10 people, up from 4 to 6 a decade ago (although many offices have a mix of small and large rooms).

  The growth of broker ancillary businesses, particularly settlement services, and technology are driving the space change. Brokers offering settlement services may use conference rooms for closings; thus, the rooms must be big enough to accommodate the principals, including their children, the settlement agent, and the sales associates. These larger conference tables start at about $1,000. You'll pay about twice that for one that comes built to handle data wiring for each seat. The alternative is to have a regular table modified to handle wiring, bringing the cost close to a wired table. Chairs run about $300 each.

  Some brokers are installing wall-mounted screens enabling them to use conference rooms for presentations and showing listings to sellers and buyers. "A 42-inch plasma is about $2,500," says Kurt Bowers, vice president of operations for Jordy Carter Furnishings. "It would have inputs for laptops, TV, and DVD." Large-scale LCD screens are nearly comparable in resolution quality now, he says. Wall mounts are $250 to $300 depending on type and functionality.

  Customers no longer need to huddle around a computer screen but can view presentations, including virtual tours, in comfort.

Adapting to Life with Gen X

QUICK TIPS

Tap Web marketing to reach new recruits.

Stay up on technology.

Keep meetings short.

Let young associates work with young customers.

The historically strong real estate market has drawn in a new generation of young practitioners, forcing brokers established in their ways to adapt to new ways of doing business. That often means putting a greater emphasis on technology, revamping recruitment and coaching strategies, and taking a new look at how sales meetings are structured.

"They don't like the sharing of old war stories," Natalie Carpenter, managing broker of the Chatham office of Coldwell Banker Residential in Chicago, says of the younger practitioners in her office. "They want bite-sized pieces of information and meetings that are short and concise."

Carpenter changed the focus of sales meetings to appeal to the younger set. Years ago, when her salespeople were a bit older and more uniform in age, motivational speakers were fitting for sales meetings, but now she invites guests to deliver presentations on how to accomplish tasks more efficiently and incorporate technology into their businesses—skills the new workers see as more central to their success.

Brokers and real estate executives, almost without exception, say the influx of new talent is a positive trend for their offices and the industry overall. But they also acknowledge challenges of adjusting to the different skill sets, ambitions, and interests of the new generation.

Generation Xers, the post-baby boomers born roughly between the early 1960s and mid- to late-1970s—varying slightly depending on which source you consult—make up the bulk of newcomers. But some of the younger rookies can even be classified as Generation Y, born in the late 1970s and early 1980s.

Their reasons for entering the business vary. Some are fresh out of school and see big opportunities in the booming real estate industry, while others choose real estate after trying out a different career path or losing a corporate job to downsizing.

Short on Experience, Long on Drive

When young practitioners lack sales experience, they compensate with quick learning and a drive to succeed, real estate executives say. Career-switchers, in particular, are well-suited to the real estate business, says Avram Goldman, CRB, president and chief operating officer for Coldwell Banker Northern California in San Ramon.

"They're used to being focused, passionate, and entrepreneurial, and they come to this industry possessing the skills and attitude needed to be top producers," says Goldman, whose company has seen many former dot-com workers transform into successful practitioners.

And most Gen X practitioners come well-equipped with technology skills they can use from the start to grow business and market themselves.

"In the old days, it took a person about 10 years to really build a solid career," says Harley E. Rouda Jr., CEO of Real Living in Columbus, Ohio. "Today, through Web marketing, new technologies, and a willingness to embrace the business quickly, they can generate income and be successful much faster."

A New Coaching Approach

Because so many new practitioners have no prior work experience in real estate, brokers are putting extra thought into training programs that channel the skills from employees' previous work experiences into productive careers selling properties.

Coldwell Banker Residential Real Estate Inc. in Coral Gables, Florida, which employs more than a dozen Gen Xers, developed a plan in which managers do one-on-one mentoring to help rookies set goals, identify a strong niche, create promotions, and develop a budget and business plan. Managers also closely supervise new practitioners through their first three transactions.

Scott Bloom, sales director for the office, likens the young employees to new lawyers. "They've passed the bar, but it doesn't mean they know how to practice law yet," he says. "It's difficult for new practitioners to know everything needed to represent people. The biggest obstacles are learning everything they can and learning it right as quickly as possible."

Bloom's company also holds group training sessions to teach new practitioners how to write purchase contracts, discuss marketing strategies, and learn negotiation tactics. Well-rounded training increases employee retention, lowers recruiting and training costs, and reduces broker liability, he says.

"Through our mentoring and training, we can better educate and prepare them to succeed," Bloom says. "If we invest in them initially, we know they'll bring money to our business in the long run."

Capturing New Business

Younger practitioners—for the most part—also have the inherent ability of relating to customers in their age group. That helps capture new business, particularly among first-time home buyers, whose average age is 32, according to NAR's 2003 Profile of Home Buyers and Sellers.

"I'm thankful for the younger salespeople," Carpenter says. "People are buying homes at a younger age and they're able to work well with people of their own generation. Gen X salespeople are bringing in clients we might not have had."

Young buyers typically start their home search online and expect their real estate salesperson to respond to them quickly through e-mails and other technologies.

"Those buyers like younger practitioners because they talk the talk," says Daniel Mancuso, executive vice president of Murphy Realty Preferred Homes in Rumson, New Jersey. "That matters when trying to capture Gen X clients. Young sellers are impressed with practitioners' use of technology. The sooner you get back to them, the more credibility you have."

Technology skills are mentioned over and over as one of the biggest assets of the new generation. It changes not only how new business is captured, but how real estate offices are run.

Gen X Brings New Tech Focus

Some brokers say less time is needed to train young recruits on how to work computer programs because they already have skills from school and previous jobs. And tech-savvy workers raise the bar for what kinds of tools and computer programs real estate companies provide to salespeople.

Carpenter says she's had to increase her technology know-how and incorporate new computers and software programs into her business, while Real Living's Rouda says it's an "ever-expanding commitment" to stay current on new technologies and offer the most up-to-date programs.

The challenge starts before Gen Xers even set foot in the office. That's because most aspiring practitioners head to the Web to do company research and decide where they would like to build their careers. Sites with interactive tools, rich information, and easy navigation will grab their attention. "The web site has to show that your business is technology friendly and that you provide the tools necessary for salespeople to succeed," Goldman says.

Real Living uses an online tool called the Real Estate Simulator to recruit new salespeople. The Simulator quizzes prospective employees to help them get a sense of the business and find out if real estate is right for them. Results are sent to a manager who follows up with the prospective salesperson.

Erik Sjowall, sales manager for Edina Realty in Maplewood, Minnesota—where nearly a third of the salespeople are between the ages of 20 and 35—says he's had success advertising on web sites like Monster.com and using outdoor signage that promoted real estate as "exciting" and "fast-paced."

When recruiting, brokers say it's also smart to ask for help from the office's younger talent. Dan Mancuso took that route and says it worked. When he asked new hires why they chose his office instead of the competition, they said they felt they'd be more understood by managers and that the company was "hipper" than others.

"The Future of the Business"

It may be hard to visualize, but today's young recruits someday will be industry veterans, heading up real estate companies and training yet another generation of practitioners that will bring their own skill sets and ways of doing business.

For now, they'll continue to shape the industry with a new emphasis on technology and insight into what younger consumers want from their real estate salesperson.

"They're the future of the business and they're going to change the face of real estate," Mancuso says of the Gen Xers. "We'll lose some of our stodgy image, and they'll help us stay current."

Gen Xers also will help preserve the role of practitioners in real estate transactions, he says.

"Buyers and sellers still don't like to negotiate for themselves on such an emotional issue as selling and buying their homes," Mancuso says. "I think the younger crowd will help keep real estate salespeople in the equation."

—Elyse Umlauf-Garneau. This article originally appeared in the November 2004 issue of REALTOR® Magazine Online.

What Career Means to Generation X

Are you tired of reading about the unfortunate, misunderstood Generation X, those born between 1965 and 1975? Are you tired of catering to these folk, only to have them leave your organization? You might have no choice in the matter.

With the U.S. unemployment rate continuing at levels near historic lows, managers have little choice but to learn how to set aside their motives, values, and goals to accept those in this generation and help them be the individual contributors to your organization that they want to be.

Here's a quiz about how you communicate with and lead Gen Xers. The goal is to start an honest self-evaluation process that will help you create win-win relationships.

Gen X Quiz

1. You're advertising for a position in your company. In the advertisement, do you:

   A. Describe the 100-year history of your stable, well-established company?

   B. Discuss the opportunities for learning new skills and working in a challenging, results-driven organization?

   C. Emphasize the benefit plan, stressing your excellent 401(k) program?

D. Use testimonials from your senior employees that describe how much they like working at your company?

E. Explain that you are looking for self-starting, motivated people that can make a difference?

2. During an interview with job applicants, what do you emphasize the most?

A. The work-out room and outside picnic tables.

B. Your flexible work schedules and job-sharing program.

C. The benefits new employees get after working for one year.

D. The company's desire for every person to learn as much as they want and be successful no matter how long they are with the company.

E. The casual atmosphere and your policy on what type of clothing is "business casual."

3. As a leader, what do you think are the most important behaviors you can exhibit?

A. Your interest in people's personal lives.

B. Your mentoring skills.

C. Your hands-off style.

D. Your ability to relate to this generation.

E. Your belief in their ability to take on varied tasks.

4. You are working on next year's training for your department. What does this look like?

A. You have a lot of training scheduled for the first six months of employment.

B. A majority of your courses can be done individually in a self-paced format.

C. A catalog lists the courses and times available, stating that anyone can take one course each quarter if they can document a job-related need.

D. Your courses are available online.

E. Employees are encouraged to look elsewhere if you don't offer the training they need.

5. How do you delegate work assignments?

   A. Assign a lot of work so people don't get bored. Make these assignments based on what they have done well in the past.

   B. Discuss the task and help them divide the work into manageable pieces.

   C. Clearly define the task and associated deadlines.

   D. Tell them they should come to you first with any questions or when they need help.

   E. Parcel out pieces of a task so they are not overwhelmed.

6. As people set out to accomplish a task, do you:

   A. Encourage them to be creative and innovative in how they accomplish a task and ask questions as needed.

   B. Give them detailed instructions and procedures for how the job has been done successfully in the past.

   C. Let them know who can be of assistance within your department and throughout the company.

   D. Discuss why the task needs to be done and help them see their value-added contribution.

   E. Require daily approvals of the work accomplished.

7. How do you go about giving feedback and performance evaluation?

   A. Let the person review the performance appraisal form so they can be prepared for their quarterly review.

   B. Plan some time every day to talk to the person about how their job is going and see if they have any concerns or questions.

   C. Provide quick, specific, accurate reflections of their performance.

   D. Give feedback when it is requested.

   E. Review their work several times each day.

8. When people participate on your project team, what are the characteristics of the team?

   A. The team includes representatives from each department so everyone knows what's going on.

   B. You are the leader throughout the scope of the project.

C. The team is empowered to make decisions and implement solutions.

D. Your project teams generally take 6–12 months to resolve their issue.

E. Members of the team are selected based on the skill or knowledge they can bring to the project.

9. How do you provide recognition?

A. Bring in doughnuts for the coffee room.

B. Have an Employee of the Quarter award.

C. Pass out T-shirts when your department achieves its goals.

D. Frequent, immediate "pats on the back" to individuals when they do something well.

E. Schedule department lunches to honor specific individuals each week.

10. When you try to have some fun at work, you:

A. Post cartoons on a bulletin board.

B. Have a "costume" day.

C. Celebrate every person's birthday.

D. Schedule fun events after work or on weekends.

E. Pass out mugs with the company logo.

Scoring

1. A = 2, B = 10, C = 6, D = 4, E = 8

Xers are most interested in a job that is challenging and rewarding. They want to add value. They're not interested in the company's history or the accolades of 20-year veteran employees. They believe in themselves and aren't looking for a long-term career with one company.

2. A = 4, B = 8, C = 2, D = 10, E = 6

Xers are looking for the "what's in it for me" to work at a company, as well as a chance to contribute. Stress the "what's in it for me" and you'll get the contribution. Give them flexible work hours and they will be more productive. Work-out rooms and picnic tables are a token start. But what does the rest of the office look like? Is it parceled out in cubicles and offices (for managers, of course), with policies on who gets how much space and what type of furniture? Is the work-out room only available during lunch or before and after work? How about any time of the day? Can you loosen up on the dress code? Can they get benefits now? One year is too long to wait.

3. A = 6, B = 10, C = 4, D = 2, E = 9

The best way to lead this group is to be a mentor so they can learn and grow. They will probably come to look upon you as a surrogate "work parent." Take an interest in their "causes" (this group has a high rate of volunteerism). The minute you say, "That's not in your job description," you will lose these folk. Likewise, the minute you say, "I remember when I was your age," they'll be turned off. Their life is totally different from yours at their age.

4. A = 4, B = 10, C = 2, D = 9, E = 6

This generation is self-motivated and wants to learn at their own pace. Training is the number one motivator with Xers because it increases their portfolio of marketable skills. So you train them and they leave? When you satisfy their thirst for knowledge, then you will reap the rewards if you let them apply their new skills on the job.

5. A = 2, B = 10, C = 8, D = 6, E = 4

Due to a shorter attention span, these people can get lost in a large project. So, help them set daily goals and tell them exactly what is expected and when it is required. Let them know "what is on the test." Then, let them manage their own time. However, don't treat them like babies who can't handle the whole task or make the mistake of assuming they need a lot of (busy) work to be challenged.

6. A = 9, B = 2, C = 8, D = 10, E = 4

Don't micro-manage these folk and stifle their creativity with "the way we've always done it." Be patient with their questions about "why" they're doing something. They're not questioning you but just want to understand the big picture and their part in it. Don't be the only person they can come to for help. Offer them a variety of people from whom they can learn.

7. A = 2, B = 10, C = 9, D = 6, E = 4

While Generation X does not want over-your-shoulder managers, they do want constant feedback. Does once a day sound like too much? It doesn't have to be a sit-down 30-minute discussion. Surely you can find a few minutes each day to talk to your people and see how they're doing.

8. A = 6, B = 4, C = 8, D = 2, E = 10

Xers have a low tolerance for meetings when nothing gets accomplished and never-ending bureaucracy rules. While they are independent workers, they crave the relationships that teams provide. But they want to contribute something to the team based on their expertise and expect the other team members to be selected based on their skills, not the prevailing political wind or because "every department must be represented." If you're not serious about empowering teams, they'll see right through you.

9. A = 6, B = 2, C = 4, D = 10, E = 8

As with feedback, Xers need recognition as proof of their ability to add value and produce results. Don't base all recognition on team or department successes; recognize the individual within the team. When recognition is for the entire department, make it a social event such as a lunch). Doughnuts left in the coffee room reminds them of the breakfast they ate alone while their parents were getting ready to go to work. Employee of the Quarter? Three months is a long time.

10. A = 4, B = 10, C = 8, D = 6, E = 2

Companies have to loosen up when they think about having fun. Ask people what would be fun for them. It probably won't be what you think is fun. Don't ask for input and not be ready to implement it. This one area might be the greatest test of your flexibility and paradigms.

Your Score

80–100 points: You're well on your way to understanding and supporting the needs of this generation. Hand them the remote control and put them in charge of their work life. Allow them to have ownership of their work by creating "businesses within your business" and pay their dues based on performance, not seniority.

60–79 points: You've started to accommodate this diverse group of people. But you may need to examine your paradigms even further. You may be talking the talk, but you're not walking the walk. This generation can see through "phoniness" quicker than any other. If you don't make drastic changes now, they won't stay around to see if you do in the next year.

Below 60 points: You are in denial that change needs to occur. Xers don't come to you with that built-in trust and respect of organizations and your authority. You earn this because of who you are and what you do.

> *—From "How in Step Are You with Generation X?,"*
> *Oklahoma-based Center for Coaching & Mentoring at*
> *www.coachingandmentoring.com. Used with permission.*

Now Comes Generation Y

Those tech-savvy Gen Y kids, the oldest born in 1980 and now in their mid-twenties, are the future of your sales staff. But do you know how to motivate them? A free day on the golf course or a gift certificate to a fancy restaurant might not get their competitive juices flowing. Some things that might, from Eric Chester, CEO of GenerationWhy Inc., in Lakewood, Colorado.

1. **XM** *radio.* Actual costs will vary, but for about $150 in startup fees and $10 in monthly subscription costs, one of your sales associates can enjoy 150 stations via satellite car radio. Each month, transfer the satellite receiver to the monthly volume leader's car.

2. *Reverse mentorship.* Give your tech-savvy newbie a chance to shadow an old pro on listing presentations, negotiating sessions, and closings. But don't make it a one-way mentorship. Have the newbie provide mentoring on tech issues that the top performer doesn't have the time to learn. The mentoring will have more impact because the rookie will feel good about giving something useful in return.

3. *Get-togethers.* For a generation whose parents whisked them off to soccer or band practice after school and wouldn't think of letting them

play unsupervised in the street, unstructured time with others is important. Occasional barbeques in the afternoon or smoothie breaks in the morning are ways to create valued connectivity to others.

4. *Relevant gifts*. Put yourself in their shoes when thinking of gifts: a coupon for snowboarding rather than golfing, a gift certificate for a comedy show rather than for dinner, an iPod mini instead of a watch. Best: Present them with all three options and let them pick which they want.

—*Robert Freedman. This list originally appeared in the March 2005 issue of REALTOR® Magazine.*

Keeping Rivalries in Check

Competition among salespeople is inevitable—indeed, there's much to be said for an office in which many of the sales associates vie to top one another in performance. With their competitive juices flowing, associates focus on growing their business, spurred to reach ever-improving numbers.

But is it productive when competitiveness between two associates in your office turns into rivalry? The answer is yes, as long as the associates continue to channel their energy into improving their sales.

And that's the rub. When rivalries turn destructive, they can jeopardize the health of your office. So stay on guard to keep rivalries from crossing the line.

When Good Rivalries Go Bad

What are the signs of an unproductive rivalry? In any organization, change often triggers unanticipated consequences. So keep a close eye on your sales team whenever a new associate comes on board, the performance of a current associate suddenly changes for the better or the worse, or new management or ownership takes the helm.

Even if there are no outward signs of change in your office, unhealthy rivalries could be brewing. Based on my own experiences both as a broker and as a sales coach and trainer and on my conversations with other brokers and executives in real estate, there are signals:

An associate begins to spread rumors about another associate.

An associate questions everything you're doing for another associate or asks a lot of questions about another associate's business, rather than asking about—or even talking to—the associate directly.

An associate begins to lobby staff and others for support against another associate.

An associate stops participating in meetings and events and avoids contact with others.

An associate suddenly becomes overprotective, using a desk lock and not sharing information.

Two associates start avoiding each other or make deprecating remarks about each other. Or, when they interact, sparks fly.

Follow a Five-Step Action Plan

How do you know when to intervene or even whether you ought to?

It's time to take action when staff members and associates begin to express discomfort over tension in the office or start to take sides in a rivalry, creating cliques.

Once you choose to intervene, there are immediate steps you should take to keep the problem from spiraling out of control.

Step 1: Get facts, not gossip. Gather all the facts you can from each party and verify the facts to the greatest possible extent.

Step 2: Express your concerns and expectations. As quickly as possible, pull in the rivals one at a time for a meeting. Voice your concerns and listen like crazy. Take notes. In both meetings, counsel the associates to focus on their goals and business plans rather than one another. If written policies and procedures were violated, review the rules with the associates.

However, it may be just as likely that the violations are of unwritten rules—that is, rules of fair play, respect, and cooperation. In these cases, you can take similar steps. If you've been vocal and clear about the culture of your office, and these unwritten rules are commonly known and generally respected, remind the associates of them. If these types of unwritten rules are not widely known or followed, your job is tougher, and it's time to lead the charge for creating a more constructive environment.

Going forward, consider putting the "unwritten rules" into writing. Even if you can't make them hard and fast rules, you can describe your office culture in concept as being one that encourages fair play, respect, and cooperation.

Step 3: Suggest getting the two together for an open discussion. In the meeting, mention that you've had individual conversations with each and feel confident that both want to work toward a more positive relationship. Let them know that they're both good salespeople whom you want to keep, but you don't want their rivalry to get in the way of their business or distract others in the office.

Step 4: Follow up within a few weeks. If the problem hasn't abated, be clear that further violation or disrespect of the rules will result in an ultimate consequence. Here's one way to reinforce your initial meeting:

> "Joan, I'm excited about your work. You're a good associate and have a great future in this business. But there's a problem. Let's take a look at our policy guidelines and talk about the unwritten protocols of our office. If the inappropriate behavior continues, I'll have to make a decision that protects the health and integrity of the office. I want you here. I believe your career will reach its potential in our organization. But, if this unhealthy rivalry continues, be prepared to tell me what office you want to transfer your license to."

Step 5: Remove the offender. If the rivalry continues to create a bad office environment for others, you have to determine who's responsible and terminate the relationship.

Unhealthy rivalries can't be left to fester. Management will quickly lose the respect and cooperation of its sales force.

How Did We Get to This Point?

Is it possible to prevent or at least deter unhealthy office rivalries? Yes, and these techniques can help you do that.

Ensure that associates focus on specific business goals. This is the best way to prevent unhealthy sales rivalries. It takes leadership on your part to help associates set and work on agreed goals.

Communicate. The more you communicate with associates regarding their work, the more likely you can prevent unhealthy rivalries, quash rumors, and temper the hard feelings of those who feel threatened. If comfortable for you, shift your office culture from one in which you manage strictly as a supervisor to one in which you also manage as a coach.

Establish pride in fair play, professionalism, and integrity. Make professionalism a part of the language and content of your meetings, training, and counseling sessions. In addition to honoring your associates' production levels, find reasons to honor them for other types of achievements, such as outstanding professional behavior, community service, marketing ideas, a tough situation handled well, or helping out another associate.

Make your company goals clear up front. During the recruiting and hiring process, establish the written and unwritten rules that encourage cooperation, fair play, and professionalism. Make clear what behavior is unacceptable.

Let staff, new and established, know that they are your eyes and ears for heading off any situation that might damage the productivity or harmony of the office. Also make it clear that you can be trusted to keep their confidence while you address any situation that they discuss with you.

Set boundaries. Strongly request that your managers, if you have any, and administrative staff refrain from socializing with the associates or behaving in a way that may lead to charges of favoritism. Train your staff to remain neutral in conflicts between associates and staff.

In the end, your job is to promote healthy competitiveness among your associates to help keep performance juices flowing. But you also must stay alert to prevent competition from degenerating into unproductive rivalries. By taking action quickly and forcefully, and by maintaining a professional environment, you can go a long way toward doing that.

—Rich Levin. This article originally appeared in the
April 2003 issue of REALTOR® Magazine.

CASE STUDY: THE NEW KID ON THE BLOCK

Sometimes all it takes for competitiveness to turn sour is bringing a new associate into your office. That's what happened in the case of two strong performers, Olivia and Samuel.

Olivia and Samuel competed strongly and amicably to be the top associate in their office. Each would watch the sales board to see how much the other had sold that month. The rivalry spurred them to try to exceed each other and raise themselves to higher levels of performance.

Then the manager hired Sue from a competitor. As Sue's production began to approach Samuel's and Olivia's, Sue positioned herself as a rival, but not in a healthy way. She was often heard to dismiss the others' success by positioning their production in an unfavorable light. "You know Olivia lives alone and doesn't have anything else to do," she would say, or, "Samuel's mother is an attorney in town who feeds him all of his business."

Even if these statements are true, the personal focus invites others in the office to take sides, straining feelings and releasing unproductive energy. That's a recipe for an unhealthy rivalry that needs to be checked quickly.

What to Do?

Take Sue aside for a chat to outline your expectations and re-emphasize office culture. Follow up with another meeting or meetings to assess her progress and show that you're on top of the situation. Within a month, determine whether she's your type of associate.

CASE STUDY: THE RIVAL NEXT DOOR

Rivalries aren't confined within offices. With interoffice rivalries, finding a solution isn't completely within your control. Unchecked, they may escalate into formal complaints and even litigation. As a broker or manager, you must address these cases on your side of the rivalry as best you can. That primarily means helping your associate stay focused on business, as in this case:

Beatrice was the top associate at a well-known local independent company, specializing in high-end homes. Then Dorothy began working as an associate for another company in the same market. She was so successful targeting the high end that she soon exceeded Beatrice as the No. 1 associate in the area. The two were continually up against each other for listings and buyers—and Dorothy often won.

The working relationship between the two began to suffer. Was it a coincidence that Beatrice didn't receive many of Dorothy's messages to show homes? Suddenly, offers on Beatrice's listings had to be presented through Beatrice and Dorothy's offers on Beatrice's listings were outright rejected instead of countered. Dorothy began to think Beatrice was out to get her and rumors were flying that she was thinking of filing a formal complaint with the board.

As Beatrice's broker, what would you do? Call her into your office as soon as you're aware of the situation. Listen, take notes, document any complaints she has about Dorothy, and be supportive. Gently refocus her back to appropriate goals.

As Dorothy's broker, you should make a similar effort to call your associate aside, listen to her complaints, and be supportive. If she's truly thinking of filing a complaint, ask her to take a day or two to consider her action. Mention that decisions based on emotion are often made in error. A day or two later, check her emotional temperature. If she hasn't cooled down and is still considering lodging a formal complaint, discuss how much time and energy that'll realistically require. Again help her maintain focus on her clients and business.

Regardless of which associate you supervise, it's in your best interest to prevent the problem from escalating into a formal complaint or litigation. How do you prevent that?

1. Call the other broker. Express your desire to solve the conflict as quickly and painlessly as possible. In most cases, the other broker will want the same outcome.

2. Discuss with the broker what each associate believes transpired and what actions, if any, need to be taken to resolve the problem.

3. If a cooperative resolution can't be identified, involve a third party, such as your local association executive. Tell the executive what has transpired, and ask that the person intercede with the other broker. Intercession by a respected third party can often bring the situation to a satisfying close.

Training Associates to Succeed

Providing training for your rookie associates is integral to your efforts to beef up profitability, because associate competence is directly tied to profitability. Rookies who don't know how to present themselves to consumers or, worse, aren't up to speed about the latest disclosures could become costly liabilities.

And the issue of new-associate training is gaining importance for the industry as some states report huge swells in licensee numbers around the country. The biggest growth in recent years appears to be in large states, such as California, Florida, New York, North Carolina, and Ohio, says Craig Cheatham, CEO of the Association of Real Estate License Law Officials. His agency says there are more than 2 million reported licensees nationwide.

When you affiliate rookies, you can't simply rely on the fact that they took pre-licensing classes. "Students just memorize concepts," says Eileen Taus, director of education for the Westchester County Board of REALTORS®, White Plains, New York. "Once they get into the industry, they need to learn the practicalities of the business."

So how do you ensure that associates absorb and use the practical skills you teach them? Successful learning emphasizes interactivity rather than lectures. It should also focus on a few key topics.

No matter your state, new recruits need to learn how to fill out and explain to customers the paperwork of real estate, including the sales contract and disclosure forms. They also need to learn the basics of working with consumers, how to develop a clientele, and how to stay out of legal trouble, including mastering the intricacies of agency.

In broad outline, these basic training courses are typically organized in a two-week program, the first week conducted in the classroom and the second week in both the classroom and the field.

You can organize your basic training in roughly four modules: paperwork, sellers, buyers, and business development.

1. *Curriculum: paperwork.* For the first day and a half, have students do nothing but practice filling out business paperwork—forms for listings, seller and buyer disclosures, the purchase contract and its addenda, and agency disclosures.

   Teaching technique: Have students complete documents based on different scenarios—for example, on a sales contract, ask them to list certain buyer requests, and see if they attach the correct contract addenda—then build discussions around their mistakes. New salespeople may be timid about discussing mistakes at first, but they'll come to see that open dialogue helps in their learning and their ability to explain the forms to others. Training is the time to make mistakes.

Some trainers opt to weave lessons in paperwork into broader modules, such as those covering buyers, sellers, and business development. The rationale: Students, in theory, are already familiar with real estate documents—they've had roughly 30 hours of these forms in pre-licensing school.

So, for example, when you discuss financing have students complete an application for FHA mortgage insurance as homework. Then review it the next day for correctness.

2. *Curriculum: sellers.*   Devote a day to covering seller issues, weaving in additional instruction on paperwork as needed. Be sure to cover:

Pricing and marketing property.

Measuring property.

Conducting market analysis.

Choosing comparables.

Analyzing properties and adjusting for differences.

Determining costs to seller and seller net on sale.

Making listing presentations.

Obtaining appointments.

Presenting yourself and your company.

Teaching technique: Help rookies write a seller presentation, including an explanation of the value of hiring them to market and sell the home and the value the company brings. That way, when they leave class, they're ready to start looking for clients. Have the class discuss aspects of the presentations, including who had a good first sentence.

In addition, use role-playing: One student acting as the sales associate practices trying to persuade another student acting as the seller to give the associate the listing contract. Such role-playing builds students' confidence in communicating their strengths as salespeople and overcoming objections.

3. *Curriculum: buyers.*   Spend a day on how to find and work with buyers. Along the way, revisit paperwork issues such as writing contracts. Among the points to cover:

Showing property.

Determining buyer costs.

Qualifying buyers and understanding the loan approval process.

Matching loan products to buyers.

Writing and negotiating offers.

Marketing buyers to potential sellers, an emerging trend. Communicate to rookies the importance of letting other associates know about their buyers and what they want by sending e-mail to local associates or talking with colleagues in informal networking sessions.

You may want to avoid teaching rookies how to show a house, because that lesson can collapse into canned salesmanship. When associates try to push a buyer into a decision during a showing, they can damage their reputation.

Teaching technique: To supplement instruction, host a panel discussion with a handful of veteran associates who work with buyers. The panel format encourages wide-ranging discussion of key issues and gives students a peek into strategies of experienced colleagues. The panels are also a good way for associates to network.

4. *Curriculum: business development.*   Spend two days acquainting students with techniques for finding clients, presenting themselves, writing ads, calling prospects, and building rapport and loyalty. More than anything, business development should focus on helping new associates overcome their natural hesitation in promoting themselves. Address the fear of prospecting and fear of rejection. And make sure they have the right vision for the business, which means not waiting for the phone to ring but staying in touch with people and building a sphere of influence.

In addition, encourage students to market their ability to counsel consumers, not just sell homes. That is, they can position themselves as service providers who help buyers find houses, help sellers move on to a new chapter in their lives, and bring people together in a transaction.

Teaching technique: With a "soft" topic such as business development, sessions should be interactive. That means using discussion, role-playing, and team breakouts, and limiting your use of media, including PowerPoint presentations and video programs. Although they can be entertaining, multimedia presentations are passive training tools that, used improperly, can reduce interaction time.

Once the basics are out of the way, often during the second week of training, managers or veteran associates in the office take over. They coach and mentor new licensees as they start to put classroom learning into practice. And really that's the heart of good training, says Ruth Marcus, ABR®, CRS®, director of training for Russell & Jeffcoat, REALTORS®, Inc. in Columbia, South Carolina. "It's all about learning by doing."

—Robert Freedman. This article originally appeared in the August 2003 issue of REALTOR® Magazine.

TRAINING FOR LIFE

For veteran associates seeking credit hours to maintain their license, company training programs generally are built around six to eight hours of core classes, usually on legal issues, including agency law.

For a class to qualify for continuing education credit, the trainer must be state-certified; large company and local board of REALTOR® programs typically are.

Beyond licensing renewal, to help veteran associates stay on top of their game, companies typically host advanced training classes covering key topic areas such as risk management, technology, selling techniques, and negotiating. Specialty classes, such as selling to seniors, understanding cultural diversity, taking safety precautions, or mastering technology, are often contracted out rather than taught in-house, because it's not cost-efficient to keep the expertise in-house, say trainers.

Westchester Real Estate Inc., a network of 10 brokerages in Westchester County, New York, partners with its local board of REALTORS® to bring in trainers on hot topics, such as selling luxury real estate, for special half-day courses. Costs to bring in a nationally known speaker typically run from $5,000 to $10,000, so partnerships help spread costs around and keep seminars affordable for associates.

The Westchester network charges associates a modest fee, mainly to give associates who RSVP an incentive to show up, says Gail Fattizzi, the network's executive director.

If your associates are seeking advanced training without having to make a substantial time commitment, direct them to online training options.

NAR launched REALTOR® University in the late 1990s to provide continuing education credit, professional development, and designation certification to practitioners in an online environment.

Classes take from 1 to 12 hours and cost $45–$295, depending on class length, complexity, and whether they apply toward a certification or designation. Topics include business planning, ethics, financing, fair housing, business valuation, and time management. There's also an Internet marketing and professionalism program called e-PRO (www.epronar.com).

MORE ONLINE

Information on training available through REALTOR® University, affiliated with the National Association of REALTORS®, and other educational resources, is available at www.realtor.org under "Education."

Managers That Sell:
When to Stay in the Game

Norman K. Brooks, broker-owner of Commonwealth Realty in Richmond, Virginia, was in the field working on one of his transactions when one of his sales associates called him on his cell phone. The associate wanted advice on two offers he'd received for one of his listings.

Brooks' ability to provide his associate an effective answer relied greatly on the fact that, after 23 years in the business and now as owner of a real estate company with about half a dozen associates, he continues to sell every day and is intimately familiar with the market.

What's more, the call shows that, even though he sells, his salespeople understand he's not competing against them but working for their benefit. "For a small company like ours, it's important for me to keep selling to know what's going on in our market," says Brooks, who launched his brokerage in 2003 after leaving a mid-sized company at which he was a partner.

But to make the arrangement work, Brooks says he must make it clear that his pursuit of sales won't crowd out his associates' efforts.

Imperative to Sell

Maintaining a good relationship with your associates as you continue selling is key for small broker-owners for another practical reason: finance. The sales you generate might be the only thing standing between the company and bankruptcy, says Bob Beck, broker-owner of Beck & Beck Realty Co. in Nashville, Tennessee.

Given the large commission split sales associates command in the market today, Beck says, few owners can afford not to sell, so it's the rare small company in which sales associates find a non-competing broker-owner. "When I started selling 35 years ago, the commission split was 50–50," says Beck, who launched his company in 1967. "Today new associates are getting 70 percent to 75 percent, and experienced associates are getting 80 percent."

To make the economics work for their small company, broker-owners rely on income from their associates' sales to cover their company overhead and rely on their personal sales to put money in their pocket, says Ronald McManamy, CRB, CRS®, broker-owner of United Real Estate Solutions in Sioux City, Iowa. "What selling broker-owners close costs nothing to generate because associates' commission income covers the brokers' costs, such as out-of-pocket expenses to prospect, market listings, and process paperwork," he says.

To Compete or Not to Compete?

Still, not everyone in the industry thinks brokers who manage should continue to sell. "Other brokers try to use the fact that I'm a selling broker against us in the competition for new recruits," says Larry Sutherland, CRB, CRS®, president-broker of Wyoming #1 Properties in Cheyenne. "They say to salespeople, 'You don't want to go over there because they're competing brokers.' The perception is, we'll take floor time, we'll take their leads, and so on. But that's not the case."

Another argument made against broker-owners who sell is that they're spread too thin and the sales associates might be the loser as a result.

But broker-owners who continue to sell paint a different picture, saying their experience and the leads they generate are a net plus to their associates. "If you're in business a long time, you generate a lot of repeat business," says Roger Cox, broker-owner of Roger Cox & Associates Real

Estate Brokerage, LLC, in Albuquerque, New Mexico. "You can only do so much yourself, so you refer additional business to your salespeople. They benefit from your sales activity."

Cox's company focuses primarily on commercial real estate and is developing and selling a 3,700-acre housing subdivision, but his associates also list residential property.

"When you get into a 20- to 25-person sales office, you have more issues to care for as a broker, and running the company should become a full-time job," says McManamy, who sold while he was a sales manager but quit selling after he became a broker-owner. His company affiliates about 60 associates.

Rules for Fair Play

Broker-owners who sell say it's a simple matter to set up your office in such a way that you and your associates avoid direct competition for customers. The arguments that brokers will take all the business don't hold up, they say, so long as brokers follow a few rules. Here are some of the ways selling broker-owners can avoid stepping on salespeople's toes.

Don't take floor calls.

Don't prospect for business. Rely instead on referrals.

Do try to sell associates' listings.

Do bring listings into the inventory for your associates to sell.

Do give leads to your associates, particularly to new associates.

Do defer to an associate when the customer is ready to become a client and both you and the associate have been talking to the same customer.

Do lead by example by digging up business when the market slows. Less experienced associates may need a model for finding customers in tough times.

The Competitive Sales Manager

For companies large enough to have them, sales managers should continue to sell as well, say brokers. But the same rules for avoiding competition should apply to them. "We have a fundamental understanding with our sales managers that if they're faced with competition from an associate, they always back down," says McManamy.

That kind of competition can occur fairly regularly, since managers often meet customers on the floor. "One of the associates might be talking to people who are still deciding whether to sell their house," says McManamy. "At the same time, the sales manager might be acquainted with the customers, too, if they came into the office when the associate wasn't there. Once the manager becomes aware that the prospects are talking to the associate, the manager formally recommends the associate and in so doing helps the associate acquire the listing."

For associates, the benefit of a sales manager who continues to sell is the manager's market knowledge. Like a selling broker-owner, a selling manager can advise less-experienced associates on key pieces of their transaction—how much to price a listing, where to look for potential buyers, how to help sellers evaluate two offers.

Once associates see the benefits of having a broker or manager who's active in the field, it becomes a non-issue or even a plus, say brokers. And that's a message they convey to recruits who might otherwise be scared off.

"We just explain to prospective associates that we're going through the same problems over appraisals, inspections, interest rates, and open houses that they are," says Sutherland. "We lead by example. And when we say that and show associates how we can work together and also help them get business from our leads, we gain greater respect from them."

—Robert Freedman. This article originally appeared in the
September 2004 issue of REALTOR® Magazine.

CHAPTER

10

Ideas for You
(A Look at What Your
Competition Is Doing)

Offering Annuities to Spur Recruitment

Avalar Real Estate & Mortgage Network
Las Vegas, Nevada
www.avalar.biz

From a start in the rich wine country of Sonoma, Marin, and Lake counties in California, Chuck Scoble has begun exporting to other states a concept that he hopes will make a big market splash. And he's not talking about Zinfandel.

Armed with a franchise approach that gives brokers and associates a share of company revenue in return for recruiting salespeople, Scoble has started building a residential real estate network that's breaking out of its California roots.

Under the incentive program, Avalar Real Estate & Mortgage Network distributes to brokers and associates about 1 percent of the revenue generated by each salesperson they recruit. Brokers and associates also are paid a small percentage from the income of each salesperson that their recruits bring on board and from the recruits of those recruits, and so on. The income percentage diminishes with each "generation" of recruits and stops at the seventh.

Starting from one office in the mid-1990s, the franchise now has a dozen companies in California and Arizona and is in talks with brokers to add affiliated franchisees in Alabama, Illinois, Nevada, and Florida. In 2004, the company moved its headquarters to Las Vegas.

On its face, the recruiting program is much like the incentives that underlie the growth of Keller Williams Realty, based in Austin, Texas, and Exit Realty Corp. International, the Canadian franchise, whose U.S. operations are based in Burlington, Massachusetts. Both of those companies offer supplemental broker and associate income based on revenue generated from sales recruits. But the Avalar program has a character of its own, Scoble says.

First, the recruiting incentives at Avalar are distributed to brokers and associates from a pool of funds set aside from revenue generated from the franchise's royalty income. This way, brokers and associates receive incentive payments regardless of company profitability levels.

Second, the system incorporates a feature that Scoble calls compression. If recruits leave the company after a certain period, the next-generation recruits move up the chain, generating supplementary income at the same percentage rate as the recruits who left.

Other incentive features at Avalar include:

A *breakage pool*. If funds remain in the royalty funds pool after supplementary income has been distributed, the extra funds are divided among senior and executive recruiters, who are brokers and associates with at least 8 and 20 recruits, respectively, to their names.

A *competitive franchise fee*. Avalar's starts at $4,400 (and can go up to $12,500). That compares to an average fee of $16,654 among 21 franchises participating in a franchise survey.

No-cost contract renewals. Renewals come with five-year terms.

A *guarantee*. Brokers are entitled to 90 percent of their fee if they want out of the franchise within the first year.

The company also permits brokers to retain their company name and their commission structure. Avalar franchises a mortgage brokerage operation with the same recruiting incentive.

So far, of Avalar's nearly 500 associates, more than 100 are earning supplementary income. For some, that income tops $100,000 a year. Says Scoble: "The earnings growth can be pretty phenomenal."

—Robert Freedman. This article originally appeared in the September 2004 issue of REALTOR® Magazine.

Complementing Traditional Associates with Salaried Division

Century 21 New Millennium
Alexandria, Virginia
www.c21nm.com

Todd Hetherington, CRS®, GRI, isn't a revolutionary out to move a residential brokerage away from its traditional reliance on independent contractors.

But he is open to change. That's why one of the Century 21 New Millennium CEO's eight offices in metropolitan Washington, D.C., employs salaried associates. The rest of his sales force of 250 are independent contractors (ICs).

Hetherington believes that to thrive in the future, the industry needs the diversity of salaried salespeople and independent contractors, particularly in multi-office brokerages. "There are areas of the business for which brokers need more control," he says. "And there's a higher level of accountability to the broker among salaried people."

Since the typical relocation transaction involves more parties and paperwork and generates less revenue than traditional sales, Hetherington chose the efficiency of a salaried model for his Kingstowne relocation office in Alexandria, Virginia, four years ago. He divides the office into three teams of about eight salaried salespeople, who are backed up by a five-person office support group.

Team spirit comes from the associates' shared military background— West Point grad Hetherington staffed up with other military pros—and from the monetary rewards he offers for high productivity. He distributes 20 percent of the office's profit to all the teams on a pro rata basis.

Associates receive a base salary, an individual bonus, the team bonus, benefits, vacation, and personal days. Base salaries are adjusted monthly according to the associate's previous 12-month rolling production average.

On a transaction basis, the office is more productive than the company's seven traditional offices. Its 25 salespeople produce roughly what 40 associates at one of the traditional offices do. In 2002, with 20 associates, the salaried office closed 500 transaction sides. The comparison needs qualification, though. Century 21 New Millennium brings 75 percent of the business to the relocation office; in the traditional offices, the independent contractors must generate 85 percent to 90 percent of their business.

Still, the salaried associates are go-getters, Hetherington says. They're expected to prospect for the other 25 percent of their business. Several associates close six to eight deals a month, earning $150,000 to $200,000 a year in income. Of that amount, 75 percent is pre-bonus income.

With increased efficiency comes increased administrative costs. Hetherington estimates that carrying 25 salaried salespeople for five months requires a seven-figure investment.

Lately, he's moved beyond recruiting military types to hiring attorneys and technology professionals, which points up another advantage of operating a mix of salaried and commission-based offices. The setup, he says, attracts a whole new pool of competent, professional recruits who might not be comfortable working on commission.

—*Matthew McDermott. This article originally appeared in the September 2003 issue of REALTOR® Magazine.*

Paying Salaries, Charging Fees

Realty Select Inc.
Lancaster County, Pennsylvania
www.realty-select.com

Ryan Hess and his partners are hoping to knock down two of the toughest challenges facing brokers today: keeping talent and competing with fee-for-service pricing.

Hess, Quentin Miller, and Ron Felpel are holding on to new talent by hiring sales associates as employees, complete with a group health plan and 401(k) retirement accounts. "We are very fortunate to have a group of associates who have stuck with us from the beginning and who really believe in the company and the vision," says Ryan Hess, broker of the company, which is located in Lancaster County, Pennsylvania, outside Philadelphia.

The company, Realty Select Inc., starts associates at a $15,000 salary with a 20 percent commission split. As they gain experience, associates trade in their salary for a higher split, up to 50 percent. The company pays marketing and technology costs.

"New associates can focus their energy on working with customers without having to worry about covering their costs," Hess says.

To attract cost-conscious sellers and create a competitive edge, the company provides listing services for $1,500 with a 3 percent commission to selling salespeople. The fee covers the listing, several open houses, and marketing—print and online—over 6 months. For extra fees that total a few hundred dollars, sellers can obtain additional marketing.

Strong volume, an emphasis on ancillary business, such as mortgage lending and title services, and a high company dollar enable the company to charge the $1,500 fee, says Hess.

The company's listing pipeline is generally full, with each associate typically handling some 30 listings a year. Plus the company sells about 30 percent of its own listings. The company also generates income through its mortgage and title services, with capture rates of 65 percent and 90 percent, respectively, Hess says.

Meanwhile, Realty Select's retained dollar per transaction (what's left after commissions, salaries, and taxes) is fairly high, at about 55 percent. That said, the company pays out a good deal to cover associate costs. But there's a positive side to that: control. "We bring costs per transaction down because our associates don't need to buy anything on their own," says Hess.

To help its mostly rookie sales force manage a high volume of business, the company takes a team approach. Experienced associates work with three to four associates and an originator from the mortgage company. The leader, accountable for team performance, helps associates stay on task. A leader who's performing well receives a cut of commissions generated by the team. The company hasn't been shy about releasing nonperformers. "Because of the volume of work," says Hess, "they have to perform."

In 2003, the company's first full year of operation, it closed 670 transaction sides—at an average $160,000 sale price—and ended the year with about 30 associates. Hess expects to keep a strong listing volume, because sellers are increasingly attracted to the low listing fee. Even if interest rates rise, he says, "we'll be a strong player."

—*Robert Freedman. This article originally appeared in the May 2004 issue of REALTOR® Magazine.*

Freeing New Associates from Pressure of Selling Fast

A-List Realty
Columbus, Ohio
www.alistrealty.com

When Mark Dandrea sold new homes for a builder in Columbus, Ohio, he showed rookie sales associates the ropes. Under his tutelage, they learned the trade without the pressure of having to hit a quota. That responsibility fell to Dandrea as the lead salesperson.

From that experience, Dandrea came to believe rookies do best when the pressure's off. So when he launched his own company in early 2002 with partner Scott Bookheimer, he sought to recreate that pressure-free learning environment by seeking out new licensees who, with other means of support, could wade into real estate as a part-time career.

"We want people to come into real estate slowly and accurately and not go after transactions to put food on their table," says Dandrea, co-owner of A-List Realty. "If you're too hungry for sales, you might be pushed into making mistakes."

To be sure, many brokers have exactly the opposite philosophy, blaming part-timers' inexperience for costly mistakes and saying the practice of hiring them reduces professionalism. But, Dandrea says, part-timers shouldn't be singled out.

"Training is the key," he says. "Whose fault is it if a person is allowed to sink or swim without proper training? It doesn't matter if you're part- or full-time."

As to professionalism, "How do people define that?" he asks. "If they mean returning calls consistently and professionally, having a thorough knowledge of contracts and paperwork, and servicing clients, our part-timers have all that."

To help part-timers build their careers, Dandrea immerses them in what he calls back-end marketing: at least once a month, contacting people they know and people who know of them and providing useful in-formation, such as area home prices. In this way they wade into the busi-ness helping family and friends and then expand outward as referrals come in. "Everyone in real estate says they do this, but at A-List, we're fanatical about it," he says.

Ultimately, whether part-timers move into full-time sales is up to them, he says.

The company pays full-time "sales directors" an 80–20 commis-sion split. Full- and part-time associates (called "partners") receive a 75–25 split. Several part-timers work with the sales directors as team members, supporting their transactions. The part-timers pass along 5 percent of commissions from their own transactions to the directors. As a result, the brokerage never receives more than 20 percent of any commission.

To stretch the company dollar, the brokerage operates virtually—asso-ciates work from home—and maintains no companywide staff. A-List provides training, signs, a web site for marketing listings, and market re-ports and materials.

In 2005, A-List hopes to open an office, rent out space, form an equity affiliation with a mortgage provider, and add support staff. Those plans rest on the company's growth projections. For 2004, the company's 15 people are on track to close $25 million in sales, nearly double what it closed in 2003.

"We're offering a significant twist on the conventional model," Dan-drea says, "offering part-timers a high split right off the bat by keeping our costs low, breaking them in slowly, and letting them decide when they're ready to jump in all the way."

> —*Robert Freedman. This article originally appeared in the October 2004 issue of REALTOR® Magazine.*

Letting Associates Take
a Company Equity Stake

Prestige Real Estate Group LLC
Denver, Colorado
www.prestigerealtygroup.com

In what might be called a Jeffersonian moment, Jack O'Connor, CRB, and Leeann Iacino, CRB, GRI, founded Prestige Real Estate Group LLC as a democracy: Independent sales associates hold ownership interest in the Denver-area company, govern it, and reap the rewards of its successes—or pay for its failures.

One sign of that strategy's success, says O'Connor, has been the company's rapid growth—from 22 associates when it launched in 1999 to 357 associates in 8 offices today. "Inviting our associates to buy into the company is what allowed us to expand so quickly," says O'Connor, a 26-year real estate veteran who, along with Iacino, left a mid-sized company to launch Prestige.

For 2004, the company's on track to generate 3,800 transaction sides, with an estimated $26 million in gross commission income (GCI). That's up from 3,000 transactions and $21 million in GCI in 2003.

Associate-owned real estate companies aren't new, but O'Connor believes Prestige stands apart from others because of its sheer number of owners. About a third of the company—108 associates—are owners, with stakes ranging from less than 1 percent to 8 percent. Associates can also take equity interests in the company's ancillary businesses.

All of these equity holders give the company a strong capital position. Even with its rapid expansion, the company has no debt and is sitting on a nice pile of cash, O'Connor says.

For the associates, ownership means additional cash flow when the company distributes profits at year's end and a share of any sales proceeds should the company be sold. Plus associate-owners have an asset they can borrow against, he says.

The other benefit to associates is control. Each year they elect representatives to an advisory committee of associate-owners, who work with O'Connor to write company policy. All major decisions, including the launch of the mortgage and title companies, are approved by the committee.

For instance, the associates wanted, and are receiving, top-of-the-line technology. On the Prestige web site, each listing receives its own URL and comes with a 360-degree home tour and more than a dozen photos. The listing's URL is included in all print ads and brochures, enabling buyers to go directly to the listing's home page.

The company offers associates a conventional commission split, generally 50–50 or 70–30, until they reach a threshold level—an average of $21,500 in gross commission income to the company—which raises their split to 90–10. Or they can opt for a 100 percent commission with a monthly desk fee, which also averages about $21,500 annually. The company sets an associate's fee based on such factors as whether the person has a team, works from home, or uses a company office.

Associates pay their own property marketing costs, capped at about $3,600 a year. Prestige pays anything above the cap, which makes netting more listings cost-effective, O'Connor says.

"Deep down, most associates want to say they're owners of their business," he says. "When you involve them, they understand what the goal is and how to get there. And they get there."

—*Robert Freedman. This article originally appeared in the September 2004 issue of REALTOR® Magazine.*

Motivating Associates through Personalization

Impact Real Estate
Niles, Michigan
www.impactrealestate.net

I s it possible to build a small but productive brokerage around the practice of individualization? With just a handful of associates, Impact Real Estate has grown into one of the busiest brokerages in its Niles, Michigan, market since its launch in mid-2001 on the idea that it can.

Individualization isn't a term that broker-owner Andrew Fletcher, ABR®, GRI, uses. Rather, the former associate at RE/MAX Four Flags Realty prefers to say "people matter," a phrase he's adopted as his company motto.

The simple statement encapsulates two key aspects of how Fletcher interacts with his associates. He identifies what makes each of them tick, and he offers compensation, training, and support choices for each of them based around those unique characteristics.

Before he affiliates associates, Fletcher administers DISC (dominance, influencing, steadiness, compliance) personality assessments to determine the kind of salesperson each associate would be—someone who's good at persuading others, for example, or whose strength is analytical.

If the person is a risk-taker, the associate might pay the company a monthly fee and take a 95 percent split. If the person seeks more financial stability, a 50–50 commission split might be appropriate.

Fletcher also tries to tailor coaching to each person's learning style. "How do they like to be communicated with? Do they like to be cajoled? Do they just want the facts? Do they want help with their life goals as well as their business goals? I adjust how I manage them based on their learning styles and needs," he says.

The individualized approach is paying off. In 2002, its first full year of business, the company closed about $11 million worth of real estate in 117 transactions with six associates. In 2003, with 15 full-time associates, the company closed about $20 million in 180 transactions, the lion's share of them in Niles. That would account for something close to 30 percent of the 547 transactions closed in that city, according to figures from Impact and the Southwestern Michigan Association of REALTORS®. Fletcher's goal for 2004 is 200 transactions. As of late March, the company had closed nearly 30.

It's Not for Everyone

Can he provide every prospective associate an individualized program? No, which is why he has dropped back to six associates. Some have found the atmosphere—Fletcher pumps in high-energy music over the office sound system, rings a bell whenever an associate gets a listing or sale, and hosts weekly motivational meetings open to salespeople from outside his office—at odds with their personality. "One associate liked the environment at first but then came to feel there was too much pressure, so she left," says Fletcher.

Today, only if prospective associates are comfortable working in that environment does Fletcher consider affiliating them. "I used to feel I could hire anyone and make that person a winner," he says. "But I learned it's better to identify the ones who want help and then do what you can to help them."

—*Robert Freedman. This article originally appeared in the June 2004 issue of REALTOR® Magazine.*

Training Associates to a T

Prudential Preferred Properties
Chicago, Illinois
www.prupref.com

Associates at Prudential Preferred Properties in Chicago are each expected to close a minimum of $3 million in volume in their first 15 months—or they're let go from active sales. The standard is realistic, say company heads David Hanna, Jim Roth, and William White, because of the rigorous training process the company requires of its affiliates.

Training's a chief reason the brokerage has closed $1 billion in volume after five years in business. Productivity is 30 percent higher on average for associates who've been through the training, says Hanna, who's CEO. Roth, ABR®, GRI, is company president, and White is chief financial officer.

With about 400 associates in 11 offices throughout the metro area, the company was on track to generate $25 million in gross commission income from 4,000 transactions in 2004, up from about $21 million in GCI from 3,400 transactions in 2003, Hanna says.

For associates, joining the company means spending a lot of time in their first 15 months learning the ropes. Training includes

- An intensive, required five-day sales seminar.
- Formal modules. Ongoing, three-hour classes held weekly cover core subjects, such as prospecting, financing, listings, and buyer brokerage, as well as non-core subjects, such as home inspections and contract negotiation. Core subjects are required.

- An accountability group. Once a week several associates, including a veteran, meet to exchange feedback on each other's performance. Veterans discuss their challenges and advise new affiliates how to reach their weekly goals. Sessions are required for new affiliates until they show they're driving forward their business and for experienced associates at risk of missing their performance goal.

- Coaching. Each rookie is assigned a manager for required one-on-one coaching for as long as deemed necessary.

- Mentoring. Experienced associates guide new affiliates through the first transaction in exchange for a percentage of the commission from the deal. Optional for rookies.

- Transition coordination. New affiliates must attend a once-a-week session with an office manager, called a transition coordinator, to learn company technology and office procedures. After that, affiliates can attend these open sessions as needed.

"Given the level of attention our associates receive and the vibrancy of our market, [associates who can't meet the production requirements] are probably in the wrong profession," says Hanna.

Since the beginning of 2004, dozens of associates have been let go or have left of their own accord, but those losses have been offset by a similar number who've succeeded under the company's system. "We're not looking to let people go, but we do expect people to apply themselves," says Roth.

The company's training regimen coupled with aggressive culling of the ranks has led to a $500,000 increase per associate in volume between 2003 and 2004, to $3 million annually, says Hanna.

To help associates keep learning, the company directs its newer associates to work out of the office rather than from home; it encourages veteran associates to do the same. "The cost savings of having people work out of their house isn't a good trade for us," says Hanna. "We want newer associates to hear and see our successful associates and to capitalize on that knowledge base."

This year, the company plans to open its 12th office and is on track to reach $30 million in GCI, says Roth. "We want our associates to start with us, grow with us, and retire with us," says White.

That's a lesson the company hopes it's teaching.

—Robert Freedman. This article originally appeared in the August 2005 issue of REALTOR® Magazine.

III

Managing Risk

Your Nightmare Scenario

With remediation specialists in airtight suits transporting materials in special containers, the scene looked like something out of a horror movie. And in a sense it was—at least for Wally Folks, GRI, broker-owner of Century 21 Folks Realty in San Antonio.

Back in 1999, one of Folks' associates worked with buyers on the purchase of a one-story brick house in the north-central part of San Antonio. The buyers thought they were getting a modest house that needed a few cosmetic upgrades. But while replacing the carpet, the buyers found a mold-infested crack in the cement slab where the previous owners had had some remodeling work done.

The creatures crawling out of the crack, as the buyers described the scene during a mediation session, were only part of the horror. The buyers alleged allergies and other health problems from the crack and another patch of mold discovered behind the kitchen sink. They wanted their lives set right. They sued the sellers, Folks, and Folks' associate. That was the beginning of a protracted liability case that occupied Folks and his associate for years, and it's what brokers and managers do their best to avoid. The collection of articles in this section offers you ideas on how to avoid negative legal scenarios like this in your office—and what to do if, despite your care, you get hit with a lawsuit.

CHAPTER

11

Legal

Living with Litigation

The liability case against Wally Folks, GRI, broker-owner of Century 21 Folks Realty in San Antonio, was every broker's nightmare, hitting just when the country's focus on mold was intensifying. After purchase, the buyers had found a mold-infested crack in the cement slab of their house, and they sued Folks, the sales associate, and the sellers.

Suddenly, Folks found himself contending with the emotional strain his associate was suffering, the prospect of a costly lawsuit, concern for his other associates' state of mind, and the need to keep business moving smoothly during a time when "fast-paced" was an understatement. And strangely enough, he was feeling sympathy for the plaintiffs.

Even if it's clear it has little or no merit, a lawsuit can be devastating to brokers and associates alike. "Most cases I defend are tenuous or groundless," says Robert Bass, a broker defense lawyer in Phoenix. Still, the financial and emotional toll can be significant.

Folks' experience, however, shows that lengthy litigation doesn't have to be crippling. The keys, he says, are to be upfront with everyone about the facts of the case, prepared with plenty of documentation, and supportive of the associate involved. Above all, it's critical to keep control of your time. Otherwise the legal action will threaten to overtake the good parts of your life.

The Attorney's Call

Few calls are less welcome than the one from an attorney representing a disgruntled party. When the attorney for the buyers of the mold-infested house called, Folks suggested they strive to resolve the complaint through mediation. The attorney agreed, and a mediator was secured.

Given the reasonable prospects for resolving the complaint, Folks proceeded with mediation without informing his errors and omissions (E&O) insurer of the matter. "I thought we were looking at something that would involve a few thousand dollars, and for that, I didn't want to get a black mark with my E&O company," says Folks.

His biggest concern: that a claim would drive up his premiums.

To prepare for the mediation, Folks and the associate sat down with a pen and a notepad to retrace the events leading up to the complaint. Folks numbered each event—starting with the associate's first contact—identified the date it occurred, and summarized it in a sentence or two. To refresh her memory about what happened when, the associate referred to documents such as the home inspection report and her own notes taken during the transaction.

"That session showed me how important it is to keep notes on everything you do," says Folks. "When you have a phone conversation, just take out your pad and start writing. It'll help you recollect what you've done."

Note taking also forces you to analyze the situation as it's happening and can be a good way to catch red flags early in a transaction.

Back to Square One

Despite Folks' high hopes, the mediation failed. "The buyers went into hysterics," says Folks. "The husband said his wife had suffered migraines and allergies and had missed work."

The buyers showed pictures of the mold, and Folks admits, "They were horrifying. I felt very sorry for them."

The buyers' attorney said his clients wanted Folks to buy back the house for $99,000, its purchase price, and fork out $63,000 to cover costs for mold remediation and matters related to the buyers' health concerns.

Faced with those demands, Folks contacted his E&O carrier and quickly learned that insurers want a call from you at the first hint of a claim.

"The first thing the insurance company did was chew me out for not calling right away," he says. "But I thought I was saving them a few thousand dollars."

Folks' insurer secured him an attorney from Austin, 75 miles from San Antonio. To clarify the chain of events that led to the complaint, the attorney spoke with Folks periodically by phone and traveled to San Antonio several times, including before each of four depositions that were taken—one for each of the sellers and one for each of the buyers.

The depositions were integral to clarifying points of contention between the parties. For example, the buyers contended that Folks' associate had told them plumbing work under the cement slab—part of the remodeling work that had been done—had a lifetime guarantee. Leakage from that plumbing was believed to have contributed to conditions that caused the mold. But in the depositions, the contention about the plumbing guarantee wasn't corroborated by the other depositions. "What came out was that the associate had turned to the seller, and the seller had said the slab, not the plumbing, was guaranteed for the life of the house," says Folks.

During the depositions, the buyers concentrated on their compensation for the cost of the house, the remediation, and their attorney. They no longer raised the health issues that had come up during the mediation. "They just wanted the house and their attorney taken care of," says Folks.

Now several years since the start of the case, Folks sees the light at the end of the tunnel. The mold has been eliminated, and mold spores have been contained. The buyers' insurance company bought the house, paid for the remediation, and sold the house to a buyer who fixes up distressed houses for sale.

—Robert Freedman. This article originally appeared in the May 2003 issue of REALTOR® Magazine.

QUALITY CONTROL TO CURB LEGAL WRANGLES

It's unlikely you'll ever eliminate lawsuits, but a quality control process can greatly reduce the likelihood of your being sued.

John Foltz, president of Realty Executives in Phoenix, implemented such a system five years ago, and he says he's cut his legal tussles to a fraction of what they once were and slashed his risk management costs—E&O insurance premiums, deductibles paid, legal fees, and settlement costs—by 70 percent.

He starts with a standardized review process. Three dedicated staff members review each of the 130 transactions his 1,300 associates generate each day.

Each transaction is reviewed to make sure four goals are met:

1. All disclosures have been properly made.
2. All inspections have been recommended or performed.
3. A home warranty has been ordered.
4. A final walkthrough has been completed.

If one of the goals hasn't been met, the associate receives a pink slip that says the commission will be held if the review finding isn't addressed.

"The slip is the only piece of paper in the office that's pink, so when associates get one, they pay attention to it," says Foltz.

The key is consistency. Each transaction is reviewed the same way each time, no matter who the associate is.

When he first implemented the procedure, he held a few checks a week. Now he almost never has to hold a check. But more important than the stick is the carrot, says Foltz, who reminds associates that the professional behavior that helps them avoid lawsuits is the same behavior that will help them attract more business.

TAKING CARE OF BUSINESS

As consuming as a legal complaint can be, it's imperative to stay focused on business and remain sensitive to the mood of the office.

Faced with a mold lawsuit, Wally Folks, GRI, of Century 21 Folks Realty in San Antonio was quick to inform the 25 associates in his office.

"We called a meeting immediately," he says. "The associate who was involved gave her story, and everyone encouraged her to hang in there."

That encouragement was critical to helping the associate—who held a GRI designation and had been in the business about seven years—deal with the emotional turmoil she was experiencing, Folks says.

"She was shell-shocked," he says. She effectively left the business for six months, coming in only for meetings with the attorney and to talk with other associates. When she did get leads during that period, she referred them to colleagues.

"She felt that she had done everything right, so she was petrified that something like this could happen to her again despite her best efforts," he says.

To keep the associate engaged in the business and office goings-on during her absence, Folks called her once a week. And in conversations and meetings, Folks and the attorney offered her reassurances.

Meanwhile, Folks kept his eye on mold coverage in the media. That enabled him to see the complaint in a larger context. "We could see this case as part of a trend," he says.

That trend is starting to cool, Folks believes, as insurance companies limit their mold coverage, lessening the incentive for people to seek mold-related damages.

Besides providing support for his associate, Folks concentrated on keeping his own priorities straight. "You have to set aside time to take care of the case," he says, "but then you need to move on to other things on your schedule. If you dwell on a lawsuit, it'll drive you nuts."

Strong time management practices can help you stay on task. And as remote as it seems from the problem at hand, paying attention to your health is integral, too. "If your health is good, that makes it easier to cope," Folks says. "You have to eat right and get plenty of rest. It's all related."

MORE ONLINE

Ideas for Minimizing Risk

REALTOR® Magazine Online maintains resources on risk management under its Brokerage Management section at www.realtor.org/realtor mag. In addition, the National Association of REALTORS®' Information Central maintains a field guide on errors and omissions insurance and agency disclosure among other risk management field guides. Access to some of the material requires a fee or a site user name and password, available only to NAR members. The field guides are at www.realtor.org, under "Library."

Addressing Top Legal Concerns

What legal issues keep brokers and their associates up at night? Here's what attorneys at state REALTOR® legal hotlines say they frequently field questions on. For each issue, we include the states we talked with and guidance from the hotline attorney. Because state law varies, always consult your own attorney about relevant law when you or your associates have questions on these topics. The interviews with attorneys were conducted in late 2003, but the issues they raise remain valid today, in late 2005.

1. *Procuring cause.* Questions about the procuring cause are regularly top among hotline calls. In many cases, callers are buyer's agents trying to make the case that they're the procuring cause and thus should be paid by the listing office, says Elizabeth (Betsy) Urbance, an attorney with the Sorling Law Offices in Springfield, Illinois, who fields calls for the Illinois Association of REALTORS®.

   Guidance: There are no hard-and-fast rules that determine procuring cause, because every transaction is different. So a hotline call won't settle the issue, Urbance says. Should the caller take the conflict to arbitration, a hearing panel will sort through the facts and circumstances of the case. As the NAR *Code of Ethics and Arbitration Manual* explains, only through a full analysis of the incidents and actions of the parties can the panel decide who's the procuring cause of a sale.

2. *Practicing without a license.* The growth of web sites that host listings and offer selling tips and signage directly to sellers is generating calls from practitioners who suspect the sites have crossed the line from being an advertising venue to providing services that properly are the domain of real estate licensees. "There's a concern that these entities have moved beyond an exemption in Illinois license law for advertisers and are engaged in brokerage," says Urbance.

   Other calls of this type tend to concern companies that manage properties for other parties. Callers are seeking clarification on what activities those companies are restricted from doing without a real estate license.

Guidance: In the case of the web sites, Urbance advises callers that such sites, unless operated by a licensee, should limit themselves to selling advertising space to consumers. Anything beyond that could amount to brokering without a license. In Illinois, the recourse for practitioners concerned about such a site is to contact the Illinois Office of Banks and Real Estate, the state's licensing agency, to file a complaint.

Likewise, restrictions on unlicensed property managers are extensive. Managers in Illinois need a license for anything that goes beyond taking care of the physical structure, including advertising for tenants and showing units, says Urbance.

3. *Multiple representation.* What happens when a buyer and seller in a transaction want the same sales professional to represent them? Dennis Schmidt, an attorney who has handled legal hotline calls for the Texas Association of REALTORS®, says practitioners are looking for upfront guidance on how to handle multiple representation, known elsewhere as dual agency.

Guidance: Multiple representation situations create an inherent conflict of interest for sales associates, Schmidt says. The conflict can be waived under Texas law, because the practitioner can act as an intermediary—that is, someone who represents both the buyer and the seller—but statutory guidelines must be followed. Among other things, both parties must consent in writing in advance, and the practitioner must not reveal information received in confidence from one party to the other. For example, the practitioner can't tell the seller what the buyer is ultimately willing to pay for a property or tell the buyer that the seller is willing to take less for a property than was stated publicly.

This confidence requirement doesn't apply to property disclosures, though. When practitioners in Texas know about a material property defect, they must disclose it to the buyer.

Schmidt reminds callers that the multiple representation requirements also are triggered when two associates from the same office end up on opposite sides of a transaction.

In Illinois, where it's known as dual agency, representing both the buyer and seller is permissible if appropriate disclosure is made and the written consent of the parties is obtained, says Urbance. Illinois has two disclosure forms. The first spells out what dual agents can and can't do and must be signed before any act constituting dual agency occurs. The second confirms consent and must be executed by the buyer and seller no later than the time the purchase contract is signed.

Dual agency isn't permitted in Illinois if the licensee has an ownership or other financial interest in the property. This restriction tends to generate a common question on the hotline: "Can I sell my own property?"

The answer is yes, as long as practitioners disclose their status as a licensee to prospective buyers and explain that they can't represent the other party.

4. *Withheld offers.* A common question in California is from buyer's agents who present an offer to the listing agent, then suspect the listing agent of withholding the offer from the seller, possibly because the agent has another buyer lined up and wants to avoid a co-broker situation.

   Guidance: "It's unethical not to tell sellers that someone wants to buy their house," says Gov Hutchinson, assistant general counsel and manager of the member legal services hotline for the California Association of REALTORS® (C.A.R.). He tells callers that listing agents clearly have an obligation to convey offers to the seller and advises callers to insist on hearing the seller's response to the offer. However, he reminds callers never to contact the seller directly, which would be a violation of the NAR Code of Ethics. It might also lead to an accusation that the licensee is interfering with the listing agent's "prospective economic advantage" or agency relationship, which could be grounds for a lawsuit.

5. *Fee disputes.* In Texas, Schmidt frequently receives calls regarding fee disputes between licensees who have cooperated in a transaction.

   Guidance: The NAR Code of Ethics provides for mandatory arbitration in these cases, and Schmidt urges callers to consider whether a compromise would be appropriate instead of slugging it out in a winner-take-all arbitration. Settlements also promote good relations between brokerage companies, Schmidt says.

6. *Sex offender disclosures.* Is a real estate licensee obligated to disclose when a registered sex offender lives nearby?

Guidance: The Texas Megan's Law provides licensees a safe harbor on disclosure, so practitioners have no duty to disclose the presence of sex offenders near the property being sold. That said, Texas licensees might want to make such disclosures voluntarily as a business decision if a continuing relationship with the buyer is anticipated, says Schmidt.

In Florida, the law isn't as clear-cut. No Florida case or statute addresses whether the proximity of a sex offender must be disclosed, says Mike Velt, deputy legal counsel for the Florida Association of REALTORS®. In advising hotline callers, Velt must parse the facts and circumstances in every call. His starting point: a general proposition of Florida law, which requires sellers and real estate licensees to disclose all known facts that materially affect the value of the property in residential sales transactions when such facts are not readily observable or known to the buyer.

Even if there's no objective proof that the presence of a sex offender affects property values, Florida law has employed a subjective standard in other contexts, Velt says, so feelings about the desirability of the property are relevant. On the other hand, the fact that the sex offender registry in Florida is readily observable on the Internet might provide a defense if a buyer were to sue, he says.

Velt's advice depends on the location of the offender vis-à-vis the property. He's inclined to recommend disclosure if the offender is next door but not if the offender is three blocks away. "Until you get a test case or legislative guidance, however, you're in that gray zone where there's no clear answer," Velt says.

7. *Lead-based paint disclosure.* What should you do to be prepared if a federal lead-paint investigator calls your office requesting a voluntary audit of all your records for the past three years?

Guidance: Brokers need to be certain that all their records are in order for residential sales transactions involving properties built before 1978, the year lead paint was taken off the market. The file must contain evidence that the proper disclosure forms were signed and that a federally required pamphlet on the subject was given to the buyer. Brokers should also examine their office policies, Urbance says, to ensure that the requirements are spelled out and being followed by all associates.

8. *Property defects disclosure.* Do your associates have to disclose property defects, even in states without a state-mandated disclosure form?

   Guidance: Yes. Common law disclosures, those arising from court decisions, still apply, says Tom Kelley of Thomsen & Nybeck, who's provided services as a hotline attorney for the Minnesota Association of REALTORS®.

   Approximately 30 states have state-mandated disclosure forms. Even if your state doesn't, attorneys often recommend creating a property condition disclosure form to protect sellers and your company from liability.

   Minnesota has a law, effective January 1, 2003, allowing property condition disclosures to be waived in some instances. Examples include new construction, which carries a statutory warranty, and investor-held properties.

9. *Mold disclosure.* Toxic mold has been a big issue on the Florida hotline for the past couple of years, says Velt.

   Guidance: There's no case law or statute in Florida imposing a duty on sellers or practitioners to disclose the presence of toxic mold, Velt says. So as in the sex offender situation, Velt says he weighs the facts and circumstances on a case-by-case basis. To minimize potential conflicts, Velt typically recommends disclosure of known mold.

   In Indiana, hotline callers are advised to complete a mold disclosure form and urge buyers to conduct their own mold inspection. These voluntary actions cut off any claim that buyers weren't advised to inspect for mold, says Richelle Cohen-Mossler, staff attorney for the Indiana Association of REALTORS®.

   The hotline in California is receiving fewer calls about disclosing mold since C.A.R. modified its standard purchase contract in 2002 to incorporate mold disclosure, Hutchinson says.

10. *Homeowners insurance.* In California, as in other states where obtaining homeowners insurance is growing more difficult, the insurance issue is showing up in calls to the hotline, says Hutchinson. Callers are asking questions like this one: "Is it true

that an insurance company can refuse to write a permanent homeowner's policy after issuing a 60-day binder?"

Guidance: Hutchinson advises callers that a binder isn't a policy and can be withdrawn. Thus, practitioners want to alert buyers early to the need to secure insurance as soon as possible. "Homeowner's insurance isn't simple anymore," Hutchinson says.

—Christopher Wright. This article originally appeared in the September 2003 issue of REALTOR® Magazine.

MORE ONLINE

Top Industry Cases

The National Association of REALTORS® tracks the industry's top legal cases in its online legal newsletter, The Letter of the Law, at www.realtor.org under "Law & Policy," and in its legal scan, which the association conducts every two years, also under "Law & Policy." The latest legal scan is through 2003. Access to some material requires a site user name and password, available to NAR members.

Test Your Antitrust Knowledge

Real estate brokers and sales associates must cooperate with one another in the sale of properties, opening the door to conduct that might be construed as violating antitrust laws. Antitrust laws are intended to promote competition and prevent the growth of monopolies. Do you know the ins and outs of antitrust? Test your knowledge with these five questions.

Antitrust Quiz

1. Two competitors in my market asked me to cooperate with them in setting a "standard" commission for the area. I refused, but subsequently started charging the same rate that they suggested. Because

I didn't overtly agree to participate in price fixing, I did not violate the antitrust law.

True

False

2. Even though my salespeople are independent contractors, I may establish the commission rate for my company and require them to charge that rate.

True

False

3. I offer an annual training session to all my sales associates and sales managers on what constitutes antitrust violations, and I keep attendance records of who participated. These records will protect me from any lawsuits even if one of my salespeople violates antitrust laws.

True

False

4. The best way to persuade sellers that they should not insist on an open listing is to tell them that the MLS will not accept open listing.

True

False

5. If one of my salespeople participates in a price-fixing discussion, my company can be held liable even if I have no personal knowledge of the salesperson's conduct.

True

False

Answers

1. False. An offer to conspire, followed by conduct consistent with the acceptance of that offer is sufficient to violate antitrust laws, even if you do not expressly agree to the conspiracy. The best way to avoid participation in an illegal conspiracy is to openly repudiate that offer and to be sure that your conduct does not reflect participation.

2. True. A broker may obligate salespeople working as independent contractors to abide by the company's commission rate without violating any antitrust laws.

3. False. Providing training in what constitutes antitrust violations will not protect your company from being named in a lawsuit. However, an antitrust compliance program and the records indicating who participated may be valuable parts of your defense.

4. False. Although most MLSs prohibit the acceptance of open listings, you should explain your reluctance to accept such a listing not because of such a rule, but because open listings operate to the disadvantage of the seller and the broker alike by making the listing less cost-effective to market.

5. True. Just as ignorance of the law is no excuse, brokers' ignorance of their salespeople's conduct is no defense to an antitrust charge. A brokerage company will be held liable for the conduct of its salespeople whether or not the principal broker was personally aware of their conduct.

—*From* Antitrust Compliance Guide for REALTORS® and REALTOR®
Associates, *Fourth Edition, National Association of REALTORS®.*

MORE ONLINE

What You Need to Know about Antitrust

The National Association of REALTORS®' Information Central maintains a field guide on antitrust law. Contents include materials on avoiding antitrust risk, staying alert to phrases that signal antitrust risk, and recommended guidelines for antitrust compliance. Access to some material requires a fee or a site user name and password, available only to NAR members. The field guides are at www.realtor.org, under "Library."

Antitrust Pocket Reference for Your Associates

Arm your sales associates with a convenient resource, the Antitrust Pocket Guide for REALTORS® and REALTOR® associates from the National Association of REALTORS®. The guide (item # 126-1093) is available online at the online store at www.realtor.org. Price varies based on order quantity. NAR members receive a price discount.

Heading Off Privacy Complaints

In this age of Internet information sharing, protecting your clients' personal and property information is more than a duty; it's a practice that ensures their trust and safeguards your reputation.

Yet there's uncertainty among brokers over what they need to do to ensure they're approaching information security appropriately—or even whether there's a legal requirement to take any action related to privacy.

With privacy issues evolving, what you're required to do depends on how you collect and use your customer information—and in some cases what state you live in. If you're in California and you operate a web site, for example, you're required to post an information privacy policy on your site, period. What that policy contains is up to you; you're required only to disclose what information you collect and how you plan to use it.

Other states are following suit. Nebraska, like California, has a privacy law for commercial sites, and at least 10 states have Internet privacy study commissions or task forces in place, according to information on the National Conference of State Legislatures web site (www.ncsl.org).

There are federal laws to consider, too. If you post an information collection policy and fail to follow it, you could be in violation of the Fair Trade Commission Act for misleading consumers. The Federal Trade Commission has enforcement powers over electronic media, e-commerce, and the Internet under several different acts, and has stepped up efforts to identify unfair and deceptive practices on the Internet, including practices related to how one collects information about consumers.

Additional laws come into play if you share your web site with any financial affiliates, such as a mortgage broker, which may be regulated under other laws.

Given the evolving nature of privacy protection efforts, it makes sense to establish procedures to protect the information you gather. But don't think you can create a policy on the cheap by adopting the language you find on other brokers' sites. Under the law, privacy policies are considered implied contracts between a business and its customers. If the language you adopt doesn't describe how *you're* collecting and using data, you could be exposing yourself to liability.

That said, here are five items to include in a policy:

1. *Notice and disclosure.* If you collect data from visitors to your site, take stock of what data you gather, how it's collected, and with whom it's shared or sold. Then write a policy around these practices.

2. *Choice and consent.* Include an opt-in or an opt-out clause. With an opt-in approach, you can't share your clients' and customers' data unless they say you can; with an opt-out approach, you can share your customers' data unless they say you can't. Many consumers feel they have more control with the opt-in approach.

3. *Access and participation.* Give your customers the right to modify or delete data at any time.

4. *Security.* Outline your methods for protecting the integrity and security of your clients' and customers' data.

5. *Redress.* Offer a dispute-resolution option, such as mediation or arbitration, for people who believe their information was used in a way counter to your stated policy. Have an attorney look at your procedure to make sure it's enforceable under the law.

Integrating data security into your business isn't just the right thing to do; it's a practice that generates consumer trust and loyalty. What's more important to your business than that?

—Darity Wesley. This article originally appeared in the
February 2004 issue of REALTOR® Magazine.

MORE ONLINE

Protecting against Identity Theft

The National Association of REALTORS®' Information Central maintains a field guide on identity theft that contains prevention resources and links to additional governmental and private resources. Access to some of the material requires a fee or a site user name and password, available to NAR members. The field guides are at www.realtor.org, under "Library."

Understanding Internet Copyright Law

A fter much planning, you're ready to upload content onto your new web site. You have marketing material you wrote describing your services and company brochures.

You have photographs you've taken of homes, plus some you've borrowed from the local chamber of commerce web site. You plan to include a few real estate–related articles you found in other magazines. Plus, you're thinking about including a short video or some background music to make your site more inviting.

But just as you're ready to go live, your 16-year-old daughter, a former "Napster addict," reminds you that you'd better determine who owns the material you're about to post. Where do you begin?

Copyright Basics

Copyright law protects much of the content—brochures, articles, photographs, audio and video recordings, and other original works—you're thinking of putting on your web site. That means the creator or other copyright owner of anything typed, printed, recorded, or available at a web site controls the right to use the information. Furthermore, the owner retains rights to copyright-protected content regardless of where the material is later used. For instance, if a printed magazine article is subsequently posted on the magazine's web site, it's still protected.

Although the person who creates material is generally the copyright owner, an employer is considered the author and holds the copyright when works are created in the course of employment. On the other hand, works commissioned by a company or individual and performed by an independent contractor are generally owned by the creator unless the agreement commissioning the work states otherwise. If you hire a writer, photographer, or web site designer, you need a contract to establish ownership. The agreement should acknowledge that the creation is work for hire and belongs to you.

Protecting What's Yours

Before March 1, 1989, original works could be copyrighted only by publishing that material, registering it with the U.S. Copyright Office, *and* using proper copyright notices. Today, however, creating work in any fixed form—typed, recorded, or posted on the Web—automatically grants its author copyright protection.

Still, U.S. law provides many incentives for registering your work. If someone infringes on your copyright—by downloading information from your web site, for example—registration provides prima facie evidence of copyright validity. Registering also allows you to sue for copyright infringement and to seek special statutory damages and lawyers' fees.

Although not mandatory, it's prudent to always include a copyright symbol on your works. A copyright notice consists of the word "copyright" or the copyright symbol ©, the first year of the work's publication, and the name of the copyright owner. Also include a copyright statement that notifies others that they must contact you to use your work.

If you find others using your work without your permission, notify them by e-mail or letter. If you don't hear back from them, or, in the case of a web site, if your material isn't removed, you may want to contact a copyright lawyer.

Complying with Copyright Law

Unless the material you reference has a clear copyright statement or you're sure the copyright has expired (generally 70 years after the author's death), you must determine whether the work is still protected by copyright and, if so, who the owner of the work is. You can locate copyright holders by checking the records at the U.S. Copyright Office (www.copyright.gov/records), and by using online search engines and library sites, such as the Library of Congress (www.loc.gov).

Some people assume that online content may be freely used and modified without permission. No. It's protected just like other forms of creative material. A link to an interior page of another web site or framing another web site as yours may require permission from the site owner as well. U.S. law isn't clear on this issue, and legal experts continue to debate the point. To be safe, many web site owners link only to the home page of another site and not to any internal pages. If you prefer to be 100 percent risk free, ask permission even to link to a home page.

Also keep in mind that scanning or digitizing a work, such as a book or photograph, is a reproduction of that work and requires permission from the copyright owner.

When you ask permission to use a copyrighted work, you'll need to provide a description of the work, where you'll be using it, how many copies you'll make, and any other information the copyright owner requests. Copyright owners may also charge you to use copyrighted material.

The U.S. Copyright Act does include a provision for "fair use" of copyrighted material. This allows you to use a small portion of a work, such as a quote, without permission. Since fair use is an ambiguous provision, if you use more than a few lines of an article or if the material you quote is a critical part of the work, play it safe and obtain the owner's permission.

If all this seems onerous, think of the time you spend writing a great marketing brochure. How would you feel if your competitors started passing it out as theirs? When you infringe on copyright, you're poaching someone else's creativity.

—*Lesley Ellen Harris. This article originally appeared in the June 2004 issue of REALTOR® Magazine.*

MORE ONLINE

Everything You Need to Know about Copyright Law

The federal government maintains an online clearinghouse on copyright law at www.copyright.gov. You can access material explaining copyright law as well as the laws themselves.

Know How to Give Legal Testimony

When you give a deposition in a lawsuit, the truth won't necessarily set you free—or even keep you out of court. As society becomes more litigious, many real estate brokers and salespeople are unwittingly submitting themselves to the perils of what appears to be a harmless deposition, only to learn too late that what they say can trap them in a lawsuit.

Giving testimony at a deposition can be risky because the U.S. legal system is naturally adversarial. Although the attorney who is taking your deposition may like your testimony and keep a promise not to bring you into the lawsuit, the other side may be so angered by your testimony, you'll be sued.

However, 10 simple guidelines will help you render deposition testimony effectively and safely.

1. *Seek advice of counsel before you testify.* There's an old saying that a person who represents himself has a fool for a client. Whenever you're subpoenaed to testify in a deposition, speak to an attorney first. Let your attorney review the deposition subpoena and discuss potential liability issues with you. For example, suppose a buyer is suing a seller because of water damage caused by a leak that the sellers had told you was repaired. You had told the buyers what the sellers told you, and thus far, you're not named in the suit. However, without the advice of counsel, you might unwittingly say something during your deposition that might lead the buyer's attorney to believe you were a part of the cover-up.

2. *Know why you're there.* A deposition is often taken to learn your version of the facts—that is, what you'll testify to at trial if called as a witness. A second reason is to develop impeachment evidence and admissions that could be used against you in a suit.

   To get a better understanding of the issues in the lawsuit, call one of the attorneys involved and ask for a copy of the complaint. Then review it with your attorney. You could also speak to the parties involved in the case, if their attorney agrees, to get a better understanding of the arguments they intend to put forward.

3. *Know why you're not there.* A deposition is *not* your chance to explain your side of the story. You may be eager to tell everyone about the disclosures you made or explain that your advice to a client was sound and there's really no merit to the case. Stop!

   The opposing attorney could introduce your additional testimony to hurt your credibility or damage your client's case. You'll have an opportunity to explain your story in court if the case goes to trial.

4. *Answer only the questions you're asked.* For example, if you're asked whether you completed a form, answer "yes" or "no." Don't explain how you use that report or how you file the information. If attorneys want more information, they can ask follow-up questions. It's also critical not to pass along as personal knowledge or fact any information you heard from others. And remember, the longer you make your answers, the longer the deposition will take.

5. *Be prepared.* Very often a deposition will concern a transaction that occurred several years earlier. Review all relevant records beforehand so you'll have an understanding of the factual background that gave rise to this lawsuit. Don't bring any notes or other documents to the deposition, however. Also remember not to take notes unless you're asked to do so by the court. Otherwise, the opposition has a right to review all your jottings.

6. *Always tell the truth.* Although telling the truth in a deposition is no guarantee of impunity, lying or playing fast and loose with the facts will undoubtedly increase your potential liability exposure.

7. *Don't be afraid to say, "I don't know."* You may feel as if you always need a right and ready answer for a client. But a deposition isn't a test you have to ace. Especially when the events in question occurred a long time ago, "I don't know" may be a more truthful answer than racking your memory for some half-forgotten fact.

8. *Stick to the facts.* We all have a tendency to embellish our statements and describe our states of mind during an incident we're recounting. In a deposition, such statements can be extremely detrimental. For example, avoid characterizing your testimony with lead-ins such as "in all candor," "honestly," or "to tell you the truth." Such statements open the chance for the opposing attorney to use your statements against you: "Weren't your other statements honest?"

9. *Act professionally.* This common sense is imperative. Wear business attire (a tie for men, a dress with jacket for women). Don't chew gum or smoke, and refrain from any off-color humor (as tempting as a good attorney joke may be). Behaving professionally will enable you to testify with confidence and increase the credibility of your testimony.

10. *Admit you're not perfect.* If you realize you've made a mistake in a deposition, all isn't lost. Correct yourself immediately if you become aware of your misstatement during the deposition process. If the mistake comes to your attention only afterward, make alterations in the transcript you'll be sent to sign. Include a note explaining your changes.

A deposition can be an intimidating process and should never be taken lightly. However, with care you can ensure that your depositions prevent lawsuits rather than bring them on.

—*Robert Tyson. This article originally appeared in the September 2003 issue of REALTOR® Magazine.*

Fair Treatment in Dual Agency

Representing the buyer and the seller in the same transaction, also known as disclosed dual agency, gives you the flexibility to assist both parties and can reduce the adversarial atmosphere of negotiations. On the other hand, it means full representation isn't available to either the buyer or seller. And because dual agency isn't always fully understood by salespeople or consumers, it can lead to misunderstandings and liability.

Because of the potential for conflicts of interest inherent in the disclosed dual agency relationship, buyers and sellers must understand its implications and give their informed consent to the relationship.

For salespeople who practice dual agency, one of the biggest challenges is keeping price and motivation confidential on both sides of the transaction so that neither buyers nor sellers lose their bargaining position.

Disclosed dual agency is legal in most states. However, nondisclosure or improper handling of dual agency can result in substantial legal liability, such as the $200,000 settlement in a 2002 Alaska case in which the salesperson didn't properly disclose a dual agency relationship (*Columbus v. Mehner*).

Even with proper disclosure, many dual agents find themselves in complex situations in which it's difficult to know how best to serve both the buyer and the seller. Consider these familiar scenarios, and recommendations for dealing with them:

> You attend the home inspection with your buyer and even though you let the inspector lead the way, you overhear the buyer saying things like, "That's fine; I can take care of that myself" or, "No problem; my brother's a carpenter." The buyer and his attorney list those same items as repairs they want the seller to make, but you know the buyer probably doesn't really *need* the repairs.

> *Recommendation:* Although the buyer may be using the repairs as a negotiating ploy, as a dual agent you really have no choice but to relay the buyer's repair demands to the seller.

> You receive an offer from a buyer client on your own listing. When you present it to your seller, he asks about the other buyers who looked at the property in the past few days: "Please call all their agents to see if their buyers are interested." The seller won't move forward with the offer until you do. Your buyer really wants this house and has asked you to let him know if there are any other offers. Yet the seller has instructed you not to tell the buyer if another offer comes in for fear it will cause him to walk away.

> *Recommendation:* The savvy dual agent can head off this type of situation by learning early on how the seller wants to handle multiple offers. Then, make sure to inform your buyer of the seller's plan for addressing multiple buyers up front, before the buyer makes an offer.

> You have two sets of buyers interested in your listing. You sign an agency agreement with the first set but refer the second set of buyers to another agent. The buyers you referred say they don't want to work with another agent because they feel the first buyers would have a negotiating advantage working with you.

Recommendation: You may hate to lose both sides of the sale, but the best alternative is to refer both buyers to other salespeople and represent only the seller in the transaction.

Protect Yourself

The only sure way to avoid conflicts arising from disclosed dual agency is to not practice this form of agency. However, there are steps you can take to protect yourself and lessen potential conflicts.

Do

Give buyers information about the property.

Disclose all material defects.

Help the buyers compare financing alternatives.

Provide information on comparable properties so that both parties may make educated decisions on the price.

Don't

Disclose confidential information about either client without permission.

Recommend or suggest a price to either party. Do a comparative market analysis and let the parties decide for themselves.

Disclose the lowest price the seller will take for the property or the seller's financial position without permission.

Disclose the highest price the buyer will pay for the property or the buyer's financial position without permission. (Might not apply in Arizona. Check with your local counsel.)

Following these simple rules won't guarantee that you'll never get caught in a disagreement between buyers and sellers in a disclosed dual agency relationship. But it'll give you the protection of knowing you did your utmost to serve both parties fairly.

—*Lynn Madison, ABR®, GRI. This article originally appeared in the July 2003 issue of REALTOR® Magazine.*

MORE ONLINE

What to Know about Agency Disclosure

The National Association of REALTORS®' Information Central maintains a field guide on agency disclosure, which includes material on disclosure forms and risks of inadequate disclosure. Access to some of the material requires a fee or a site user name and password, available to NAR members. The field guides are at www.realtor.org, under "Library."

Using the REALTOR® Trademark Correctly

The National Association of REALTORS®' victory in late 2004 defeating a legal challenge to the uniqueness of the REALTOR® trademark is a reminder of the need for continual care and vigilance in preserving this valuable asset. NAR's trademark protection efforts can be traced back almost to the first time the REALTOR® marks were used in 1915. Then, as now, the purpose of these efforts is to assure that the terms REALTOR® and REALTORS® are used only to identify members of NAR and aren't synonymous with generic terms, such as "real estate practitioner." The importance of this trademark program was demonstrated during the recent case, *Zimmerman v. NAR*, 2004, when the Trademark Trial and Appeal Board that decided it cited NAR's trademark protection efforts and members' observance of NAR's trademark rules as critical elements in its decision in NAR's favor.

At the heart of the association's trademark program is a comprehensive set of rules describing the proper use of the REALTOR® marks, which include the term and trademark symbol. The rules are organized around five limitations on the use of the marks, which apply to virtually all uses.

1. *Membership limitation.* Only individuals who hold the category of REALTOR® membership in a REALTOR® association are auto-

matically licensed by NAR to use the REALTOR® marks to identify themselves. And to do so, they must follow NAR's rules, which
allow the marks to be used in conjunction with, but not as part of,
members' names and the name of their real estate businesses. A
correct usage would be "John and Betty Smith, REALTORS®,"
while a usage such as "Your Professional Realtor" would be incorrect. The marks should be separated from the name of the member
or the member's company name with appropriate punctuation,
such as a slash, dash, or comma. Members may continue to use the
REALTOR® marks for as long as they remain association members
in good standing.

2. *Real estate business limitation.* Members are authorized to use the
REALTOR® marks only in connection with their real estate businesses. Although members may be involved in other lines of business, their use of the REALTOR® marks is restricted to real estate
brokerage and management, mortgage financing, appraising, land
development, and building.

3. *Context-of-use limitation.* Perhaps the most difficult to understand,
this limitation requires that the marks be used only to refer to a
person's status as a member, not to an occupation. For this reason,
uses such as "No. 1 REALTOR®," "Your REALTOR®," or "Professional REALTOR®" are incorrect. Such uses are improper because
the REALTOR® marks are supposed to distinguish between members and nonmembers. They're not intended to promote one member over another.

A simple rule of thumb to use when trying to determine
whether a particular use of the REALTOR® marks is proper under
this limitation is to substitute the phrase "member of NAR" for
the term "REALTOR®." If the meaning of the sentence doesn't
change, you're probably using the term correctly. If the meaning
changes, you'd need to substitute the words "real estate broker" or
"real estate salesperson" in order to comply with correct trademark use. For example, a sentence such as "REALTORS® will
benefit from the lower interest rates" is incorrect because all real
estate brokers and salespeople, not just members of NAR, would
benefit.

Another common context error is using descriptive words or
phrases with the REALTOR® marks. NAR's bylaws expressly

prohibit this practice. For example, "residential REALTOR®" is improper because "residential" is a descriptive word being used to modify the term REALTOR®. Geographic descriptive terms, such as the names of communities, cities, and states—for instance, Wisconsin REALTOR®—are also prohibited. Geographic descriptions may be used in the names of state and local REALTOR® associations, however.

4. *Geographic limitation.* Members are allowed to use the marks anywhere they go, but they must include the address of their place of business on materials in which the REALTOR® marks appear. This limitation applies to materials such as business cards, brochures, and web sites.

5. *Form-of-use limitation.* REALTOR® marks must be used consistently and in ways that distinguish them from the words and symbols around them. The preferred format for REALTOR® is all uppercase letters, followed by the federal registration symbol (®). The term should never be used in all lowercase letters: realtor. In some special circumstances, such as newspaper articles, however, the marks may be used with only an initial capital letter—Realtors, for example—as long as the term refers to a member or members. Internet domain names and e-mail addresses also are treated as special exceptions. These options don't require the use of capitalization, punctuation, or the federal registration mark. Thus, a company named First National Realty, REALTORS®, could use the URL www.firstnationalrealtyrealtors.com. However, the company is subject to the other rules. For example, it couldn't use the domain name bestrealtors.com for the reasons described in No. 3.

By observing these rules and properly using the REALTOR® marks to identify your status as an NAR member, you'll help to assure that the REALTOR® marks always retain their special significance and the value they hold today.

—*Laurie Janik. This article originally appeared in the*
October 2004 issue of REALTOR® Magazine.

MORE ONLINE

NAR's Membership Marks Manual

The National Association of REALTORS®' policy on using the REAL-TOR® mark is contained in *Membership Marks Manual,* available at www.realtor.org by entering the term "trademark manual" in the search bar. In addition, you can purchase for distribution to your sales associates *On Your Mark: A Trademark Pocket Reference for REALTORS®* from REALTOR VIP® Publications at the NAR Ethics & Policy section of the REALTOR® VIP site at www.realtor.org.

Avoiding a Breach:
Fiduciary Duties Clarified

You know the drill: When acting as an agent, you owe fiduciary duties to your buyer and seller clients. Frequently, however, it takes court decisions to outline the parameters of those duties. Three recent cases offer guidance to help clarify our understanding of fiduciary duties.

A decision by a Washington state court of appeals examined whether a buyer's agent breached his fiduciary duty when the purchase offer he prepared on a $1.6 million commercial property included a legal description of the property that was incorrect in a number of material respects.

The agent obtained the description from a database compiled from tax records maintained by the county assessor's office. The database incorrectly indicated the square footage to be 27,260 when it was only 20,141. The database description also indicated that the seller owned three lots, when he actually owned two lots and the east 26 feet of the third.

After purchasing the property, the buyer discovered the discrepancies and sued his agent for, among other claims, breach of fiduciary duty. The agent argued that, on the basis of a state statute, he had no duty to verify the information obtained from the database. The statute expressly provides that, unless the parties agree otherwise, the licensee owes no duty to inspect the property or to independently verify the accuracy of any statement by a source the agent reasonably believes to be reliable.

The court found that the statute didn't protect the agent in this case because the agent had acknowledged that the information in the database, including square footage data, could be inaccurate. Therefore, the agent had a duty to verify the information obtained from the database. His failure to act on this red flag constituted a breach of his fiduciary duty to the buyer.

In New York, an appellate court recently examined a case in which a seller claimed that a listing broker steered a prospective buyer away from the seller's lot because it wasn't listed with the broker.

The seller, a real estate developer and subdivision owner, had listed six lots in the subdivision with the broker but intended to sell several other lots independently. The seller claimed that when a buyer expressed interest in a lot that wasn't listed with the broker, the broker told the buyer the lot wasn't for sale. The broker then successfully sold that buyer one of the lots listed with him. The seller claimed the broker's conduct constituted a breach of fiduciary duty, requiring the broker to forfeit his commission.

The court held that a broker's fiduciary duty to protect the principal's interests and to refrain from taking any action adverse to the principal's interests extended only to the transaction that formed the agency relationship. Since the broker didn't represent the seller on any of the unlisted lots, the broker's fiduciary duty didn't extend to those properties. The court therefore concluded there had been no breach of fiduciary duties.

In a third case, an Ohio appellate court addressed a claim brought by a couple, who said their buyer's agent had breached her fiduciary duty by refusing the wife's repeated requests for information about the ethnic diversity of the neighborhoods the agent suggested.

The court recognized that it's in the best interest of salespeople and brokers not to disclose information about a neighborhood's racial composition in order to avoid fair housing claims of unlawful steering. The court further recognized that since what constitutes a satisfactorily diverse neighborhood is subjective, responding to such a question puts an agent in an untenable position.

These factors led the court to conclude the agent had no fiduciary duty to disclose the racial composition or ethnic diversity of a neighborhood to a potential buyer, even when the buyer requests such information. The court noted that a buyer's agent could accommodate a specific request by a buyer who indicated a preference for housing on a racial basis. However, if challenged in court, the agent would face a heavy burden proving that the buyer's request was independent from any encouragement by the agent.

To avoid breaching your fiduciary duties to clients, remember, among other things, to protect their interests within the scope of your engagement, to verify unreliable information, and to uphold fair housing laws.

—*Laurie Janik. This article originally appeared in the*
January 2003 issue of REALTOR® Magazine.

Commission Rules for Departing Associates

You're moving on to another brokerage. As you tie up loose ends, don't lose sight of the biggest transitional issue: how much compensation you're entitled to receive from your soon-to-be-former brokerage.

Are you entitled to commissions based on your transactions that were in the works when you left? Is the broker entitled to reduce the amount you receive because another associate must complete your pending transactions?

In theory, you can determine the answer to such questions by reviewing the terms of the agreement between you and your brokerage. What you negotiated—or failed to negotiate—when you joined the company will now determine what sort of compensation you're entitled to receive.

If the terms of the agreement are ambiguous, a court will decide how much, if any, compensation you'll receive. Courts have enforced oral contracts when the terms are undisputed. But an agreement that fails to spell out very specific terms about compensation can invite legal disputes.

Be Specific to Avoid Litigation

Take a 2002 Ohio case. In *Kitchen v. Welsh Ohio LLC*, a written agreement stated that a departed sales associate was entitled to receive a share of brokerage fees on any transactions "made that aren't closed" before the associate left the company. The contract further specified that if the sales associate left pending transactions or listings that required further work, the broker or the associate would arrange for another individual in the company to perform the required work and that individual "shall be compensated for taking care of pending transactions or listings."

A dispute arose because the language in the contract failed to specify whether the broker or the departing sales associate would compensate the individual who completed the transactions.

The trial court and later the Ohio court of appeals based their decisions in part on testimony by an expert witness for the broker who said it was industry practice to deduct the expenses from the departing sales associate's share of compensation. The departed associate also admitted during his deposition that he thought the cost of taking care of pending transactions would be deducted from his share of the fees. Therefore, the ambiguous provision was interpreted as a charge against the sales associate's compensation.

Say What You Mean

If vague contract language can result in a commission dispute, using a specific word that doesn't convey the meaning you intend can create its own set of problems. In a New York case (*Goldsmith v. J.I. Sopher & Co. Inc.*, *1998*), a salesperson sued to recover commissions from his former brokerage. The agreement between the parties specified that the salesperson was entitled to receive a percentage of the gross commissions generated by salespeople under his direction that were "collected" by the brokerage.

Based on that language, the court awarded the salesperson his share of all compensation received by the brokerage prior to his departure. But the court denied him a percentage of commissions received by the brokerage after his departure, even if those sums were earned during his tenure. The reason? Those sums hadn't been "collected" prior to his termination, the court said.

Make It Enforceable

It's also critical to ensure that compensation terms included in an agreement are enforceable. In a 1998 Connecticut case (*Lawler v. Blazawski*), a broker and a departing sales associate agreed that the associate would receive commissions on transactions that were nearing completion. Additionally, the agreement stated that some of the associate's existing listings and contracts that were in negotiation would become the property of the associate's new broker.

When the broker failed to follow through on this agreement, the sales associate sought to recover compensation for his listings that sold as well as on those that didn't sell. The salesperson argued that if the unsold listings had been transferred to his new broker, as agreed, they would've sold.

The Connecticut Appellate Court found the sales associate's claim speculative. Additionally, it ruled that the broker and salesperson couldn't enter into an agreement regarding the transfer of the listings. Such an agreement would have to have been made between the two brokers, and the salesperson's new broker wasn't a party to the agreement.

The lesson to draw from each of these cases? Review carefully the language in the agreement you sign with your brokerage so that it says precisely what you intended in very clear terms. Courts will enforce what you wrote, not what you meant to write.

—Laurie Janik. This article originally appeared in the May 2004 issue of REALTOR® Magazine.

COMPENSATION QUESTIONS

When you join a brokerage, immediately square the terms of your compensation agreement. Here are some questions to ask a broker before you sign on:

What compensation will I receive when I leave?

For which transactions will I receive payments?

Will I or the broker assume the expenses of bringing pending transactions to close?

MORE ONLINE

Learning from Departing Sales Associates

It's never easy when associates leave, but you can gain valuable intelligence about improving operations going forward by conducting exit interviews. REALTOR® Magazine Online maintains materials on conducting exit interviews and handling terminations amicably under "Retaining top personnel" in its Brokerage Management toolkit at www.realtor.org/realtormag.

Employment Law: Who's Exempt?

Although most real estate salespeople work as independent contractors, affiliated with a brokerage, there are many others in this business—managers, receptionists, assistants—who are considered employees under federal and state employment laws. Whether you're a broker who hires management and support staff or a salesperson with one or more assistants, you need to know how employment laws governing wages, overtime, and record keeping pertain to you.

Many of these laws aren't new, but the recent issuance of new regulations defining exempt and nonexempt employees makes this a good time to review key provisions of federal labor law.

Unlike real estate licensees working as independent contractors, who are covered by special Internal Revenue Service (IRS) regulations, workers in other aspects of the real estate business aren't considered independent contractors unless they meet extensive tests created by the IRS. Some of the principal factors that determine whether a worker is an employee include the amount of control the company has over the worker's hours, where the worker does the job, and the manner in which the work is performed. Generally speaking, if an employer gives specific directions as to when and how work is to be done, the worker is an employee.

To help companies determine whether a worker is an independent contractor, the IRS has created Form SS-8 (available at www.irs.gov). The form, which is necessary to complete only if you have a question about the tax status of a worker, poses a series of questions on the work performed and the behavioral and financial controls the company has over the worker.

Behavioral-control criteria include how the work is assigned, the location where the work must be done, and who determines how the work should be done. Financial-control criteria include who provides equipment for the worker; how expenses are reimbursed; and whether payment is made as a lump sum, commission, or hourly wage.

Exempt versus Nonexempt Status

Once an employer has established that a worker is an employee, the next question is whether that worker is exempt or nonexempt from federal overtime requirements. Exempt workers don't qualify for overtime pay. Last August the U.S. Department of Labor issued new rules defining exempt employees. Under these rules, employees in real estate activities could possibly qualify under either an executive or an administrative exemption from overtime. To qualify for an executive exemption, an employee must

Be compensated on a salary basis and be paid at least $455 per week. According to the regulations, a salary is a predetermined amount of pay that constitutes all or part of the employee's compensation. It may not be reduced based on the quality or quantity of work performed.

Be managing the enterprise or a recognized department or subdivision of the enterprise.

Direct the work of at least two or more full-time employees or their equivalent.

Have the authority to hire and fire other employees or have a strong influence on these decisions.

To qualify for an administrative exemption, an employee must

Be compensated on a salary or a fee basis at a rate of at least $455 per week. Employees are paid on a fee basis if they receive an agreed-upon sum for a single job, regardless of the time required for its completion. Payments based on the number of hours or days worked aren't considered payments on a fee basis.

Have primary duties that require office or nonmanual work directly related to the management or general business operations of the employer.

Exercise discretion and independent judgment with respect to matters of significance.

For a complete summary of the regulations, go to www.dol.gov.

If employees don't qualify as exempt, they're entitled to overtime pay for work time exceeding 40 hours in any workweek. The Fair Labor Standards Act requires that you pay nonexempt employees one and one-half times their regular pay rate for overtime.

Discrimination and Immigration

Employment law, like fair housing law, prohibits discrimination on the basis of race, religion, national origin, ethnicity, age, or gender. Title VII of the Civil Rights Act prohibits an employer with 15 or more employees from asking questions about any of these protected factors during a job interview or from deciding a worker's promotion, salary, or termination based on any of these factors.

Companies with 15 or more employees must also comply with the Americans with Disabilities Act, which requires employers to make special accommodation for workers with a disability.

Organizations with one or more employees must comply with the Immigration Reform and Control Act of 1986. This law requires companies to verify that the employee is either a U.S. citizen or an alien legally authorized to work in the United States. Under the act, employers must complete the Immigration and Naturalization Service's I-9 form within three days of hiring a worker and keep it for three years after the employee has left.

Workers prove their legal status by providing forms of identification listed on the form. For more information, go to http://uscis.gov and look under "Immigration Forms, Fees, and Fingerprints."

—Doug Hinderer. This article originally appeared in the January 2005 issue of REALTOR® Magazine.

RECORD KEEPING BASICS

Maintaining appropriate records on employees is sound employment practice. Keep these records for at least three years after employment terminates.

Employee's name, Social Security number, and address.

Date of birth, if the employee is under 19 (ensures children don't work more than they're allowed by law).

Gender and occupation.

Time and day of week that workweek begins.

Hours worked each day and the total for the workweek.

Basis on which the employee's wages are paid (hourly, salaried).

Regular hourly pay rate.

Total daily or weekly regular earnings for the workweek.

Total overtime wages for the workweek.

All additions to or deductions from wages (Social Security, insurance, and so on).

Total wages paid for each pay period and date of payment (such as once a week or twice a month).

MORE ONLINE

Know Your Workplace Requirements

REALTOR® Magazine Online maintains resources on risk management under its Brokerage Management section at www.realtor.org/realtor mag. In addition, management manuals from the National Association of REALTORS® are available for sale (with pricing discounts for NAR members) at the REALTOR®.org store at www.realtor.org. Titles include *The Risk Aversion Trio* (Item #126-375), which includes "Workplace Law and Office Policies."

12

Risk Management

Avoiding Pitfalls

When one of his clients was hit with a complaint alleging misrepresentation during a home sale transaction, attorney David Scott weighed in with a simple piece of advice that made the difference in how the lawsuit ended: Check your files and all your desk drawers for written records verifying what you disclosed.

So, when the sales associate produced a cover sheet showing that he had, as claimed, faxed the home buyer information on the house's water supply, the judge closed the case in favor of the associate. "The judge said to the buyer, 'You may not have received the information, but the sales associate sent it, and here's the proof he fulfilled his duty,'" says Scott, whose practice is in Nashville. "You'd be surprised how many cases turn on proof that a simple document was sent."

Allegations of misrepresentation, including failures to disclose, have long been the No. 1 complaint against real estate sales associates, say attorneys who represent associates in professional liability cases.

Probably 90 percent of liability cases against associates involve misrepresentation, and 90 percent of those charge negligent misrepresentation, says Paul Stephen Drayna, an attorney in Seattle. Negligent misrepresentation occurs when sales associates say something they believe to be true based on what the client, often the seller, says—the water heater is five years old, for example—but the statement turns out to be false.

Although courts overwhelmingly tend to decide in favor of sales associates in these cases—probably 80 percent to 85 percent of the time, says Drayna, based on the cases he's handled—the complaints keep coming. That's because unhappy parties to a transaction, usually buyers who've discovered a problem with the house after purchase, don't feel satisfied until they've sought damages. "Many times, all the person really wants to do is vent," says Drayna.

Despite your odds of success, prevention is key because defending yourself, even in cases you ultimately win, costs time and money and can lead to increases in your errors and omissions insurance premiums.

What's more, to avoid the costs and uncertainty of a trial, E&O insurers even prefer to settle lawsuits your associates are likely to win. But settlement can negatively affect your professional reputation and even attract more lawsuits. "Some brokers feel that if you settle a claim, even if it's frivolous, you encourage more frivolous lawsuits," says Drayna.

Consider four top risk-management issues that attorneys suggest you advise your associates about.

1. *Dual agency.* A big portion of misrepresentation claims come out of dual agency transactions, says Drayna, who makes this claim based on his experience rather than any hard statistics. Problems tend to arise when sales associates, acting as the listing agent, attract a buyer and propose to represent the buyer in addition to the seller.

   Even assuming appropriate disclosures are made, if buyers discover something wrong with the house after purchase, they're more likely to file a complaint than if they had separate representation, says Drayna. That's because they're more likely to question whether they were represented adequately.

   Dual agency is permitted with appropriate disclosure in all states but three—Colorado, Florida, and Kansas—according to the *Real Estate Agency Annual Report* for 2003, prepared for NAR Government Affairs by the Legal Research Center Inc. But Drayna calls it "a lightning rod."

   Risk reducer: Associates should limit dual agency to instances in which they have an established relationship with both parties rather than with just one of them, Drayna recommends.

2. *Seller disclosure.* Having sellers disclose the condition of their property on a standardized form—a requirement in New York and some

30 other states—can give sales associates a false sense of security, says Richard Evans, an attorney in Rochester, New York.

In Evans' state, the form tells buyers they're not to rely on the disclosures as an affirmative representation of the actual condition of the property, he says. Instead, they're to verify conditions on their own with the help of professionals, such as a home inspector.

Even with that disclaimer, unhappy buyers are filing claims alleging the listing agent and even the buyer's agent in some cases should have known the seller disclosure was inaccurate, says Evans. In court, judges often rule in favor of the buyers, he says.

"Buyers are coming in saying, 'Why didn't you point out this property condition to me?'" says Evans. "And judges are saying, 'If the condition's discovered, you're liable.' The seller disclosure form isn't stopping disgruntled claims."

NAR supports the use of seller disclosure forms as a tool for associates to help reduce, but not necessarily eliminate, their liability.

Risk reducer: Make sure your associates tell buyers upfront that the form reflects property condition only to the best of the seller's knowledge, the disclosures aren't to be relied on, and it's advisable to inform themselves by hiring an inspector, says Evans.

3. *Loan and investment fraud.* Your associates can get caught up in such fraud unwittingly if they're not careful about when it's okay, and when it isn't okay, to meet certain demands by vendors or other parties to a transaction, says Steve Willoughby, president of Steve Willoughby Seminars in Casper, Wyoming.

Your associates should be wary if a mortgage broker asks them to rewrite a purchase agreement to mischaracterize the nature of a purchase to obtain more favorable loan terms than they otherwise could, says Willoughby, whose company hosts seminars on risk management and other topics for real estate professionals in Idaho, South Dakota, and Wyoming.

Drayna warns of characterizing the purchase of an income-producing property, such as a bed-and-breakfast or a boarding house, as a residential purchase. One scenario he's aware of involved a boarding house near a university that, at the mortgage broker's suggestion, was characterized as a duplex. And indeed, from the outside, the property looked like a duplex because that's what it was originally developed as.

Lenders typically make financing available on better terms for residential purchases than for income-producing properties. Or they might not make a loan at all on an income-producing property. If the practitioner writes up the purchase agreement as a residential purchase knowing the deal is being mischaracterized by the mortgage broker or loan officer, the practitioner could be found to have committed loan fraud.

The same concerns about mischaracterization apply if associates help investors who ask to be listed as owner-occupants in the loan documents, says Willoughby.

Risk reducer: Anytime you're asked to mischaracterize the nature of the purchase, that should be a red flag to you that you risk committing fraud and should refuse to do that, says Drayna. Associates should get as much in writing as possible—that the buyer intends to occupy the property, for example. If the buyer doesn't intend to occupy and won't say that in writing, then you don't want to work with the person. "Typically you don't find out about loan fraud until after the owner defaults and people start reviewing files," says Willoughby. "If you have everything in writing, you're protected."

4. *Unauthorized practice of law.* Alert your associates to be cautious of requests by the buyer or seller to append unique language to a standard purchase agreement. "Anytime your associates find themselves putting pen to a blank piece of paper, rather than just filling in blanks or checking boxes in a contract, that should be a red flag they could be engaging in the unauthorized practice of law," says Drayna.

In one case Drayna is familiar with, a buyer of a property occupied by a tenant wanted a clause written into the purchase agreement that he could terminate the agreement if, among other things, the seller couldn't evict the tenant in time for the closing.

Risk reducer: If there's no legal language in your company's collection of standard forms referencing what the buyer or seller wants in the contract—and in Drayna's example there wasn't—the most prudent course of action is for the associate to advise the buyer or seller to hire a lawyer to draft language, says Drayna.

Saying You're Sorry Works, Too

Whatever situation your associates find themselves in, they can't go wrong asking for advice from you, other experienced brokers, an attorney, or the legal hotline hosted by their state association of REALTORS®, if one is offered. In many cases, commonsense advice such as keeping a good paper trail is all they need.

And sometimes saying "I'm sorry" works wonders. In one case Drayna was involved in, in which the plaintiff sought both damages and an apology, the sales associate didn't believe he'd done anything wrong and couldn't be coaxed into issuing an apology. Yet that was the main thing the plaintiff wanted, Drayna says.

Given the power of an apology to defuse a tense situation, make it part of your standard practice to wield it when a conversation is heated. If someone calls your associate and alleges he made a mistake, you might avoid a lawsuit simply by finding out the facts, saying you're sorry for the problem and, even if you don't believe your associate did anything wrong, taking accountability and searching for a resolution," he says. "That could include refunding a commission or relisting a property at a reduced rate."

Such a proactive response might not only forestall a lawsuit, it might help you keep a client.

—Robert Freedman. This article originally appeared in the December 2004 issue of REALTOR® Magazine.

Proper Documentation Keeps You out of Legal Trouble

If you've been in the real estate business any length of time, your transaction files are probably bursting out of their drawers. Even if you need to make room for the next client's pile of paper, don't give in to the temptation to toss or thin out old files. Doing so puts you at a huge legal disadvantage if a dispute arises.

With so many state and federal regulations and statutes governing legal disputes, it's difficult to provide a record keeping rule of thumb.

In addition, because tax laws and regulations such as disclosure provisions usually stipulate a time frame for keeping documentation, which again can vary from state to state, it may be necessary to keep some records longer than others. For example, sellers and their agents must keep federal lead paint disclosure forms for three years after a transaction closes. In many states, time limits for filing lawsuits for misrepresentation can vary from two to four years after a sale is completed. Fraud can be claimed several years after it's discovered, and often the period of time for filing a claim doesn't begin until the alleged fraud is detected. Suits concerning contracts can be filed up to 10 years after a transaction.

The best advice is to keep all transaction files for at least 5 years and major contracts, such as the listing agreement, purchase contract, and disclosure forms for 10 years.

An easy test for what to keep and what to throw away is to ask yourself, "If I'm sued and an attorney subpoenas this file, does it contain everything I need to prove I did everything right?"

Among the items that should be retained in your transaction files for at least five years—and longer if possible—are:

The principal documents that are part of the transaction, such as the listing agreement, purchase offer, counteroffers, agency relationship disclosure, property defects disclosure, escrow instructions, and repair agreements.

State- or area-specific documents and addenda recommended by your state and local association, franchise, or brokerage. For example, California requires an addendum in which an inspector certifies that water heaters in earthquake-prone areas are strapped in place.

Also retain completed and signed documents that your errors and omissions carrier suggests you provide to buyers or sellers. These might include special supplements advising buyers of their inspection rights or notifying buyers that they have the option to investigate for mold.

Backup documents that demonstrate that the property was priced properly and promoted legally. These include comparable sales data, sales brochures on the property, the MLS listing, property advertisements, and a list of other properties the buyer was shown prior to this accepted offer. These documents can be invaluable if you're charged with a fair housing violation.

Documents that pertain to the physical condition of the property and land, including land surveys, inspections (current and previous, if the sellers kept them), the preliminary title report, permits, receipts from the seller for repairs made before sale, and current repair receipts for agreed buyer-requested repairs. These types of documentation will be valuable if questions arise about disclosure of known defects.

Receipts from buyers that they had received any required disclosure pamphlets on lead-based paint, mold, earthquake safety, flood warnings, and so on.

Correspondence, e-mail, faxes, and notes of phone calls and conversations between the principals and the sales associates, as well as with third parties, such as escrow or title agents, inspectors, or repair people. For example, if you received two offers for a property, be sure you have documentation of the date and time offers were received, replied to, and accepted as well as how you presented each offer.

Any prior offers and their respective documents and correspondence.

A log of transaction activities and forms, with the date each was executed. Also remember to retain faxes and e-mail that reflect when documents were sent.

During the transaction, be sure documents are properly signed and dated. Documents should be signed and dated by all parties—sellers, buyers, and real estate practitioners—affected by them. For example, the listing agreement is a contract between the seller and the listing agent, so both parties should sign and date it. Just before the closing, check your files to ensure no critical document is missing. Keep checklists—one for buyers, one for sellers—so that you won't overlook anything.

Some of the documents you save may overlap, but if you end up in court, you'll quickly learn that repetition is a good thing. Buyers told in three different documents of their option to inspect for mold will have a hard time convincing a jury that they didn't understand that they had that option. Another important point to remember is don't rely on your brokerage office's files for transaction information. Keep your own records, and you'll be sure you have them when you need them.

An added benefit of long-term record keeping: Buyers move every three to seven years on average. When you call for a listing appointment on a property you've once sold, you'll be ahead of other practitioners if you're able to quickly pull out all the pertinent data. Finally, remember, when in doubt, keep it.

—Barbara Nichols. This article originally appeared in the
November 2004 issue of REALTOR® Magazine.

MORE ONLINE

Ideas for Minimizing Risk

REALTOR® Magazine Online maintains resources on risk management under its Brokerage Management section at www.realtor.org/realtor mag. In addition, the National Association of REALTORS®' Information Central maintains a field guide on errors and omissions insurance and agency disclosure among other risk management field guides. Access to some of the material requires a fee or a site user name and password, available only to NAR members. The field guides are at www.realtor.org, under "Library." Also, the National Association of REALTORS® makes available for purchase a risk management guide called *Don't Risk It: A Broker's Guide to Risk Management* at the REALTOR®.org store at www.realtor.org. A purchase discount is available for NAR members.

Improving Customer Service

A curious thing happened when Debbie D'Valentine, CRS®, started putting listing information on her company's web site a few years ago. The online information was great at generating customer traffic, but few of the sales associates at her company, Tomie Raines Inc., in Lansing, Michigan, could take time to answer customer inquiries quickly; instead, they continued to direct their attention to their established clients.

The result: a less than exemplary service experience for online customers. Her solution: customer-relationship management.

She required all of her sales associates to complete a day-long training session to become certified as customer-service specialists through a program offered by Quality Service Certification (QSC) Inc. (www.quality certified.org) in San Juan Capistrano, California. QSC also offers online training.

Now all 145 of her sales associates follow a system for determining up front what their clients expect of them and measuring how well their service met those expectations.

D'Valentine's receptionist, a licensed associate, also took the training, allowing D'Valentine to expand her role. As Internet customer-service coordinator, the former receptionist is now responsible for developing a relationship with customers coming to the company over the Internet, answering their questions quickly, and then referring them to an associate when they're ready to transition from casual shopper to committed client.

"Usually customers in the information-gathering stage don't want to be pressured," says D'Valentine. "But they do want their inquiries answered quickly and professionally."

Improving Service

Ramping up the quality of your customer service can be as simple as making sure that a live person always answers the phone and that your associates obtain feedback from clients shortly after a transaction is complete, says real estate brokerage management consultant Joe Klock Sr. of Key Largo, Florida.

D'Valentine opted for a structured system, which gives her a way to start all of her associates out on the same foot and learn the same lessons. As she affiliates new associates, she sends them through the online version of the training, too.

The structured approach also enables her to obtain a consistent measurement of how well her associates are doing. If an associate consistently scores low, she and the associate can discuss the circumstances and map out an improvement plan.

"When an associate isn't providing good customer service, you tend to hear about it anyway," she adds. "But now we can quantify the issue and see where the person is weak." The consumer surveys address such performance areas as communication and marketing plans.

An aggressive customer-relationship management program can generate push back from associates, especially top performers who feel they wouldn't generate as much business as they do if their customer-service skills were weak, says Larry D. Romito, CRB, president and CEO of Quality Service Certification.

Many do provide good service, he says. But some top performers build their business by being good prospectors and good closers—qualities that don't necessarily translate into good customer service.

"Only one in three buyers and sellers, when asked after closing, indicate that they're very likely to use that salesperson again," says Romito, citing a statistic his company generated through its client feedback surveys. "The service that real estate professionals provide shouldn't be so hit-or-miss."

What are critical components of customer-relationship management? According to Romito and Klock, your associates should:

Determine up front what clients expect, then match the level of service to that expectation. Some clients expect their salesperson to talk with them daily and walk them through every aspect of the transaction; others want certain services taken care of, but otherwise prefer to be left alone.

Obtain feedback on how well service matched client expectations. Salespeople can get feedback more reliably if it's solicited as soon after the transaction as possible, when the experience is fresh in the client's mind.

And you should:

Institute a companywide customer-service program to see how your company is performing as a whole.

Consider working with a third-party vendor that would provide customer-service training and obtain feedback so performance measurement is consistent and objective.

Offer coaching for associates whose customer-service performance is weak or declining.

Encourage associates to tout completion of customer-service training and strong customer-service ratings in their marketing.

Brokerages can and do get by just by measuring their sales performance year after year. But by measuring customer-satisfaction levels, too, you can up your sales numbers by retaining customers who in the past may have slipped away.

—*Robert Freedman. This article originally appeared in the March 2004 issue of REALTOR® Magazine.*

MEASURING CUSTOMER SERVICE: WHAT'S IT COST?

Making sure someone in your office is always available to answer the phone or reminding your associates to obtain customer-service feedback from clients might not cost you anything. But if you take a systematic approach to customer satisfaction, expect to budget for it.

Debbie D'Valentine, of Tomie Raines Inc. in Lansing, Michigan, paid Quality Service Certification Inc. of San Juan Capistrano, California, $9,500 for training 140 associates, plus $5,428 for certifying them. Going forward, D'Valentine will pay an annual $50 certification renewal fee for each of her current associates and $149 for each new associate who's trained and certified online.

The certification program also involves surveying costs. QSC uses a third-party company to survey client satisfaction shortly after transaction completion and includes the results in a database. The cost: $3.50 per survey, which is billed to the brokerage monthly.

CUSTOMER SERVICE AS PART OF YOUR BUSINESS CULTURE

The National Association of REALTORS®' Information Central maintains a field guide on customer service that walks you through ideas on adding value through consistency in your high-touch efforts. Access to some of the material requires a fee or a site user name and password, available only to NAR members. The field guides are at www.realtor.org, under "Library."

Lowering E&O Premiums through Customer Service

Thanks to booming home sales, southern powerhouse Crye-Leike Inc., REALTORS®, saw its sales volume grow from $3 billion to $3.7 billion in a year-to-year comparison not too long ago. Yet the premiums on its errors and omissions (E&O) insurance have nudged upward only marginally in that time.

Company Vice President and General Manager Steve Brown, ABR®, CRB, who's based in Memphis, believes Crye-Leike's use of risk-mitigation seminars for its salespeople and the addition of a customer-service component to its web site have had much to do with the bottom-line-friendly premium rate the company has been enjoying.

"We've had nominal premium increases in our past few policy periods," says Brown, whose company in late 2004 had 2,850 sales associates and brokers in 80 offices in Arkansas, Florida, Georgia, Kentucky, Mississippi, and Tennessee. Brown won't disclose what Crye-Leike is paying in monthly E&O premiums.

For most brokers, E&O premiums are a major expense each month. Estimates vary by carrier and by state, but typical, basic premiums range from $200 to $400 per associate per month, say insurance executives. So earning discounted rates through risk-management practices can be a big money saver.

E&O insurance providers have long granted clients discounts on their premium and deductible amounts for taking risk-management measures that could lead to fewer claims against company sales associates. These measures include systematic use of industry-standard contracts and disclosure forms and regular training for licensees on best practices for minimizing risk. Past claims history also plays a big role in a company's premium structure.

Increasingly, though, insurance companies are also looking at how companies integrate customer service into their risk-management practices. Brown and other brokers say they're taking customer service even more seriously than in the past, and their efforts are part of the reason premium increases have been lower than they'd otherwise be, they believe. They can't confirm that, though, since insurance providers don't disclose internal underwriting decisions to their clients.

Beyond Risk Management

Customer service involves practices aimed at customer satisfaction and not, as with risk management, claims reduction.

"Last year we added a toll-free customer-service phone number on our web site that lets customers and clients call us directly if they have a complaint," says Brown. "If we head off these disputes more quickly, we're far more likely to avert a claim."

Toll-free numbers are great, but for real estate E&O insurance brokerage Arthur J. Gallagher & Co., systematic customer-service programs are even better. Insurance brokers help match clients with suitable insurance products. For the past year, the Itasca, Illinois-based insurance broker has been collecting claims and other data from several large real estate brokers that have implemented a customer-service program through Quality Service Certification Inc., a customer-relations management company in San Juan Capistrano, California. The exercise is intended to demonstrate a correlation between companywide implementation of a customer-service program and reduced claims likelihood. Crye-Leike isn't part of that effort.

Until the data is collected, the connection is anecdotal, not empirical. But John Fuhrman, senior vice president at Arthur J. Gallagher & Co., believes the data will show a strong correlation. "Insurance companies are [already] starting to get the idea that improved customer service and focus on risk reduction in the real estate management process will, over time, lead to better results from an E&O standpoint," he says.

Once the data is collected, Fuhrman will go on a "road show" to several large insurance companies to make the argument that real estate companies that implement customer-service programs should have systematic access to discounted rates on E&O insurance products.

"It's not always the case that underwriters have the flexibility to account for a broker's customer-service program," says Fuhrman. "We're seeking a more formalized process."

The QSC program, launched in 2000 and now being used by about 500 brokerages, representing some 15,000 associates who've gone through the training, is built around the idea that customer service can be systematized. That enables brokers to build risk-reduction via customer satisfaction directly into office procedures in a measurable and repeatable way.

"Customer service shouldn't be hit or miss depending on the inclination of individual associates. It should be a process salespeople follow to manage their customers' expectations," says Larry D. Romito, QSC president and CEO.

Early Results

Even without complete data, the first fruits of Gallagher's customer-service claims reduction effort are in. Last June, National Union Fire Insurance, a member company of American International Group Inc., a major U.S. insurance provider with operations in more than 130 countries, announced it would take into account a broker's QSC program. Since then the insurance company has written policies factoring in the certification, but a spokesperson for Gallagher said in late October it was too soon to estimate the volume because the program was still just getting off the ground.

Fuhrman can't say how much of a discount insurance providers will give the QSC brokers he's working with, but he believes it will be in the double digits. One or two insurance products reflecting the reduced premium structure could be ready from insurers by the second quarter of this year, he believes.

For Gallagher it won't be just any broker with a customer-service program who'll be eligible for the discounts; it'll be those who offer the QSC program. The reason: "The Quality Service Certification model makes it easier for us to convey the message to underwriters that this group of brokers has a consistent customer-service process," says Fuhrman.

Systematizing Quality Service

Under the QSC program, a brokerage hires QSC to provide initial training to its associates in widely accepted customer-service techniques such as setting expectations and maintaining open lines of communication. QSC uses a third-party provider to obtain feedback from the associate's clients shortly after closing about how well the associate met customer-service goals. The broker also offers a guarantee to clients that if they're not satisfied, they're entitled to amends, typically a cash credit to buyers and, for sellers, the opportunity to rescind a listing agreement.

The broker uses analyses of the feedback to identify customer-service areas that are consistently found to be weak, both among individual associates and in the company as a whole.

Associates and brokers who take the initial training have the option of being certified in customer service (by taking a test and paying a fee). They maintain that certification by scoring above a certain minimum performance level.

Among the details to be worked out: The amount of E&O discount might be tied to the percentage of associates in a company who become certified. A company with 75 percent of associates certified would receive a deeper discount than one with only 25 percent certified.

Gregory Scott, president of the Beazley Co., with 550 associates in 25 offices in Connecticut, who's used the QSC program since 2002, says he can't directly tie any effect to his E&O premiums. But he believes the program has helped keep his claims low, and that's kept his premiums from rising.

"With many claims, people are just aggravated about the transaction and are left with a bad taste in their mouth," he says. "That's where a systematic approach to customer service can make a difference."

"At the end of the day, satisfied customers are far less likely to sue," Fuhrman says, "so instituting a system in that regard should lead to fewer claims and thus lower premiums over time."

—*Robert Freedman. This article originally appeared in the January 2005 issue of REALTOR® Magazine.*

RISK MANAGEMENT MEANS E&O CREDIT

You take risk-management practices, such as careful documentation by your sales associates, seriously. So does that mean you'll pay less in errors and omissions insurance premiums than you otherwise would? The answer is yes, say insurance specialists, but how much less can vary greatly by state and by individual insurance underwriters.

As a rule of thumb, expect to receive a discount of 5 percent to 10 percent off your base premium for each of some half-dozen risk-management practices you institute, says Joan Schmalz, executive vice president of insurance provider Geo. F. Brown & Sons Inc., in Chicago, a REALTOR® VIP Alliance Program partner.

And expect to reduce your total premium between 15 percent and 50 percent, says Terry Cooper, vice president of sales at Pearl Insurance, based in Peoria Heights, Illinois. Pearl provides insurance administration for American Home Shield, also a REALTOR® VIP partner.

The amount of the discount, if any is granted, will vary greatly by state, because each state imposes its own rules on how much flexibility underwriters have. And underwriters themselves exercise flexibility within their internal company guidelines on how to apply discounts, says Schmalz.

Risk-management practices that typically qualify for discounts, or premium credits as they're sometimes known, include:

Attendance by brokers and associates at loss-mitigation or risk-management seminars and state-required continuing education courses, including those covering risk management.

Use of industry-standard contracts and disclosure forms.

Absence of claims by the brokerage in the past few years, typically the past five.

Purchase by the broker's clients (or by the broker on behalf of clients) of home warranty policies.

The home warranty policy is considered key to claims reduction because it gives buyers who discover an undisclosed property condition after closing the financial means to get it fixed. Without that, they're more likely to make a claim against the brokerage, says Schmalz.

MORE ONLINE

Tap Customer Service Resources

The National Association of REALTORS®' Information Central maintains a field guide on customer service that walks you through ideas on adding value through consistency in your high-touch efforts. Access to some of the material requires a fee or a site user name and password, available only to NAR members. The field guides are at www.realtor.org, under "Library."

The Right Amount of E&O Insurance

No matter how careful you are, don't underestimate the importance of professional liability insurance. People sue even when they don't have much of a case, and the financial drain can be crippling. Here are two actual cases and tips on how to prevent these nightmares from happening to you.

Case 1: Three months after a closing, Kate received this letter from her buyer clients: "Remember when you recommended an engineer to look at those cracks in the basement? Well, they're getting worse, and we think you should have insisted on us hiring an engineer to look at the defect."

Kate immediately went to the buyers' home to examine the cracks. The cracks had definitely expanded, so Kate arranged for an engineer. The buyers seemed satisfied.

A year later, Kate and her broker, Dan, were now in litigation, with the buyers claiming that Kate had a "duty to insist on an engineer." Legally, Kate had no such duty, and the case ultimately would be settled. But in the meantime, there were court costs, depositions, and attorneys' fees.

Dan's defense costs were covered by his insurer, because he filed a claim as soon as he learned about the case. Kate's coverage was denied, however, because she hadn't filed a claim when she received the initial letter. Kate had feared filing a claim would cause her premiums to increase. Was she right to worry? No. If your state has an endorsed or mandatory insurance program, you should be able to file a claim without fear of a premium increase. Generally, the carrier must insure all licensees in the state regardless of claims history—but check your carrier's practices and the terms of its policy.

Case 2: Aaron, a broker, listed his best friend's grossly overpriced property. Since it was probably worth $300,000, a listing at $625,000 was crazy, but, Aaron told himself, who knows?

Monica, a relatively new salesperson in Aaron's office, was on floor duty when the buyers entered. They viewed Aaron's new listing, and Monica's heart raced when they indicated that they loved it and would like to write a contract, full price, all cash.

Back at the office, Monica drafted the offer letter and presented it to the buyers for their signature. Aaron took it to his friend, who signed it.

When he returned to the office, Aaron told Monica to deposit the $25,000 earnest money check. Oops. In her excitement, Monica had indicated on the offer that the earnest money was a check, but she hadn't actually received a check. The buyers, who were from out of town, didn't have a check with them. Not to worry, they'd sign an earnest money note due in three days, which would give them time to get home to send the check.

Nervously, Monica told Aaron, who then called the seller, who indicated that this plan was just fine. However, the buyers left town and never sent the earnest money. The deal didn't close. The friend sued Aaron and Monica for $25,000.

Negligence? Yes. Proper action would've been to amend the contract to provide for the plan for earnest money payment.

Covered by insurance? Yes. This claim was well within the coverage limits of $100,000 under many state policy minimum limits used by so many real estate professionals today.

However, the seller then amended his claim from $25,000 to $325,000. Apparently, the seller had sold the house as a FSBO (for sale by owner) for $300,000 and wanted the entire "benefit of the lost bargain." He had no legal case, but it didn't matter. The attorneys' fees to prepare to defend against his suit would be high, and the potential existed—no matter how slight—for a large settlement or judgment.

The seller and his attorney delayed, danced, and tried everything to drag the case out. More than a year later, we finally settled for $25,000. By then, my attorneys' fees were more than $45,000.

To avoid this type of nightmare scenario, heed the following advice:

Understand that every real estate salesperson is at risk for a crazy case, so make sure you're covered.

Know your policy limitations. Most salespeople have no idea who their carrier is, what the coverage limits are, and what the rules for timely filing of claims are.

Make sure you have enough insurance. My rule of thumb: Coverage should be the same amount as the largest deal you do in a year, with a minimum $250,000. The $100,000 level is just for those who don't sell much real estate.

Always buy state-endorsed coverage if it's available. (Often it provides coverage up to $100,000 for about $100 a year.) Also, if your company offers a policy, buy it. Should you have a claim, the primary policy (state-endorsed or -mandated) will cover you first, and then the company policy will kick in.

Remember: No one expects to file an E&O insurance claim. But the entire purpose of the insurance is to protect you from the unexpected crisis. It's well worth the cost: After you're sued, you won't be able to buy coverage at any price.

—*Oliver E. Frascona, GRI. This article originally appeared in the May 2003 issue of REALTOR® Magazine.*

MORE ONLINE

Recommended Reading on E&O Insurance

Access additional guidance in "Five Tips for Selecting the Right E&O Carrier" and "Fourteen E&O Policy Exceptions" at the Risk Management section of REALTOR® Magazine Online, www.realtor.org/realtormag.

Making Dispute Resolution Work

No matter how carefully you fill out every disclosure form and follow every agency rule, at some point in your career, you may be party to a lawsuit or be threatened with one. When that happens, it's critical to have a disciplined, nonemotional method for deciding whether to settle the dispute through mediation or take it to court.

The steps involved in making a settle-versus-litigate decision are outlined by John S. Hammond, Ralph L. Keeney, and Howard Raiffa in their book, *Smart Choices: A Practical Guide to Making Better Decisions* (Broadway, 2002). They use the acronym PrOACT to describe the five steps of a rational decision.

1. *State the problem:* What's the decision you have to make?

2. *Determine the objectives:* What business and personal wants and needs—justice, compensation—do you intend to satisfy as a result of litigation?

3. *Consider the alternatives:* What's your range of potential choices?

4. *Assess the consequences of each choice:* What are the benefits and costs of each alternative?

5. *Compare trade-offs:* How do the pros and cons of each choice coincide with your personal preferences?

Using this decision-making process to decide whether to accept a final offer or reject it and go to trial is a choice between certainty on the one hand and continued litigation and ambiguity on the other. But because outcomes are uncertain doesn't mean they can't be quantified and weighed rationally. You and your attorney can prepare a risk profile of your decision.

1. *Define uncertainties.* First, identify the unknowns involved in litigation or mediation. Ask yourself which facts you wish to present as evidence. What testimony—good and bad—will the witnesses offer?

2. *Assign probabilities to outcomes.* Next, determine a variety of possible outcomes to the litigation and the settlement process. It's seldom as simple as just win or lose, so you'll need to assess the likelihood of each outcome. The probabilities should total 100 percent.

To assign these probabilities, you and your attorney must examine each material issue, weigh the evidence, and make a realistic prediction about the outcome of each contention. An effective evaluation should also factor the probability of a loss and its consequences.

For example, assume a buyer has sued both you and a seller after escrow has closed in a dispute over plumbing leaks that caused a mold infestation. Both the seller and the broker are required to disclose known latent defects to the buyer. The buyer claims that both you and the seller knew about the mold, which cost $75,000 to repair. The buyer also claims personal injury damages of $50,000 from a mold infection. Both you and the seller deny knowledge of the defect in the plumbing, although the seller acknowledged that there was discoloration on the bathroom wall, which you advised him to paint over.

In court the buyer could win up to $125,000 if the jury believes that you and the seller knew about the leak and failed to make the disclosure. If the buyer loses, you could still have to pay the expenses of trial, amounting to $10,000.

Instead, should you offer, say $50,000, to settle? Will the buyer accept the offer or go to trial and try to win more and risk possibly losing $10,000 in court costs? Each side should analyze the problem by mapping out the benefits, risks, and consequences of settling or going to court.

Ask a Tree

A clear, graphic way to view and analyze the risks of such an issue is by creating a decision tree. The authors of *Smart Choices* say this method of displaying the interrelationships among options and uncertainties provides a blueprint for making a complex decision.

First, the attorney and client must decide whether to accept the settlement or go to court. In making the decision, the attorney should advise the client about possible outcomes. In the decision tree in the sidebar, the attorney believes there's a 30 percent chance of winning and a 70 percent chance of losing. In addition, the client must factor in all the legal costs and expenses that will be incurred to reach a verdict.

The outcomes at trial, the next phase, are uncertain. But because probabilities and estimated costs can be assigned to each alternative, the client can assess both the benefits and potential costs of making each choice.

In making the settle-litigate decision, you and your attorney must also consider your tolerance for risk. If you feel that the possible emotional and financial cost of losing outweighs the potential upside of winning, you may decide to settle—even if chances are good that you'd win the case.

Combining the risk profile of going to trial with your risk tolerance can help you and your attorney make a reasoned decision about whether to litigate, mediate, or settle out of court.

—Myer Sankary. *This article originally appeared in the July 2004 issue of REALTOR® Magazine.*

LAWSUIT DECISION TREE

You've been sued. What next? With your attorney, create a decision tree quantifying the probabilities of various outcomes to determine the pros and cons of your options. Remember to assign dollar values to each outcome, then to discount the amount you could lose during litigation based on the probability of that outcome. If you expect to lose $100,000 but there's only a 70 percent probability you'll do so, discount that loss to $70,000. Then add the expected costs of litigation to see what the loss really means to you.

You've Been Sued

Offer settlement. If it's accepted, the probability of paying that award: 100 percent

Go to court. Consider the probability of

Winning	30 percent
Losing	70 percent

If you lose, the probability of paying a

Low award	30 percent
Medium award	10 percent
High award	60 percent

Source: Smart Choices, Hammond, Keeney, Raiffa (Broadway, 2002), modified here with a real estate example.

MORE ONLINE

Negotiating Differences to Avoid Conflict

Find ideas for negotiating resolvable differences in the brokerage management toolkit at REALTOR® Magazine Online at www.realtor.org/realtormag.

How to Handle Multiple Offers

Frank was ecstatic. He had a full-price contract for one of his listings, submitted by another broker in his office. Even better, it looked as if another set of buyers was coming in with a backup offer. And, since Frank, with the sellers' permission, had told the sales associate working with Buyers No. 2 about the first offer, the backup was sure to be for more money. The sellers loved having two offers, too. If something went wrong with one, they'd still sell their home.

Sure enough the backup contract came in for $2,500 over full price. Frank even added a rider to the second offer, using a form available in his brokerage office, which stated, "This contract is conditional upon a senior contract between Buyers No. 1 and seller not closing on or before September 28, this year. In the event the senior contract doesn't close, this contract shall be in first position."

Because he was friendly with the associate working with Buyers No. 1, Frank told that associate about the backup offer and urged him to "make sure your people don't let this one go."

A few days later, the sellers called. They'd decided that despite the signed contract, they wanted to sell their home to Buyers No. 2 and make more money. Couldn't Frank just drag his feet until Buyers No. 1 went away? Although he felt funny about the request, Frank agreed. After all, he was the sellers' agent, wasn't he? He was supposed to be looking out for their best interests.

So when the lender working with Buyers No. 1 called to arrange an appraisal, Frank told him that the sellers didn't want to do it this week because they had out-of-town guests. After the lender set up another time for the appraiser to see the house, Frank stalled again by missing the appointment. Now, time was too short for Buyers No. 1 to obtain a loan approval before the contract expired.

Unhappy that they were losing their dream home, Buyers No. 1 went to see an attorney. The attorney decided that Frank had "tortuously interfered" with the buyers' right to purchase the home by delaying the loan. That is, he had allegedly breached the duty of care he owed to the customers, resulting in a loss. The attorney promptly recorded Buyers No. 1's purchase contract with the county to show that the buyers had an interest in the property and sued for specific performance. Things weren't looking good for Frank. But what had he done wrong? He'd simply followed the sellers' instructions.

When Frank called the sellers, he found they, too, had heard from Buyers No. 1's attorney. The attorney told them that because Frank was their agent, they might be liable for his actions. (This sort of vicarious liability isn't in effect in all states. But in most cases, if the sellers knew about the actions of the agent, the sellers can be held liable.) Frank also learned that the sellers no longer remembered telling him to drag his feet.

As he hung up the phone, Frank figured things couldn't get any worse. Not a moment later, an attorney representing Buyers No. 2 called to say that if the first contract didn't close by September 28, Buyers No. 2 were entitled to buy the property. To protect her clients' interests, she had also recorded their contract and was initiating a suit for specific performance. Frank wondered why he'd ever thought having two buyers for a property was so great.

Frank sighed and picked up the phone to call his own attorney. After a short conversation, he found he'd made mistakes all through the transaction. Next time, he'll:

Tell Buyers No. 1 that Buyers No. 2 exist. Buyers No. 2's offer won't come into play until the contract with Buyers No. 1 is no longer in force.

Tell Buyers No. 2 that Buyers No. 1 exist and that the backup offer is conditional on the contract from Buyers No. 1 failing.

Be sure to include a clause in the backup offer to the sellers indicating that it's conditional on the purchase contract with Buyers No. 1 failing to close.

State clearly in the backup offer contract that if Buyers No. 1 initiate litigation in relation to the backup offer, the sellers can terminate the backup offer.

Never play favorites with buyers, regardless of what the sellers say. Article 1 of the Code of Ethics states that even though REALTORS® represent their client, they must treat all parties to a transaction honestly.

Multiple contracts can be a great backup if you handle them properly. If you don't, they can turn a deal into a nightmare.

Editor's note: The information presented here doesn't necessarily reflect NAR's opinion, and contract wording here may not be appropriate for your needs. Check with an attorney in your area.

—Oliver E. Frascona, GRI. This article originally appeared
in the September 2004 issue of REALTOR® Magazine.

MORE ONLINE

Presenting Offers the Right Way

The National Association of REALTORS® makes comprehensive guidance on multiple offers available to its members in "Presenting and Negotiating Multiple Offers," a white paper on REALTOR®.org. On the home page, search "presenting and negotiating multiple offers."

Upholding the Standard of Care

We've all heard the term standard of care, but do you know what it means for you as a real estate professional? Every occupation has a standard that's determined by law or evolved by custom. Restaurant servers, for example, are legally required to wash their hands after visiting the restroom. As a restaurant customer, you also expect servers to deliver food in a timely fashion and as expected: Hot food should be served hot, and cold food should be served cold. You've come to expect this standard of care, even though it may not be required by law.

So how do you ensure that you're properly upholding the standard of care for real estate professionals? You need to recognize all of the sources that determine the standard.

Congress. You're required to comply with federal laws applicable to your profession. Such laws include the federal Fair Housing Act and the Residential Lead-Based Paint Hazard Reduction Act.

States. State legislatures may add to your standard of care by augmenting federal requirements. For instance, your state or local fair housing laws may protect additional classes of individuals, or a local law may mandate that you disclose a death that occurred on a property. Congress may also permit states to set rules for carrying out a federal requirement.

Many states also define a general standard of care required of real estate practitioners. Typically, this statement of duty outlines the conduct expected of a reasonably prudent agent based on the requirements and training necessary to obtain and maintain a real estate license. Generally, the definition is intentionally vague to allow for the continual evolution of federal and state legislation and case law.

Some states define expectations of conduct in considerable detail; others don't. California requires that sellers provide a defects disclosure statement on all one- to four-unit residential properties. The agents for the buyer and seller are required to walk through the property and note observations about defects on the sellers' disclosure form. Other states have seller disclosure requirements but impose no obligation on agents to conduct a visual inspection or to sign the form. And Florida doesn't even require a seller's disclosure statement.

Departments of real estate. Usually, licenses are regulated by a state department of real estate, whose interpretations of conduct under the law also create a standard of care. California's department, for instance, publishes reference books that explain laws in more detail than the civil code.

Contracts. The standard of care in real estate is also determined by contracts—the specific promises agreed to between parties as well as the representations or information supplied to parties. For example, an agent has a contract with sellers when listing their property or with buyers when agreeing to represent them in a purchase. In each case, practitioners and the people they represent agree to perform certain acts in good faith.

Individual expectations. The standard of care in real estate can also be affected by the experience and skill of the professional and the client or customer. A court may find that agents who advertise a certain scope of due diligence for clients or claim a certain expertise on the basis of professional designations have expanded their standard of care. Similarly, a first-time buyer may require a greater level of care than an experienced purchaser.

The Code of Ethics. The National Association of REALTORS® conduct manual also defines standards of care. In fact, courts often look to the Code to determine the industry standard, regardless of whether a real estate licensee is a member of NAR.

State REALTOR® associations. By revising purchase contracts and disclosure forms to conform to new laws or events affecting the local area, your state association evolves your professional standards. The California Association of REALTORS®, for instance, recently added disclosures regarding mold and mildew to the transfer disclosure form.

State associations may also recommend the use of forms and procedures not required by state law, such as seller disclosure statements, recognizing that they are a valuable protection for buyers, sellers, and salespeople.

Local associations. Issues of concern at the city and county level, such as properties located in an airport flight path or near planned rapid-transit construction, may prompt your local board to recommend forms and disclosures.

Geography. California mandates disclosures regarding seismic zones, and some Gulf and East Coast states require disclosure of hurricane-prone areas.

It takes work to learn what's required of you in your profession. So do the work now and adhere to those requirements, or you may find yourself learning about standard of care in court.

—*Barbara Nichols. This article originally appeared in the April 2003 issue of REALTOR® Magazine.*

MORE ONLINE

Understanding Your Duties

Resources are available to help you get a handle on the increasingly complex standard of care for real estate practitioners. The National Association of REALTORS® Property Disclosure Pocket Guide (#126-343-RM) is available for a fee (with NAR member discount) at the REALTOR®.org store at www.realtor.org. Access the complete NAR Code of Ethics at REALTOR®.org by searching "2005 code of ethics and arbitration manual."

What to Know about Synthetic Stucco

Like asbestos and radon before it, synthetic stucco, or exterior insulation finish systems (EIFS), rings loud alarms with anyone involved in buying and selling homes in certain parts of the country. News stories and lawsuits have linked the product to water intrusion behind exterior walls, which in turn rots sheathing and other building components, and makes many afflicted homes virtually unsalable.

Although few if any real estate practitioners have been held liable for EIFS defects, the publicity surrounding the EIFS controversy in recent years has increased the likelihood that you might be expected to know about the defective nature of EIFS.

EIFS didn't always have such a bad reputation. In the 1980s, thousands of houses throughout the United States were clad with EIFS (pronounced "eefs"). This multilayered system of synthetic board and finish adhered to wood or gypsum sheathing was attractive and insulated dwellings more effectively than many other products. It's still used in European homes and in commercial building worldwide.

One principal difference between EIFS's acceptance in Europe and here is that in Europe, the systems are applied to masonry. In the States, they're often applied to wood or gypsum. Because there's no moisture barrier over the wood or gypsum sheathing, the system can allow moisture to intrude through less-than-perfect window and door edges or through cracks in the exterior or rooflines, causing the underlying wood or gypsum to deteriorate. EIFS houses become moisture magnets quietly rotting underneath their facades.

A second problem with EIFS systems sometimes can arise because applying EIFS correctly is expensive and complicated. Some general contractors and appliers took shortcuts and ignored many of the EIFS manufacturers' written instructions, which added to the risk of moisture intrusion.

As a result of these problems, home owners have been overwhelmingly successful in recovering for damages resulting from EIFS. In many jurisdictions, use of EIFS has effectively been banned. Likewise, some states require that prospective purchasers of EIFS homes receive written disclosure forms.

Are You at Risk?

To date, real estate brokers and sales associates have largely been spared the agony and expense of participating in the EIFS litigation wars. For several reasons, that good fortune may change.

First, because EIFS homes are aging, the time limits for bringing litigation against the principal parties—manufacturers, builders, and subcontractors—are expiring. This means that home owners will be looking for other parties to hold liable if they experience problems with synthetic stucco.

Second, many EIFS houses are changing hands from initial owners to subsequent buyers. If disclosure is inadequate, these sales trigger new opportunities for litigation directed at sellers, real estate professionals, and home inspectors.

Defenses exist to such allegations. For example, a defendant inspector could argue that many EIFS application defects (and the resulting damage) wouldn't be apparent through a visual examination. Similarly, real estate sales associates could assert that they're under no obligation to provide information to buyers about EIFS unless they're aware of some specific problem with the property.

Prevention Is the Cure

Your best defense? Prevention. An ounce is worth the proverbial pound of cure in averting litigation.

Demand adequate information from the seller. If you represent the buyer, insist on obtaining all relevant, available information about a stucco home from the seller even if your state doesn't require disclosure. Is the system traditional stucco or is it EIFS? Have repairs been performed? Have moisture readings or other inspections been conducted? Although low moisture readings are no guarantee that there isn't a problem with EIFS, one or more high moisture readings definitely indicate the need for investigation.

Avoid potentially misleading representations about the condition of the EIFS or the underlying framing. For instance, stating that the house is "dry" or that the EIFS application defects have been "repaired" is an invitation to the courthouse. There's no way to verify reliably the condition of all the wood under the siding without removing that siding. Nor does any accepted EIFS repair protocol exist. In fact, many engineers contend that an EIFS house can't be repaired, short of stripping the structure completely of its EIFS exterior.

Encourage the buyer to obtain an EIFS inspection. Buyers' best inspection option would be to hire a structural engineer rather than a home inspector because the more invasive testing methods engineers use are more likely to find moisture problems. As is the case when recommending any vendor, offer buyers several names to choose from. Also advise the buyers that if they use an invasive test, they may have to return the property to its prior condition.

Transfer any potential responsibility back to the buyers. Direct buyers to resources (www.stuccolaw.com, www.eifsalliance.com, and www.building defects.com) designed to inform them about the product and the surrounding controversy.

Although there's no formula that will inoculate you—or any other party—from EIFS litigation, these recommendations should limit the chance of a successful lawsuit against you.

—*Gary W. Jackson. This article originally appeared in the January 2004 issue of REALTOR® Magazine.*

What to Know about Stigmatized Properties

My clients were easy to work with. I'd helped them sell their first house, and now we were looking for a larger one for their growing family. One Sunday I took them to a vacant colonial on a quiet road. They liked it, but the next day the wife called me and, in a voice as reedy as a child's, asked, "You know, about 10 years ago when we first moved here, wasn't there something about a house on that road . . . ? That's not the one, is it?"

No, I assured her, that wasn't the house where the murders had occurred, and if it had been *that* house, I certainly would've told them.

But if it had been *that* house, *should* I have told them? And what would I have risked if I had? Unfortunately, there's no easy answer.

Stigmatized properties are homes where a real or rumored event occurred that didn't physically affect the property but could adversely impact its desirability. Events and circumstances that might have a psychological impact include murder, suicide, criminal activity, occupants infected with human immunodeficiency virus, and even a reputed poltergeist.

Most states have laws that mandate disclosing known physical defects in a property. As of 2001, 31 states had laws listing events or circumstances not considered material facts, according to NAR's legal affairs department. In many cases, salespeople and brokers are exempt from disclosing these stigmas in real estate transactions. What those laws consider "psychological"—as opposed to material facts that need to be disclosed—varies considerably from state to state.

The statute in my home state of Connecticut says that neither property owners nor their agent can be held liable for failure to disclose to a property's prospective buyer or lessee that such property is stigmatized. Agents are directed to suggest that buyers with any questions about potential stigmas refer them directly to the owner in writing.

Practitioners who work in states that don't offer specific legal guidelines face a tougher dilemma. There's very little case law dealing with disclosing information on stigmatized properties.

Disclosure decisions are even more difficult in cases where a sales associate is unable to verify the facts of a reported problem or even determine whether it occurred. And inquiries regarding HIV and other illnesses connected with the home must be handled with extreme caution. Persons with HIV are protected as handicapped under federal fair housing law. Rather than putting yourself in a position in which you could be showing a preference for or against a protected class, you should inform buyers that they'll have to make any inquiries on this topic on their own. This way you remove yourself from the equation.

Even if your state has a statute that exempts you from having to disclose stigmatized property, these laws usually don't prohibit disclosure.

And such a statute doesn't allay the uncomfortable feeling that you're "holding out" on your buyer clients. If you're like most of the real estate salespeople I know, you're torn between the fear of losing your buyer clients' trust and that of facing a lawsuit from owners who don't want the stigma disclosed.

The list of such dilemmas in this area is seemingly endless: As a seller's agent, telling buyers about a property's stigma without the sellers' permission could be a breach of fiduciary duty. But if the buyers you're working with as customers ask you directly about a property stigma, you run the liability risk of misrepresentation if you fail to tell the truth about what you know.

As a buyer's representative, you'd probably have a fiduciary obligation to inform your clients of anything you know about a property even if such disclosure is exempted by state law. So what to do?

Routes through the Maze

If you list or show a stigmatized property, NAR's legal department suggests you:

Check with your real estate commission or your legal counsel to determine your state's laws on disclosure. Some states have separate laws addressing disclosures relating to stigmatized properties. In other cases, guidelines are part of the state's seller disclosure laws.

Where there's no statutory guidance, try to determine whether the stigma is based on rumor or fact.

If it's a fact, consider how material it is to the transaction—how sensational was the event; how long ago did the event occur; would it be likely to have an impact on a buyer or affect the purchase price?

If you have the listing, discuss disclosure with the owner. If the owner refuses to allow you to disclose, evaluate whether you want to retain the listing.

If you represent buyers, disclose any known facts about the property unless there's a prohibition on such a disclosure in your state. Even where disclosure isn't mandatory, it's often advisable.

The house where the murders took place on that quiet road in Connecticut was eventually put up for sale and went without offers in a brisk market until the listing expired. The new listing broker advised the owner to divulge the property's history in writing. In time, a family moved in, giving the house a new chance to be nothing more than a home.

—Raine Zygmunt. *This article originally appeared in the December 2003 issue of REALTOR® Magazine.*

MORE ONLINE

Knowing What to Disclose

Disclosure guidance is available from the National Association of REALTORS® in *Property Disclosures Pocket Guide* (Item #126-343-RM), a REALTOR® VIP publication, at the REALTOR®.org bookstore on www.realtor.org. Discount pricing is available for NAR members.

What to Know about Mold Liability Risks

There's no definitive evidence linking mold to brain damage, reproductive problems, or cancer, according to a widely covered 2004 report issued by the Institute of Medicine, an arm of the National Academy of Sciences. But that doesn't mean mold liability claims and buyers' concerns about mold have dried up. Indeed mold claims show no signs of slowing, even though court rulings have been inconsistent. There've been some spectacular awards as well as some dismissals in high-profile cases.

More troubling is that the insurance industry has greatly reduced its mold claims burden. Many states have approved exclusions to or caps on mold liability in home owners' and property-casualty insurance policies. In numerous jurisdictions, new statutes and court decisions have also reduced general contractors' potential liability. Thus, buyers who've discovered mold problems in their homes have been forced to seek other avenues of recovery, including lenders, sellers, and, in a few cases, real estate professionals.

Suits that name practitioners tend to be related to fraud, claiming, for instance, a broker had knowledge that significant amounts of mold were present in a home but withheld that knowledge from buyers.

Also because buyers tend to think of you as an expert—even though you aren't legally expected to have special knowledge about mold and, therefore, shouldn't offer opinions on mold's potential risk—you could be sued for negligence or negligent misrepresentation.

Unfortunately, even inserting a hold-harmless clause in purchase contracts or listing agreements to limit your liability won't prevent buyers from naming you in a suit. Courts typically don't find such clauses enforceable anyway.

Two Kinds of Damages

In mold-related litigation that involves real estate practitioners, the plaintiff may try to recover under two general categories of damages: (1) property repair and mold remediation and (2) personal injury.

Property damages would be awarded based on the amount of work required to repair the damage or correct construction defects and remove the mold. If mold is confined to a small area, eliminating mold may cost only a few hundred dollars. However, if mold is widespread in a home either because of faulty construction systems such as poorly installed insulation or because it has circulated through the HVAC system, remediation may require removing walls and become quite expensive.

Home buyers may also sue for personal injury damages based on harm to their health. Most health experts agree that mold can lead to allergenic and respiratory problems such as coughing, wheezing, or congestion. A recent Duke University Medical Center study also established that exposure to mold in damp buildings is an important risk factor for childhood respiratory illness. And despite the recent National Academy of Sciences report, some experts contend that ongoing research will eventually establish connections between mold and serious health problems. Still, the basis for significant personal injury claims is hotly contested.

Perhaps the greatest risk for high-cost liability in mold cases today arises when parties have engaged in fraudulent activities. Parties who conceal hazardous contamination or who recklessly oversee or approve a shoddy mold cleanup expose themselves to punitive damages that can be far more costly than negligence claims.

Curb Your Risk

Follow these four steps to lessen your liability:

1. If you know about the existence of mold, provide this information to the buyer and seller in writing.

2. If you see signs that might indicate water intrusion into a home, suggest that the buyer hire a certified industrial hygienist or other expert to examine the home for water damage or mold growth. As with any other defect or potentially hazardous condition, don't make representations or indicate you have expert knowledge.

3. Encourage homeowners to obtain an insurance claims history for their house from the Comprehensive Loss Underwriting Exchange (CLUE) at 866/527-2600 or www.choicetrust.com. This report can reassure buyers that water intrusion or other occurrences that might trigger mold haven't taken place. However, the report won't reflect water damage that hasn't been reported to insurers.

4. If sellers decide to remediate mold on their property, encourage them to be sure the process is carefully documented to show the scope and quality of the work performed by the contractor. Also direct them to give the documentation to potential buyers.

The overriding conclusion to draw from the evolving climate of mold litigation is don't bury your head in the sand. Recognizing the vulnerability of entities with deep pockets, the Mortgage Bankers Association has formed a mold task force to explore how lending practices could be altered to protect banks from mold-related losses. Likewise, don't discount the possibility that you could be a mold defendant. You'll only be more vulnerable to legal action.

—*Gary W. Jackson. This article originally appeared in the December 2004 issue of REALTOR® Magazine.*

MORE ONLINE

What You Need to Know about Mold

The National Association of REALTORS®' Information Central maintains a field guide on mold liability. Contents include materials available from state associations of REALTORS®, how to find expert mold resources, and tips on mold prevention. Access to some material requires a fee or a site user name and password, available only to NAR members. The field guides are at www.realtor.org, under "Library."

Mold Pocket Reference for Customers

Provide sellers and buyers with helpful mold resources from the National Association of REALTORS®, *A Guide to Mold, Moisture, and Your Home* (Item #141-24) and *The Facts About Mold* (Item #141-30), both available at the REALTOR®.org store at www.realtor.org.

Protecting Your Name
against Identity Thieves

Darlene Little, CRB, ABR®, senior vice president at Rubloff Residential Properties in Chicago, was preparing to leave for a vacation to Canada when an intruder pushed his way into her home and stole her purse. The thief got away with her credit cards, checkbook, driver's license, passport, and Social Security card. Little immediately cancelled her credit cards and alerted her bank. But within a few months, an unknown woman had used her name and identification to obtain a driver's license and to purchase everything from baby diapers to a new car. Frustrated and angry, Little was left with thousands of dollars in bills and a serious blow to her previously impeccable credit. She had become a victim of identity theft—a growing problem, affecting 700,000 Americans, according to some industry experts.

Identity theft occurs when someone uses your name or your personal or credit information to conduct fraudulent transactions. Victims may be denied credit or medical benefits, have their wages garnished, find liens placed on their property, or even be arrested for someone else's crime. The Federal Trade Commission (FTC) estimates that victims of identity theft spend an average of 175 hours trying to clear their names.

Having your purse or wallet stolen is the most obvious way that a thief can usurp your identity. But about one in five victims knows the identity thief as a relative, roommate, neighbor, or coworker, according to the FTC ID Theft Data Clearinghouse report. These "friends" walk off with personal information you innocently leave in your desk, file cabinet, or briefcase. Store clerks, mortgage and credit application processors, and medical records workers can copy address and financial information from credit card receipts, checks you wrote for purchases, loan applications, and health records. "Dumpster divers" rifle through your discarded credit card receipts. E-commerce sites and computerized information services sometimes fail to provide adequate protection for the personal data you've supplied to them in good faith.

Play It Safe

Clearly identity theft can come from anywhere, but there are actions you can take that will make it harder for thieves to clone your identity.

Contact creditors if you haven't received your bills. Identity thieves may file a change of address notice to reroute your mail to them.

Scrutinize your credit card and other financial statements to ensure all transactions are your own. Immediately report anything unusual.

Shred or tear up credit card receipts, unused "convenience checks," and ATM receipts.

Don't give out your credit card number, Social Security number, or bank account information over the phone or on the Internet unless you initiate the contact or have a business relationship with the company.

Put a lock on your mailbox, and deposit your mail in a postal mailbox rather than leaving it in your own box for the carrier to pick up.

Order copies of your credit report at least once a year, and search for unauthorized activity. The three major credit reporting companies are

Experian (www.experian.com), Equifax (www.equifax.com), and Trans Union (www.transunion.com).

Carry only credit cards and identification you actually need. Audit your purse or wallet and remove unnecessary items such as multiple credit cards.

Shop and conduct financial transactions online only if you're sure the site or your browser encrypts, or scrambles, data. Newer versions of Explorer and Netscape come equipped with 128-bit encryption, which is considered stringent. On web sites, look for a security statement or a lock symbol (often in the lower right corner of the browser window) to indicate that the site encrypts data.

Create unique passwords and personal identification numbers (PINs) that don't use publicly available data, such as your mother's birth name. And never keep these passwords in your wallet.

Take Action

If you do think you may be a victim of identity theft, act quickly. The thieves will.

Contact your local police department. Creditors may require a police report as proof of a crime before absolving you of wrongful debts. The Fair and Accurate Credit Transactions Act (H. 2622), which has passed the House, provides for more effective ways to put fraud alerts on your credit reports and makes it easier for banks to distinguish and block fraudulent changes to your credit. In late September a similar bill was being marked up and was expected to pass the Senate.

Cancel your credit and debit cards and get cards with different account numbers and passwords.

Close your checking account and open a new one. Report stolen checks to check verification companies such as Chexsystems (www.chexhelp.com) or TeleCheck (www.telecheck.com).

Contact the fraud units of each of the major credit reporting agencies, banks, credit card companies, and utilities about the possibility of identity theft. Ask credit reporting agencies to place a fraud alert on your account and send you a copy of your credit report.

Make a written request that credit reporting agencies correct any errors you find in your report.

Document your actions, including the names and phone numbers of people with whom you speak.

Be prepared for creditors to ask you to fill out fraud affidavits. One example is the ID Theft Affidavit form available through the FTC web site (www.consumer.gov/idtheft), which is endorsed by a growing list of companies. This site is also full of other useful ideas for reducing your exposure to identity theft and, if the worst happens, to clearing your good name.

—Isham Jones. This article originally appeared in the
December 2004 issue of REALTOR® Magazine.

MORE ONLINE

Combating Identity Theft

The National Association of REALTORS®' Information Central maintains a field guide on identity theft. Contents include tips for protecting against identity theft and the latest crime trend statistics. Access to some material requires a fee or a site user name and password, available only to NAR members. The field guides are at www.realtor.org, under "Library."

Knowing Loan Fraud

It's often done with the best of intentions, but manipulating contracts, appraisals, sources of down payment, and sale prices to help buyers qualify for a higher loan amount—even if it's suggested by the lender—may make you guilty of loan fraud. Loan fraud occurs when a lender makes an inappropriate loan, because the property is overvalued or the lender has a false picture of the buyer's financial position. Some experts estimate that as many as 1 in 10 mortgage loan applications contain some misrepresentation.

Here's how it can happen: Sally is a good real estate salesperson. She just wants to close the deal and to make everyone happy. But the seller is desperate to sell, and the buyer needs "just a little help on the down payment." So Sally writes a contract for $100,000, contingent on a 90 percent conventional loan. Both parties sign it. The contract includes a clause that reads, "Seller to credit Buyer with $1,000 for a drapery allowance." So far, Sally looks good. She's written all the terms of the deal—including the payment the seller is making to the buyer—in the contract.

Then the loan officer tells Sally to take the clause discussing the drapery allowance out of the contract and do it as a separate "side" agreement. "If there's any money being given to the buyer for draperies, it shouldn't be in the contract because then the loan won't correspond to secondary market guidelines," he says. "Just bring me a new contract, and I'll pretend I never saw the first one." Sally, who trusts the loan officer, rewrites the contract and gets the parties, who trust Sally, to sign again. The loan officer destroys his copy of the original contract, and the transaction closes with the second contract.

Now the ugly part. The buyer misses a payment. The lender conducts a routine audit and finds out about the "kickback" of funds to the buyer. This payment was part of the transaction but wasn't disclosed on the HUD-1 statement, says the lender. Next thing Sally knows, the FBI is at her door, pointing out that the incentive payment isn't in the contract. The buyer and seller say Sally promised that the side agreement was okay. The loan officer swears he never would've told Sally to leave it out and that he "never saw a prior contract." Sally spends thousands in legal fees, loses her real estate license, and barely avoids criminal charges.

If the buyer in the story hadn't missed a payment, the issue probably never would have come to light. But that doesn't make it legal or ethical. Nor does it lessen your liability if you're the one with the bad luck to get caught.

What are some other types of unintentional mortgage fraud that can creep up on even good real estate practitioners like Sally?

The delayed second mortgage. Since the seller wants to move, he agrees to lend the buyer $10,000 to complete the purchase. The buyer signs a note to the seller to be recorded after closing and receives $10,000 from the seller to use as the down payment. The purchase contract shows that the buyer bought the property for $100,000 and put $10,000 down. The second mortgage from the seller isn't mentioned in the contract written by the sales associate.

The lender makes what it thinks is a 90 percent loan of $90,000 and receives the $10,000 from the buyer to contribute as the down payment. Only after the closing does the broker finish the transaction by recording the note as a junior lien on the home.

The forgiven second mortgage. To help the buyer qualify for a higher loan amount, the seller and the sales associate agree to write a second purchase contract, raising the sale price from $90,000 to $100,000. The buyer gets an $80,000 conventional loan. Both the 80 percent conventional loan and the seller-carried $10,000 second mortgage are included in the contract.

The property appraises at $100,000, the buyer puts down $10,000 in cash, and the deal closes. At closing, the seller signs an affidavit that there are no liens on the property other than those stated in the contract. Shortly after the closing, the seller marks the second mortgage paid in full—even though no payments were made—and records a release.

The owner-occupant investor. An investor wants to qualify for the more favorable mortgage terms available to owner-occupants, so he completes a loan application stating that he will live in one of the units in the building. The broker knows the application isn't correct but says nothing.

The practitioners in these stories could've avoided problems if they'd followed these simple rules.

Put *everything* in the contract.

If the loan officer tells you to "take it out of the contract" or "do that outside the closing," ask for that direction in writing and keep the document.

Remember, the loan originator isn't the final arbiter of what's acceptable. It's the lender that finally holds the loan.

If the parties persist in using illegal loan procedures against your advice, document your advice to your client in writing.

Remember: Your desire to help clients or to get a deal closed could put you on the wrong side of the law and lose you not only a commission, but your license and your reputation.

—*Oliver E. Frascona, GRI. This article originally appeared in the October 2003 issue of REALTOR® Magazine.*

Understanding Buyer Rep Lead-Paint Disclosure Duty

When it comes to lead-based paint, the rules are clear—unless you're a buyer's agent. The federal Residential Lead-Based Paint Hazard Reduction Act of 1992 requires sellers or lessors of single-family and multifamily properties built before 1978 or their agents to disclose the possible presence of lead-based paint to any prospective buyer or renter. The law has been in effect since 1996. Disclosure includes giving prospects a U.S. Department of Housing and Urban Development (HUD) pamphlet on lead-based paint, providing any records of lead testing, and giving buyers 10 days to conduct a lead-paint inspection of the property after the purchase contract is signed.

There's no mention of obligations by a buyer's agent. However, regulations adopted jointly by HUD and the U.S. Environmental Protection Agency (EPA) to implement and interpret the lead-based paint act indicate that the disclosure requirements also apply to buyers' agents unless they're paid entirely by the buyer (a rare occurrence).

Because regulatory agencies may promulgate rules only within the scope of the statute and can't extend rules beyond what's covered in the statute, the validity of applying the EPA and HUD disclosure requirements to buyers' agents is questionable. This inconsistency leaves brokers and sales associates who represent buyers uncertain about their lead-paint disclosure duties.

Despite questions about its legal rights to do so, the EPA has sued or threatened to sue buyers' agents who failed to comply with the disclosure requirements of the act. One recent EPA claim filed under the act involved a single-family residence and included both the salesperson and the broker. Such suits are unusual for the EPA, which traditionally has sued only property owners, not salespeople or brokers, and has concentrated its enforcement activities primarily on multifamily properties.

Making matters worse, an EPA enforcement proceeding, which carries penalties of up to $11,000 per violation, is often not covered under errors and omissions insurance. That's because the EPA seeks not compensatory damages but penalties or fines.

Three court decisions—two in federal court and the recent Griffin ruling in an Illinois appellate court (*Griffin v. Bruner*, 2003)—have all held that the act doesn't apply to buyers' agents. In the Griffin case, the Illinois court went so far as to state that the law doesn't apply even if that agent shares in a commission paid by the sellers. In disagreeing with the EPA's position, the Illinois court stated that the EPA regulations create "an inconsistency [that] flies in the face of the clear statutory mandate of [the act]." However, the EPA isn't bound by a state court's decision on the interpretation of its regulations. Nor does the Illinois decision have to be followed by another state.

The two federal court decisions on the role of a buyer's agent in lead-paint disclosure (one in Illinois, one in Maine) tend to establish and reinforce the position that buyers' agents may not have to comply with these requirements.

Playing It Safe

Faced with these inconsistencies, how do brokers and sales associates meet their responsibilities under the law? To avoid any risk of failure to comply with the act, buyers' agents should be proactive and either provide or ensure that sellers' agents have given the buyers all the forms, pamphlets, and disclosures required under the act before the contract is signed. Buyers' agents may also want to confirm that the buyers have signed the acknowledgment stating they've received the required forms and pamphlet. This not only meets the EPA's requirements but also is in the best interests of the buyer clients. The buyers' rep should also ensure that the 10-day inspection period, or the buyers' waiver of that period, is spelled out in the purchase contract. If any disclosures of lead-based paint are made, the buyers' agent may want to suggest that buyers have an inspection and consult an attorney.

To ensure that both buyers' and sellers' agents understand and comply with lead-paint disclosure regulations, brokers should create a disclosure checklist (see "Lead-Based Paint Disclosure Checklist") and require sellers' agents, sellers, and buyers to date and initial every item on the checklist as it's completed. In addition, brokers should provide training to all associates on the act and its regulations.

Although the role of buyers' reps under the lead-based paint disclosure law is unclear, there's no need for concern so long as brokers and associates are proactive. The safest course? Develop systems that ensure buyers have received the appropriate lead-based paint disclosures (both federal and any required in your state) before they sign a contract. That way, you'll have happy clients, content regulators, and less contact with those pesky lawyers.

> —*Newton C. Marshall. This article originally appeared in the August 2004 issue of REALTOR® Magazine.*

LEAD-BASED PAINT DISCLOSURE CHECKLIST

To comply with federal lead-based paint regulations, make sure you follow this checklist during the transaction and have buyers, sellers, and sellers' agents sign off on each item.

Inform the sellers of their obligation to disclose any known lead-paint hazards in the home.

Obtain signed acknowledgment that sellers have been informed of their need to disclose known lead-paint hazards.

Obtain completed lead-based paint disclosure form of known hazards from sellers, and have buyers sign the form to indicate that sellers have provided them.

Provide any available records or reports pertaining to the presence of lead-based paint or lead-based paint hazards.

Obtain any supplemental reports that show testing of the property or other activity relating to the property, if applicable.

Provide prospective buyers with the federally approved pamphlet on lead, "Protect Your Family from Lead in Your Home." (It's available in packages of five from the National Association of REALTORS® by calling 800/874-6500 or by visiting the REALTOR®.org store at www.realtor.org.)

Inform buyers that they have 10 days to conduct a property risk assessment for the presence of lead-based paint or hazards.

Where applicable, obtain a waiver of risk assessment from buyers.

> ## MORE ONLINE
>
> *How to Handle Lead-Based Paint Risk*
>
> The National Association of REALTORS®' Information Central maintains a field guide on lead-based paint issues. Contents include disclosure requirements and liability concerns. Access to some material requires a fee or a site user name and password, available only to NAR members. The field guides are at www.realtor.org, under "Library." Also, NAR makes available for purchase lead protection guides called *Protect Your Family from Lead in Your Home* (Item #141-40) and the *Lead-based Paint Reference Guide* (Item #141-558) at the REALTOR®.org store at www.realtor.org. A purchase discount is available for NAR members.

Liability for What You Don't See

What you don't see can hurt you—that is, if it's something you should have seen. Real estate sales associates are required to disclose any known or readily observable property defects to buyers and sellers. Failing to disclose a defect that they knew about or should've noticed during visits to a property could lead to charges of negligent misrepresentation or fraud.

Likewise, a real estate practitioner could be held liable for negligent misrepresentation for providing a material fact to a buyer without actually knowing if the fact is true. For example, do you actually know that the roof was replaced three years ago, or are you just repeating what the seller told you?

In acting as a conduit of information between the buyer and seller, be careful to make clear which facts you've verified. And be sure you put all those disclosures in writing. Memories of verbal disclosures may be faulty when a buyer decides to sue.

Nor is ignorance a defense. If you, as a real estate professional, *should* have known about a material defect that could influence a buyer's decision to purchase or cause the buyer to offer a lower price, and didn't disclose it, you may still be liable for innocent misrepresentation. The NAR Code of Ethics obligates REALTORS® to discover and disclose adverse factors reasonably apparent to someone with expertise in the areas authorized by their real estate licensing authority.

That doesn't mean you have to become a general contractor to stay out of court. No buyer expects you to climb into attics or crawl under houses. However, real estate sales associates do have a duty to use their powers of observation in a reasonable and orderly way to spot flaws or potential flaws that are clearly visible.

You should also avoid relying too much on inspectors' reports or contract clauses that limit your liability. They are no guarantee that you won't be held liable for disclosure errors. Likewise, simply advising buyers to investigate a property's condition doesn't eliminate your duty to disclose accurately and completely.

Eyes Wide Open

So what clues should you look for when you're visiting a property?

Start outside. Is a retaining wall leaning? Does the front yard slope down toward the house? Is the cement or tile around a pool cracked and lifting? Are there horizontal cracks on walls near the foundation? Is the brick cracked on the chimney? Are patios raised above their entry doors?

Now look inside the structure. Are the floors not level or the tile cracked? Is there any sign of mold or mildew on walls or floor, or a moldy odor? Are there stains on the ceilings? Is the house warm even with the air-conditioning on?

After you complete your first walk-through, remind sellers, if you're their agent, about the importance of full disclosure. In addition, question the sellers about their disclosures if you observe potential defects that they haven't noted. If you're the buyers' rep and see inconsistencies in the sellers' disclosure statement and your observations, discuss them with the sellers' agent.

Pen at the Ready

In some states, you're required to complete a property condition disclosure form. Whether or not you're required to, it's a good idea to write up your findings. But never analyze what you see; just note the defect. For example, if you note "stain on the ceiling," don't try to guess if it was caused by a broken pipe or a roof leak. Leave that to the expert inspector. It's also a good idea in your walk-through to concentrate on the major items of buyer concern—roofs, foundations, and mechanical systems—since they're most expensive to fix. Don't waste your time making notes about scratches on cabinets and loose doorknobs; nobody has ever sued over those. Finally, don't make a statement such as "the house is perfect." No house, not even a brand-new one, is.

Whether you represent the buyer or the seller, looking over the property and providing the findings in writing is a smart way to reduce your liability and protect yourself and your client. Make it your mantra to "ask, look, and recommend." Otherwise, what you don't see, and don't disclose, might hurt you in court.

Four Disclosure Musts

1. Look over the house more than once; no one sees everything the first time.
2. Be sure buyers sign and date a receipt stating that they received the disclosure.
3. Don't hesitate to refer buyers to other experts based on the information contained in the disclosure forms.
4. Disclose "nonvisual" information you should know, such as prevalent problems in the area and its homes (example: residents typically get water in their basements on rainy days).

—*Barbara Nichols. This article originally appeared in the April 2004 issue of REALTOR® Magazine.*

MORE ONLINE

Avoiding Fair Housing Violations

Tips for staying on the right side of the law on fair housing matters are included in the brokerage management toolkit at REALTOR® Magazine Online at www.realtor.org/realtormag. Among the content: what some real-life fair housing violations look like, keys to reducing fair housing liability, contract clauses to avoid, and documents your associates' transaction file must have.

About the Contributors

Michael Abelson "Behavioral Testing: Hire Recruits That Fit In," page 137, is associate professor of management at Texas A&M University, College Station, Texas, and a real estate management consultant.

Michael Antoniak "Helping Associates Work Better, Faster, Smarter," page 75, is a freelance writer based in Dowelltown, Tennessee, with interest in technology issues.

Mariwyn Evans "Why Associates Work Where They Do," page 133, is senior editor at REALTOR® Magazine, published by the National Association of REALTORS®.

Gabriella Filisko "Shrink Your Washout Rate," page 121, is a freelance writer and lawyer based in Chicago. Her freelance interests include real estate and legal issues.

Oliver E. Frascona, GRI "The Right Amount of E&O Insurance," page 258, "How to Handle Multiple Offers," page 263, and "Knowing Loan Fraud," page 280, of Frascona, Joiner, Goodman and Greenstein P.C., Boulder, Colorado, became an attorney after working as a real estate professional. He speaks and consults nationally.

Robert Freedman "Boosting Your Bottom Line," page 3, "Taking Control of Your Accounting," page 8, "Preparing for a Financial Turn for the Worse," page 11, "Calculating Associate Compensation—The New Rules," page 13, "Running Multi-Office Loan and Title Companies," page 19, "Growing without Adding Staff," page 21, "Disaster-Proofing Your Brokerage," page 23, "Dealing with a New Competitor," page 28, "Go Commercial—and Help Your Residential Business," page 30, "Increasing Foot Traffic through Your Door," page 36, "Handling Negative PR," page 45, "Business Models: New Approaches to Profitability," page 64, "Business Models: Full-Service vs. Limited-Service," page 70, "Starting Up in a Big

Rival's Backyard," page 94, "Providing Liquidity to Net Customers," page 96, "Catering to City Dwellers on a Country Purchase," page 99, "Making Downtown Revitalization a Niche," page 100, "Tapping Technology for That Whizbang Effect," page 102, "Attracting Clients through a Blend of Business and Art," page 103, "Serving the Hispanic Investor," page 108, "What the Timeshare Niche Is All About," page 110, "Working with Others to Leverage Buying Power," page 112, "Making Your Storefront Interactive," page 113, "The Next Level for Apartment Locator Services," page 115, "Attracting and Keeping the Best," page 126, "Inclusionary Recruiting: Brightest under the Rainbow," page 142, "Four Steps to Rookie Success," page 146, "Work-Life Balance: Got Health?" page 148, "Keeping Associates Attuned to Safety," page 153, "Helping Associates Cope with Personal Crises," page 157, "Office Design That Keeps Associates on Top," page 163, "Now Comes Generation Y," page 178, "Training Associates to Succeed," page 184, "Managers That Sell: When to Stay in the Game," page 189, "Offering Annuities to Spur Recruitment," page 193, "Paying Salaries, Charging Fees," page 196, "Freeing New Associates from Pressure of Selling Fast," page 198, "Letting Associates Take a Company Equity Stake," page 200, "Motivating Associates through Personalization," page 201, "Training Associates to a T," page 203, "Living with Litigation," page 207, "Avoiding Pitfalls," page 242, "Improving Customer Service," page 249, and "Lowering E&O Premiums through Customer Service," page 253, is senior editor at REALTOR® Magazine, published by the National Association of REALTORS®.

Joseph A. Haas "Adding Home Styling to Your Services," page 97, "Learning from the 'Fixer-Upper' Franchise," page 105, and "Building a Big Following in a Small Town," page 107, is based in Arlington, Virginia. His freelance interests include housing issues.

Lesley Ellen Harris "Understanding Internet Copyright Law," page 222, is a copyright and licensing lawyer who teaches and writes about copyright law.

Doug Hinderer "Employment Law: Who's Exempt?" page 238, is senior vice president of human resources of the National Association of REALTORS®.

Gary W. Jackson "What to Know about Synthetic Stucco," page 269, and "What to Know about Mold Liability Risks," page 274, is an attorney with Lewis and Roberts, Charlotte, North Carolina. He represents owners in construction defect cases throughout the United States.

Laurie Janik   "Using the REALTOR® Trademark Correctly," page 230, "Avoiding a Breach: Fiduciary Duties Clarified," page 233, and "Commission Rules for Departing Associates," page 235, is general counsel of the National Association of REALTORS®.

Emily Johnson   "Winning the Publicity Game," page 38, is vice president of Chicago-based Taylor Johnson Associates, a media relations and marketing agency that focuses on the real estate industry.

Isham Jones   "Protecting Your Name against Identity Thieves," page 277, is a former staff attorney for the National Association of REALTORS®.

Larry Knapp, CRB, e-PRO   "Growing Your Business," page 54, is president and COO of Alain Pinel, REALTORS®, Saratoga, California.

Rich Levin   "Keeping Rivalries in Check," page 179, is a licensed real estate broker, president of Rich Levin Training & Coaching, Rochester, New York, and head of the coaching division at Mark Leader Courses, Toronto, Canada.

Lynn Madison, ABR®, GRI   "Fair Treatment in Dual Agency," page 227, heads up Lynn Madison Seminars, Palatine, Illinois.

Newton C. Marshall   "Understanding Buyer Rep Lead-Paint Disclosure Duty," page 283, is a partner at Hinshaw & Culbertson LLP, Chicago, and represents real estate professionals in litigation.

Matthew McDermott   "Spinning Returns from Your Investment," page 80, "Supporting Your Systems without Spending a Lot," page 84, and "Complementing Traditional Associates with Salaried Division," page 195, is a business development specialist with the National Association of REALTORS®.

Barbara Nichols   "Proper Documentation Keeps You out of Legal Trouble," page 246, "Upholding the Standard of Care," page 266, and "Liability for What You Don't See," page 286, is a REALTOR®, general contractor, and an expert witness, consultant, and national expert in risk management. Nichols, based in Los Angeles, has authored an audio training course for real estate practitioners entitled, "How to Stay out of Court." She can be reached at 760/753-4066.

Shelley Rossi   "Achieving Work-Life Balance," page 159, is director of public relations of John L. Scott Real Estate, Seattle, Washington.

Myer Sankary "Making Dispute Resolution Work," page 260, is a mediator in Sherman Oaks, California, and lectures on legal negotiation at USC Marshall School of Business and before meetings of the California Bar Association.

J. Lennox Scott "Achieving Work-Life Balance," page 159, is chairman and CEO of John L. Scott Real Estate, Seattle, Washington.

Pat Taylor "Boosting Your Bottom Line," page 3, is a freelance writer based in Moore Haven, Florida. Her freelance interests include land use issues.

Robert Tyson "Know How to Give Legal Testimony," page 225, is principal of the law firm Tyson & Mendes, San Diego, where he specializes in defending real estate and other professionals.

Elyse Umlauf-Garneau "Adapting to Life with Gen X," page 168, is a freelance writer based in Chicago. Her freelance interests include real estate sales issues.

Darity Wesley "Heading Off Privacy Complaints," page 220, is a licensed real estate broker, privacy and information security lawyer and consultant, and CEO of Privacy Solutions Inc., San Diego.

Christopher M. Wright "Getting the Most Bang for Your Ad Buck," page 47, "Scenario Planning: Take Your Future in Hand," page 59, "Unplugging Your Associates," page 87, and "Addressing Top Legal Concerns," page 212, is a freelance writer based in Arlington, Virginia. His freelance interests are in business, finance, music, and technology issues.

Raine Zygmunt "What to Know about Stigmatized Properties," page 271, is a referral agent for William Raveis National Relocation Management, Southport, Connecticut, and author of *The She-Wood*, a mystery novel about a real estate salesperson who must sell a stigmatized property.

About the
National Association
of REALTORS®

The National Association of REALTORS®, "The Voice for Real Estate," is the largest professional trade association in the United States, representing more than 1.1 million members, including the residential and commercial real estate industry professionals in the association's institutes, societies, and councils.

The NAR membership is composed of residential and commercial brokers, salespeople, property managers, appraisers, counselors, and others engaged in all aspects of the real estate industry. Members belong to one or more of some 1,600 local associations and boards and 54 state and territory associations. They are pledged to a strict code of ethics and standards of practice.

Working for America's property owners, NAR provides a facility for professional development, research, and exchange of information among its members and to the public and government for the purpose of preserving the free enterprise system and the right to own real property.

The term REALTOR® is a registered collective membership mark that identifies a real estate professional who is a member of the National Association of REALTORS® and subscribes to its code of ethics.

More online: You can read about the mission, organization, and history of NAR under "About NAR" on the home page at REALTOR®.org (www.realtor.org).

About the REALTOR® Code of Ethics

"The term REALTOR® has come to connote competency, fairness, and high integrity resulting from adherence to a lofty ideal of moral conduct in business relations. No inducement of profit and no instruction from clients ever can justify departure from this ideal."
—From the Preamble of the Code of Ethics and Standards of Practice of the National Association of REALTORS®.

The REALTOR® Code of Ethics is a hallmark in efforts by the National Association of REALTORS® to help maintain the professional success of its members. To keep their good standing in the association, REALTORS® complete training in the Code of Ethics every four years and are subject to disciplinary action for failure to complete the training or for conduct that's not in accordance with the Code, which is updated regularly by the Board of Directors of the association.

The Code of Ethics is organized into 17 articles and hundreds of standards of practice through which are enumerated the duties of REALTORS® to their clients and customers, the public, and other REALTORS®. The preamble is reproduced here, and the Code in its entirety is published annually in the January issue of REALTOR® Magazine and maintained online at REALTOR®.org in the resource portion of "About NAR."

Preamble of the Code of Ethics and Standards of Practice of the National Association of REALTORS®

Under all is the land. Upon its wise utilization and widely allocated ownership depend the survival and growth of free institutions and of our civilization. REALTORS® should recognize that the interests of the nation and its citizens require the highest and best use of the land and the widest distribution of land ownership. They require the creation of adequate housing, the building of functioning cities, the development of productive industries and farms, and the preservation of a healthful environment.

Such interests impose obligations beyond those of ordinary commerce. They impose grave social responsibility and a patriotic duty to which REALTORS® should dedicate themselves, and for which they should be diligent in preparing themselves. REALTORS®, therefore, are zealous to maintain and improve the standards of their calling and share with their fellow REALTORS® a common responsibility for its integrity and honor.

In recognition and appreciation of their obligations to clients, customers, the public, and each other, REALTORS® continuously strive to become and remain informed on issues affecting real estate and, as knowledgeable professionals, they willingly share the fruit of their experience and study with others. They identify and take steps, through enforcement of this Code of Ethics and by assisting appropriate regulatory bodies, to eliminate practices which may damage the public or which might discredit or bring dishonor to the real estate profession. REALTORS® having direct personal knowledge of conduct that may violate the Code of Ethics involving misappropriation of client or customer funds or property, willful discrimination, or fraud resulting in substantial economic harm, bring such matters to the attention of the appropriate Board or Association of REALTORS®.

Realizing that cooperation with other real estate professionals promotes the best interests of those who utilize their services, REALTORS® urge exclusive representation of clients; do not attempt to gain any unfair advantage over their competitors; and they refrain from making unsolicited comments about other practitioners. In instances where their opinion is sought, or where REALTORS® believe that comment is necessary, their opinion is offered in an objective, professional manner, uninfluenced by any personal motivation or potential advantage or gain.

The term REALTOR® has come to connote competency, fairness, and high integrity resulting from adherence to a lofty ideal of moral conduct in business relations. No inducement of profit and no instruction from clients ever can justify departure from this ideal.

In the interpretation of this obligation, REALTORS® can take no safer guide than that which has been handed down through the centuries, embodied in the Golden Rule, "Whatsoever ye would that others should do to you, do ye even so to them."

Accepting this standard as their own, REALTORS® pledge to observe its spirit in all of their activities and to conduct their business in accordance with the tenets set forth [in the Code of Ethics].

Company Index

Subject Index